BARACK OBAMA AND AFRICAN DIASPORAS

Dialogues and Dissensions

Paul Tiyambe Zeleza

ayebia

An Adinkra symbol
meaning *Ntesie matemasie*
A symbol of knowledge
and wisdom

Ohio University Press,
Athens

Ayebia Clarke Publishing Limited gratefully acknowledges Arts Council SE Funding

Copyright © 2009 Ayebia Clarke Publishing Limited
Copyright © 2009 *Barack Obama & African Diasporas: Dialogues & Dissensions*
by Paul Tiyambe Zeleza

First co-published in the UK by Ayebia Clarke Publishing Ltd
and in the USA by Ohio University Press in 2009
Ayebia Clarke Publishing Limited
7 Syringa Walk
Banbury
Oxfordshire
OX16 1FR
UK
www.ayebia.co.uk

Ayebia ISBN 978-0-9555079-6-0

Distributed outside Africa, Europe and the United Kingdom and exclusively in the USA by
Ohio University Press
19 Circle Drive
The Ridges
Athens, OH 45701
www.ohioswallow.com

Library of Congress Cataloging-in-Publication Data
Zeleza, Tiyambe, 1955–

    Barack Obama and African diasporas : dialogues and dissensions / Paul Tiyambe Zeleza.
    p. cm.
    Includes bibliographical references.
    ISBN 978-0-8214-1896-3 (pb : alk. paper)
    . 1. African diaspora. 2. Obama, Barack. 3. Africa—Foreign relations—United States. 4. United States—
    Foreign relations—Africa. 5. Africa—Foreign relations. I. Title.
    DT16.5.Z45 2009
    305.896—dc22   2009036319

Distributed in Africa, Europe and the UK by TURNAROUND Publisher Services at www.turnaround-uk.com

Co-published and distributed in Ghana with the Centre for Intellectual Renewal
56 Ringway Estate, Osu, Accra, Ghana.
www.cir.com

British Library Cataloguing-in-Publication Data
Cover Design by Amanda Carroll at Millipedia, UK.
Cover artwork by Getty Images.
Typeset by FiSH Books, Enfield, UK.
Printed and bound in the UK by CPI Mackays, Chatham ME5 8TD.

Available from www.ayebia.co.uk or email info@ayebia.co.uk
Distributed in Africa, Europe, UK by TURNAROUND at www.turnaround-uk.com

Ayebia Clarke Publishing Ltd wishes to acknowledge the support of Arts Council SE Funding

About the Author

Paul Tiyambe Zeleza was born in Zimbabwe and grew up in Malawi. Educated in Malawi, Britain and Canada, he has taught in several universities in the Caribbean, Kenya, Canada and the United States. His appointments have included Professor of History and Principal of Lady Eaton College at Trent University in Canada, Director of the Centre for African Studies and Professor of History and African Studies at the University of Illinois at Urbana-Champaign, and the Liberal Arts and Sciences Distinguished Professor and Head of the Department of African American Studies at the University of Illinois at Chicago. He is currently Dean of the Bellarmine College of Liberal Arts and Presidential Professor of African American Studies and History at Loyola Marymount University in Los Angeles. He has published scores of essays and two dozen books including *A Modern Economic History of Africa,* winner of the 1994 NOMA Award, *Manufacturing African Studies and Crises,* which received the 1998 Special Commendation of the NOMA Award, and the *Encyclopedia of Twentieth Century African History,* winner of several awards. As a creative writer he has authored three books including a novel, *Smouldering Charcoal,* and a collection of short-stories, *The Joys of Exile.* He has also served as the President of the African Studies Association (2008-2009).

Praise for *Barack Obama and African Diasporas: Dialogues and Dissensions*

In *Barack Obama and African Diasporas,* distinguished Professor of History and African American Studies, Paul Tiyambe Zeleza, brings together in one volume twenty-seven essays whose scope is truly impressive, engaging matters African, Pan-African, Diasporic, and global. Africans have lived for generations keenly aware of how the larger world impacts on Africa. The need for African voices on African issues is crucial. In this book we are treated to the reflections of one of Africa's most erudite scholars. This is a must read for those interested in African affairs, Pan-Africanism, and Africa's relations with the wider world.
                                                    – Emmanuel Kwaku Akyeampong,
      Professor of History and African Studies, Harvard University, USA.

To Cassandra and Natasha from whom I have learnt so much about the Diaspora, its historical experiences, current challenges, future possibilities, and multifaceted engagements with Africa.

Contents

Acknowledgements

I would like to thank friends and colleagues scattered around the Pan-African world and the thousands of anonymous readers of *The Zeleza Post* who were the first public for these essays and whose comments and critiques have nourished my intellectual imagination, my curiosities about the world, my commitments to global social justice, and my passion for Africa's regeneration. In particular, I would like to thank Cassandra R. Veney for her constant encouragement, my publisher Nana Ayebia Clarke for her vigorous support and faith in the project, my fellow bloggers at *The Zeleza Post* for their exemplary pursuit of engaged scholarship, and those colleagues who gave me critical personal and professional support at the Pennsylvania State University and the University of Illinois at Chicago where I wrote these essays.

Introduction: For the Love of Africa and Public Intellectualism

Africa is a much-maligned continent; its peoples perhaps the most disparaged, compared unfavourably with the rest of the world on almost every measure. Ever since the continent's tragic encounter with Europe in modern times – beginning with the Atlantic Slave Trade, through colonialism, to these postcolonial times of neo-liberal globalization – African peoples and phenomena have always been measured according to Euroamerican master references. From humanity to history, civilization to culture, ethics to economics, temporalities to technologies, sociality to sexuality, Africa is constantly found lacking; lagging behind Euroamerica.

This is the burden that has challenged progressive African intellectuals on the continent and in the Diaspora for generations: how to effectively defend and promote the historicity of Africa and the humanity of Africans; how to empower Africans at home and abroad and emancipate their beloved continent and countries of residence from, on the one hand, centuries of Euroamerican material violence and Eurocentric cognitive conceits and, on the other, continental and Diaspora Africa's own traditions of disorder and unproductive power and complicities with global marginalization. In short, how to address three fundamental issues that have confronted African and African Diaspora intellectuals: parity, purity, and personhood – equality with Europe, difference from Europe, and humanism denied by Europe – and how to realize the three perennial quests of Pan-African nationalism: self-determination, development, and unity.

My scholarship has been animated by a burning desire to try to understand Africa on its own terms, while simultaneously situating it

1

within worldly representation and recognition; to affirm an African identity and presence in the world – that Africa is both a unique and normal part of the world, that Africa and the world have been central to each other, that they have mutually constituted each other for better or for worse. Discourses of Africa tend to be polarized between the celebratory and condemnatory. There is a world of difference between being critical and contemptuous, between discussing and debating Africa seriously and superficially dismissing and demeaning it. We need to transcend these discursive binaries if only because the histories of Africa and the world are too entangled, too complex, too messy for the neat dichotomies preferred by Afrocentricists and Afropessimists.

The imperative for a genuinely critical engagement with Africa's multiple worlds – Africa in the world and the world in Africa – is compelling indeed. This is the inspiration behind this collection of essays: the need for discerning analyses of developments that affect Africans and African Diasporas. A similar principle and passion undergird *The Zeleza Post*, an online site that I established which seeks to provide 'informed commentary and news on the Pan-African world', where these essays were first posted. The Internet has become the ubiquitous public square of our age, an indispensable medium for knowledge production and consumption, for intellectual and social conversation among communities within and across national borders. But the power of the age-old print media remains palpable, hence the decision to publish these essays in this book to give them another life, another audience.

The proliferation of outlets for knowledge production, dissemination, and consumption offers immense opportunities for public engagement for academics wishing to escape the stifling confines of their scholarly towers. It is one of the supreme ironies of contemporary academic cultures in the richer countries that as academia has expanded and become more professionalized, academic communities have become more self-referential, and organic links between them and the public have frayed. The result is that academic knowledge production even in previously accessible fields and disciplines have become more specialized, more theoretical, less comprehensible to disciplinary outsiders, and less concerned with providing an intelligible understanding of the world. In the meantime in the poorer countries, including many in Africa, fiscal assaults on universities have undermined the reproduction of academic labour and the production of scholarly knowledge, and reduced public engagement to peddling consultancy reports.

Pressures from within the academy against engaged scholarship are matched by the growing complexity and challenges of the contemporary world which cry out for clarification, for comprehension. This is to argue that the need for public intellectuals has never been greater than it is now. All too often, today, the term 'public intellectuals', certainly in the United States, refers less to academics with organic links to social movements than to those who are in the public limelight, who tend to be called upon on television and in the mainstream print media to comment on whatever issue the media thinks is important. Many of them can best be described as publicity intellectuals rather than public intellectuals.

Public intellectuals are fascinated by ideas and address pressing questions and issues of the day in an accessible way. They are passionate about writing and commenting seriously on important public matters. Intellectuals are of course not confined to academia. Despite a shared fidelity to ideas, it can be said that intellectuals and academics differ in terms of their audience, craft, and aesthetics. The audience of academics is disproportionately composed of other academics and students, while intellectuals seek to speak to a wider educated public. Academics also tend to be specialists who know a lot about a little and whose curiosity is confined to narrowly designated areas, while intellectuals are generalists who enjoy the freedom of roaming curiosity and revel in the power of untrammelled social thought.

As I have written elsewhere, public intellectuals, in my view, are those who provide actionable knowledge, offer social critique for social action, and exhort action for social aims. They are thinkers who are unafraid to prick power and to prod the conscience of society against injustices. They cultivate and practice a critical sensibility, framed around self-reflection, scepticism, refusal, imagination, and unlearning. In other words, they exercise reflexive engagement about the social and political implications of the knowledge they produce; are committed to a constant interrogation of categories and metaphors of discourses circulating in the public sphere, including their own; refuse to surrender to despair; seek to sustain a resistant position; believe in social agency and the possibilities of change; and systematically strive to unlearn privileges and oppressive discourses in order to reclaim silenced and subjugated knowledge.

As an academic I have always been drawn more to the intellectual delights of interdisciplinary inquiries than to disciplinary introspection because, as I note in my autobiographical essay, 'In Search of the Diaspora: A Personal and Intellectual Odyssey,' presented when I was made the Liberal Arts and Sciences Distinguished Professor at the University of Illinois at Chicago, interdisciplinarity better reflects the chaos, messiness, complexity, and indivisibility of real social and physical phenomena than do the compartmentalized disciplines. Also, I am convinced that while advances in knowledge occur within the traditional disciplines, they are even more likely in the intersections, the liminal spaces, between the disciplines. In short, interdisciplinarity offers a creative, cognitive space in which new questions can be asked, new approaches developed, new understandings advanced, and from which new fields and even disciplines can emerge.

Many academics of my generation were educated, as I also observe in the aforementioned essay, to remake Africa's place in the world and the place of the world in Africa, to lift Africa from internal underdevelopment and external dependency bequeathed by the unrelenting and cruel assaults of slavery and colonialism. This is the emancipatory epistemic impulse that runs through our work, including mine despite its interdisciplinary range. In other words, many of us who followed academic careers aspired to become intellectuals, not just academics. We wanted to pursue engaged scholarship, to be the continent's critical and transformative public intellectuals. From the 1960s to the 1980s the heated debates between 'radical' and 'committed' scholars, who espoused revolutionary philosophies and programmes, and 'reactionary' or 'reformist' scholars, who supported the status quo or sought piecemeal changes, testify to the seriousness with which the role of intellectuals was seen and discussed.

Since those turbulent days in the immediate aftermath of colonization, African universities and intellectuals have faced multiple crises and challenges, one of whose manifestations has been the growing migration of African intellectuals to the global North. I am a part of that story. Increasingly, and perhaps inevitably, as migrants many of us cast our intellectual gaze on both Africa and the global North. The globalization and diasporization of our intellectual horizons is reflected in this collection, which offers critical commentaries on contemporary controversies and developments of interest to people in the Pan-African world.[1]

For me the Pan-African world encompasses the world as a whole, for not only is Africa a major part of the world, peoples of African descent are scattered across the globe, so that what happens in any particular region affects both Africa and African peoples wherever they may be. Thus these essays deal with events and issues that have occurred over the past three years which provoked me to comment, if only because I wanted to make sense of them and share my understandings with a much wider public than the small academic audiences that might be exposed to my scholarly work. The twenty-seven essays range from those dealing with political events in Africa and the continent's many challenges, to the possibilities and pitfalls of entertainment, to those focusing on Diaspora and global affairs as well as intellectual and ideological movements of significance to the Pan-African world.

The incredible story of Senator, now President, Barack Obama brings out the intricate ties that bind Africa, the Diaspora, and the world. The son of a Kenyan father who was a foreign student in America and a white American mother, his personal and political biographies poignantly combine the intimate histories of Africa and Europe in the making of the Americas, in the construction of the modern world. This has not been a happy history of course, based as it was on slavery and segregation in the Americas and colonialism in Africa. It is, in fact, precisely because of these sordid histories that the candidacy, then victory, and finally the inauguration of Barack Obama so fired the American, Pan-African, and world imaginations.

The elevation of a Diasporan African to the presidency of the most powerful country in the world marked a watershed in the cruel history of Euro-African relations that began half a millennium ago and is characterized by the savagery of racism and the dehumanization of peoples of African descent. The symbolism of this historic moment was palpable, although its full substance remains to unfold. It is part of the remaking of the Pan-African world that began with the abolitionist movement, followed by the struggles for independence in Africa and the Caribbean, the civil rights movement in America, and crowned by the demise of apartheid in South Africa. It is a long story written in blood and tears, full of heroism and sacrifice.

The collection opens with an essay written the day after Obama was elected president of the United States, 'President Obama: 'America Finally Grows Up' and ends with an essay written eleven days after he was inaugurated, 'Waiting for the Obama Dividend: The Future of US-Africa Relations.' Altogether, there are nine essays focusing on issues concerning the Diaspora and its engagements with Africa. Four were written at critical junctures in President Obama's audacious journey to the Whitehouse. The first, 'Barack Obama and African Diaspora Dialogues and Dissensions' follows the declaration of his candidacy. This essay seeks to place the early heated debates about Obama's blackness in the context of the shifting terrain of intra-Diasporan relations as waves of migrations to the United States from the continent and other parts of the Diaspora increased. The second, 'The Political Wonder That is Obama,' written after his amazing victories in the Democratic Party's primaries on Super Tuesday, attempts to explain the extraordinary Obama phenomenon that had captured the American imagination and why he seemed destined to win the party's nomination.

In 'The Dawn of the Obama Era: In Memory of the Ancestors,' I commemorate the magical moment of Obama's presidential inauguration. Both this essay, and the first, 'President Obama: America Finally Grows Up', seek to explain the meaning and implications of the Obama presidency for the United States, the Pan-African world and the world at large. If they sound too celebratory, it just shows I was caught up in the euphoria of the moment, for it was indeed a moment, however fleeting, of both extraordinary promise and homage to all those generations of enslaved Africans whose humanity and hunger for freedom sustained the protracted struggles that made this historic moment possible. The last essay, 'Waiting for the Obama Dividend: The Future of US-Africa Relations,' is more cautionary, warning against investing the Obama era with profound transformative power and possibilities for Africa and the Pan-African world more generally.

I offer a spirited plea in the essay 'In Defence of the New Diasporas and Brain Mobility,' the urgent need to turn the 'brain drain' into 'brain gain' through 'brain circulation'—the construction of mutually beneficial linkages between Africa and its Diasporas. And in 'Remembering Martin Luther King: Beyond the Sanitization of a Dreamer,' I appeal for a fuller reading and appreciation of the great civil rights leader's radical life and work in place of the oversimplified icon who has been appropriated by all and sundry including conservatives who opposed and despised him during his lifetime.

But the story of the African Diaspora these past few years has also had its more familiar side of horrific injustices and passionate struggles. 'The Political Wrath of Hurricane Katrina' reveals and analyses the racialized dimensions of this appalling natural and man-made disaster in New Orleans in September 2005, whereas the other, 'The Postcolonial Uprising in France,' exposes pervasive racism in France that provoked the national riots in November 2005 and deconstructs the myth of French republicanism.

Africa continues to harbour its own demons waiting to be exorcised, dreams of democracy and development remaining to be fulfilled. The second set of seven essays on African political and economic developments include 'The Agony of Zimbabwe,' which examines Zimbabwe's disastrous descent into political tyranny and economic decay almost unimaginable at the time of independence in 1980—in my view this very lateness of the country's decolonization helps explain the conjunctural dynamics of the crisis. But for every Zimbabwe that descends into political authoritarianism and economic meltdown, there is a Liberia that rises from the ashes. In 'Madam President: The Changing Gender Dynamics of African Politics' I celebrate the election of President Ellen Johnson-Sirleaf in Liberia. The essay tries to place this historic event in the context of intensifying struggles for women's empowerment in Africa and the rest of the world.

The struggles and victory against apartheid is one of the great stories of the late twentieth century certainly for the Pan-African world. In 'Clouds over the Rainbow Nation: South Africa and the Zuma Saga' I turn my gaze to post-apartheid South Africa's complex and difficult transition. The essay cautions against South African exceptionalism, warning that the struggles for power in the ANC and the populist politics favouring the disgraced former Vice-President Jacob Zuma reflect a familiar postcolonial path that the rainbow nation ought to pay attention to as it pursues its protracted transition into a normal post-apartheid society. South Africa is revisited in 'The Racialized Complexes of Xenophobia,' which discusses the roots of South Africa's appalling xenophobic attitudes towards and even violence against other

Africans. In 'The 2007 Kenya Elections: Holding a Nation Hostage to a Bankrupt Political Class' I bemoan the postelection political crisis that gripped Kenya, a country on which I wrote my doctoral dissertation and worked for many years, and the underlying factors behind it that go beyond the superficial fixations of the media on 'tribalism' as the proverbial cause of African crises.

Other essays that deal with Africa's developmental and governance challenges include 'The Power, Possibilities and Perils of African Nationalisms,' which reaffirms the importance of progressive nationalism for Africa, and argues that African nationalism has yet to fulfil the last four of its five historic and humanistic agendas: decolonization, nation-building, development, democracy, and regional integration. The question of Pan-Africanism, which bred the numerous territorial nationalisms of decolonization, but has yet to be consummated in regional integration within and across the continent and unity between Africa and its Diasporas around the world, is investigated in 'The Contemporary Relevance of Pan-Africanism.'

Life in Africa is clearly not confined to these weighty political and economic concerns and challenges. It involves the ordinary rhythms of daily life including leisure. A set of two essays broach this subject. And few forms of entertainment can compete in their power to enthral crowds and passions across the continent as football, the theme of 'The Africa Cup of Nations: For the Love of Football and Leisure,' written on the eve of the 2008 Africa Cup of Nations tournament in Ghana. The essay dissects the role of leisure in the construction and performance of social identities and the importance of the field of leisure studies in understanding African societies, imaginaries, and modernities.

But there is a darker side to the entertainment industry, most poignantly captured in the often warped and self-serving interest in Africa shown by western celebrities, who use decontextualized African misfortunes to shore up flagging careers or give themselves the moral gravitas of humanitarianism. The celebrity culture of this mercy industrial complex harkens back to the imperialist production of African spectacles of misery in the nineteenth century that were used to justify colonization. As pointed out in the satirical essay, 'Angelina Jolie Discovers Africa,' which I wrote after seeing an atrocious interview with Jolie on CNN, celebrities have become the new self-appointed missionaries trekking to the benighted continent to save it from itself and its seemingly biblical agonies.

The next set of eight essays focus on matters of global concern, beginning with 'The Republicanization of America: An African's Observation on the 2004 US Elections,' which seeks to explain the rather bewildering victory of President Bush and its terrible implications for the world including Africa. This essay comes after the opening essay in the collection to remind readers of President Obama's horrible inheritance, the disastrous presidency of George Bush, regarded by many as one of the worst in US history. President Obama's presidency effectively brings to a close the republicanization of America that began in the late 1960s, whose apotheosis was the Bush presidency, to roll back the gains of the civil rights movement.

At the beginning of 2006 there was widespread furore in the Muslim world over the publication of Danish cartoons defaming Prophet Muhammad, which is scrutinized as a clash of fundamentalisms, rather than civilizations, in 'Cartoons as Weapons of Mass Provocation.' Several months later the world was confronted by the destructive barbarism of another Middle East War fuelled by the competing nationalisms in the region spawned by European imperialism, which is the subject of 'The Arab-Israeli Conflict Revisited: Back to the Madness of War.'

There are few institutions as powerful in overseeing development in the global South including Africa as the World Bank, which was embroiled in a scandalous crisis in early 2007. This is the focus of 'Love, Lies, Wolfowitz, and the World Bank,' which connects the personal corruption of the Bank's president and the structural corruption of the Bank's operations in undermining sustainable development. The prospects for African development have brightened considerably in recent years, not least because of Africa's growing economic ties with China, a topic discussed in 'Dancing with the Dragon: Africa's Courtship with China,' which critically interrogates western hypocrisies, Chinese interests, and African expectations. This subject is elaborated on in 'Africa's Global Summits: The Rise of the Continent or Back to the Scramble?' Also belonging to this group of essays is 'The Whiteness of Airports,' which examines inequalities in the global travel and tourism industry, and 'The Curse of Oil Returns and the Search for New Energy Futures' that focuses on rising oil prices and the world's energy challenges.

Few of these essays deal with the two passions that define me on a daily basis, as an educator and a parent. This is the subject of one of the essays. I have become increasingly concerned about the rising costs of university education everywhere including the United States where I have been living for the past fourteen years, which reflects the marketization of higher education engendered by neo-liberalism. This is making it increasingly difficult even for middle-class families to send their children to college. I took the opportunity of celebrating the graduation of my two children in May 2007 to reflect on the class, racial, gender, and trans-national dynamics of American university education in 'The Class of 2007: The Rising Costs of Middle-Class Certification.' The picture is quite sobering. Nevertheless, the importance of a college education in general, and a liberal arts education, in particular remains as crucial as ever.

Many of these essays were written in immediate reaction to the events or issues under discussion. At the end of each essay I have indicated the date on which it was written. The temptation to revise the essays was great but in the end I decided to leave them as they first appeared to capture the flavour of the moment they were first posted on *The Zeleza Post*. This can of course be quite hazardous, but eschewing the advantages of hindsight is revealing of both my state of mind at the time of writing and the tenor of prevailing public discourse. If nothing else they show my efforts to enter and perhaps contribute to an ongoing public conversation on issues and events of utmost importance to the Pan-African world. That, perhaps, is all we can do as academics who aspire to being public intellectuals: offer intelligent comments that seek to make sense of the burning questions of our times in order to effect progressive change. I hope you will find the essays individually and collectively as illumining as I found pleasure in writing them in a passionate effort to understand our exceedingly complex world that is so desperately in need of social justice and human decency.

Chicago, February 2, 2009.

References

1   Among my books focusing on the issues of knowledge production and the challenges of Africa's globalization, development, and democracy, the following are particularly

pertinent: *African Universities in the 21st Century, Volume 1: Liberalization and Internationalization, Volume 2: Knowledge and Society* (Dakar, Pretoria: Codesria Book Series, University of South Africa Press, 2004); *The Study of Africa. Volume 1: Disciplinary and Interdisciplinary Encounters,* Volume 2: *Global and Transnational Engagements* (Dakar: Codesria Book Series, 2007); *Human Rights, the Rule of Law and Development in Africa* (Philadelphia: University of Pennsylvania Press, 2004); *Rethinking Africa's Globalization, Volume 1, The Intellectual Challenges* (Trenton, NJ: Africa World Press, 2003); *The Roots of African Conflicts: The Causes and Costs* and *The Resolution of African Conflicts: The management of Conflict Resolution and Post-Conflict Reconstruction* (Oxford: James Currey; Ohio: Ohio University Press; Pretoria, SA: University of South Africa Press, 2008).

Chapter 1

President Obama:
America Finally Grows Up

On November 4th 2008, Barack Hussein Obama was elected the 44th President of the United States of America. America and the world witnessed an historic victory in an historic election by an historic candidate. He was inaugurated on January 20, 2009. It was an amazing night: exhilarating in its significance and symbolism, electrifying in its sheer pleasure and possibilities; a rare moment when everything seemed to transcend, if only fleetingly, the cruel hierarchies and schisms of race, class, gender, and nationality. I was there, at Grant Park in downtown Chicago, when the young senator from Illinois, accompanied by his beautiful family, ascended the stage before an ecstatic crowd of a quarter of a million people.

Obama won a landslide victory. His long coattails carried the Democratic Party to undivided power in Washington. Following their traumatic defeat, the Republicans indulged further in the infighting that characterized the waning days of the McCain-Palin election campaign, fuelled in part by angry defections by leading conservative intellectuals appalled at Palin's selection.

As I walked to the park with friends, the city roared with an excitement I had not seen in the two years since my relocation there. Car horns honked with musical abandon, the crammed streets danced with history; strangers greeted each other with screams of 'Obama!', vendors sold Obama T-shirts and memorabilia, and everywhere I saw tears of incredulity. In the park Jesse Jackson, Oprah Winfrey, and many others cried with happiness unknown since this country was founded as an imperfect union of European masters and African slaves. Elsewhere Condoleezza Rice, the current Secretary of State and her predecessor,

Colin Powell also choked with tears. Now, a black man was about to speak as the President-elect. It was awe-inspiring indeed.

Obama's striking presence and splendid speech lifted the spirits and imaginations of an audience and a world hungry for change. Exhausted by the ravages of the Bush years, this hunger was also the legacy of the original crime of slavery, and the aggressive reflexes of unbridled capitalism and imperialism at home and abroad. "It has been a long time coming," the newly elected president declared. The crowds chanted, "Yes, We Can!" At last America appeared ready to grow up and return to the world chastened by its calamitous and unwinnable wars in Iraq and Afghanistan, and ready to abandon Bush's misguided unilateralism.

Obama is the first African American to reach the pinnacle of power in the world's richest and most powerful country. Since the 1960s African Americans have been breaking one barrier after another in fields as diverse as sports and entertainment, academia, the arts, and business. In politics, African Americans have become mayors, members of Congress, cabinet secretaries and governors, but the presidency seemed impregnable: a fortified zone for white males, certainly not open to a junior black senator with an exotic name who had only recently attracted attention with an inspiring speech at the 2004 Democratic Party Convention. His vision of the indivisibility of the so-called blue states and red states – a metaphor for the need for both political and racial reconciliation – struck an instant and powerful chord.

As well as being the first African American President of the United States, Obama is the first northern liberal Democratic President since John F. Kennedy. Lyndon Johnson, Jimmy Carter and Bill Clinton were all southerners. He won the biggest mandates in the popular vote and electoral vote since President Johnson. Educated at the Ivy League schools of Columbia and Harvard, and a former law professor at the renowned University of Chicago, he is an accomplished writer and sharp thinker; a man whose preference for mature dialogue with the electorate contrasts sharply with the anti-intellectualism of George Bush or Sarah Palin. And Obama is the first post-'baby boomer' president. He was only a child when the cultural wars that have wrecked American political discourse and civility broke out, and whose unproductive polarizations he seems to disdain.

This has been an historic election because it represents a potential realignment of American politics; a reversal of the republicanization of

America. The Republican Party's anti-civil rights southern strategy and its political stranglehold over national affairs has suffered a major, maybe even permanent, defeat. President Johnson clearly understood that with the passage of the Civil Rights Act of 1964 and the Voting Rights Act of 1965, which finally enfranchised African Americans, the Democratic Party would lose the South for a generation. If the Republican era emerged in the late 1960s out of the fragmentation of the liberal Democratic coalition – dominant since the catastrophe of the Great Depression – this election has been a referendum on the modern Republican era, and may usher in a new epoch of American politics. The victory of Obama and the Democratic Party thus represents a repudiation of this period in modern American history; the demise of the Republican agenda that has held sway for four decades, notwithstanding brief interludes under the Democratic administrations of Presidents Jimmy Carter and Bill Clinton.

Created under Richard Nixon and consolidated by Ronald Reagan, Republican political and electoral hegemony was crushed under George W Bush as the marriage between neo-liberalism and neo-conservatism reached its destructive apotheosis. The Bush Administration, arguably one of the worst in American history, squandered any superior Republican claims as custodians of the economy, national security, or moral values. The economy slowed as budget surpluses left by the Clinton Administration turned into huge deficits; national debt doubled to $10 trillion; the rate of job creation declined while the ranks of those without health insurance increased; and wealth was distributed upwards with regressive tax policies that widened the gap between the rich and the rest. The economy finally cratered in the Wall Street meltdown of September 2008, which accelerated America's slide towards recession and unleashed fears of the worst economic crisis since the Great Depression. Suddenly, bankers and other high priests of capitalism became converts to the virtues of state intervention as they stretched out their greedy hands for a public bailout of nearly $1 trillion.

In the meantime, the overstretched military had become bogged down in two major wars including the long, costly and bungled war in Iraq. Unilateralism, combined with the shameful scandals of Guantanamo and Abu Ghraib, had left the United States more despised than feared, and more vulnerable to terrorist assault and global censure than ever before. Compassionate conservatism lay buried in the aftermath of Hurricane

Katrina which had revealed the gross incompetence of the administration, the callousness of neo-liberalism, and the explosive mix of race and class. Personal and political shenanigans including corruption, cronyism, and contempt for the law exposed the hypocrisy and moral bankruptcy of many a Republican leader, while their party resorted to cynical manipulation of social issues from abortion to gay rights. With such a tarnished record and a widely loathed President Bush who suffered record low approval ratings, the Republican Party's chances of winning the elections were severely compromised. Such were the depths of the president's unpopularity that he was virtually quarantined from the campaign. Hardly any Republican candidate wanted to appear in public with him, not even the Republican nominee, John McCain.

Senator McCain did not help his own candidacy as he desperately sought to solidify support among the Republican base that had eluded him during the primaries and for much of his political career. The longer the campaign ran, the more the candidate became unstuck, until the electorate saw a grumpy old man given to erratic behaviour, dishonesty, condescension, a sense of entitlement, and bad judgement. He changed his message with impetuous frequency, and pandered to populist fears, rightwing pundits, racist paranoia, unfavourable polls, and unpredictable events. There was no consistent narrative, no clear indication of what a McCain administration would actually do beyond pursuing the discredited Republican mantras of national security, low taxes, and divisive patriotism.

This was revealed quite glaringly and alarmingly in his inept response to the financial crisis and his self-serving fictitious suspension of his campaign, and most damagingly by his reckless and cynical choice of the clearly unqualified and overzealous Sarah Palin, who succeeded in firing both the Republican and Democratic bases and dragging the ticket down as her negatives piled the more her ignorance and fanaticism were exposed. Cynical campaigning turned into a farce when the Republicans discovered Joe the Plumber and elevated him into the putative everyman of white America; the bulwark against Obama's redistributionist economics of 'welfare' and 'socialism' (codes for undeserving racial minorities and Democratic profligacy). Joe the Plumber's proverbial fifteen minutes of fame came after earlier charges that Obama palled around with domestic terrorists seemed to leave no traction; indeed they appeared to backfire for

16

their meanness and irrelevance. The choice of Professor Bill Ayers, a 1960s radical, as Obama's terrorist comrade revealed the unfinished cultural wars of the 1960s, especially the bitter struggle over Vietnam in which the two, McCain and Ayers, represented the lingering conflict between the soldier and the anti-war activist.

The more the public saw the two campaigns – the McCain-Palin ticket and the Obama-Biden ticket – the more the latter took the shine for calm competence, for steady and safe, even inspired, leadership.

But it would be gravely mistaken to attribute Obama's historic victory simply to a vote against Senator McCain and the Republicans. It was a tribute to his, and the Democratic Party's, own actions and agency. Obama's personal and political biographies made him an extraordinary candidate, while the organizational novelties of his incredible campaign against the formidable Clintons during the Democratic primaries proved to be the very best preparation for the presidential elections.

Senator Obama was the compelling candidate because he represented better than all his opponents the quintessential America of the twenty-first century; an America that grows evermore diverse and undergoes profound changes in its demographic, economic, spatial, social, and ideological dynamics. This is to suggest that there are different Obamas that appeal to various constituencies, and this is what, in part, lies behind his amazing political attractiveness, his charisma, the 'Obama mania' that has gripped the United States and the rest of the world.

There is Obama the black man, who embodies the dreams of African Americans. The fact that Obama is not a descendant of enslaved Africans explains the early discourses in black communities as to whether he was 'black enough', which disappeared as soon as he became a credible electoral hope with his stunning victories in the Iowa caucuses and on Super Tuesday. It also accounts for his popularity among many whites comfortable with a black man untainted by unrequited memories of slavery and looking for a postracial future.

As the son of a foreigner, Obama invokes the cherished migrant narrative of American history in which non-African Americans tend to see themselves as descendants of brave or heroic migrants who often came with little but left their offspring with the possibilities of the American Dream. Thus, the migrant narrative serves to ennoble American history, while simultaneously cleansing it of the forced migrations of enslaved

Africans. Nowadays, it also provides a convenient mode of distancing between the historic and new African Diasporas.

Biracial Obama, the offspring of a black Kenyan man and a white Kansas woman, appeals to people of mixed race, whether those from contemporary inter-racial marriages, or people from much older unions who are tired of the one-drop rule and anxious to embrace their dual or multiple racial heritages. The biracial identity was given official recognition in the 2000 Census, a reflection of the fact that the US is moving away from its historic black-white racial system into a multiple racial system common in parts of Latin America and Africa, and in keeping with the country's growing diversity as a result of increased migrations from Asia, Latin America and Africa. As a biracial, Obama escapes exclusive black appropriation and identification and is more acceptable to whites than a typically 'black' candidate would have been.

For their part, recent African immigrants identify with Obama as one of them, a beacon of hope for their own offspring, a man whose life trajectory offsets the pains and perils of migration and affirms its opportunities and promises. This explains the enormous enthusiasm Obama's candidacy has generated among the new African immigrants, many of whom for the first time began to actively participate in the American political process. Obama's victory, it is safe to predict, will lead more African immigrants in the United States to become citizens, which will help to strengthen the often fraught relations between African Americans and the new African immigrants.

Obama mania extends to Africa itself and especially Kenya, the homeland of the new President's father. People across Africa have been following the elections with unusually avid interest. When Senator Obama's victory was announced celebrations broke out across Kenya and elsewhere on the continent. Indeed, the entire world seems to have been electrified by this historic achievement, which has recovered some of the goodwill, the moral capital, US squandered so recklessly during the Bush years. President Obama's global appeal springs in part from the fact that he is transnational in a way that none of his competitors in the primary and presidential elections were: he was brought up in Indonesia and has close relatives scattered on several continents. The world has invested in Obama hopes of a more benevolent and multilateral America. For cosmopolitan Americans anxious for global respect, Obama offers an invaluable ticket to the world.

President Obama's historic victory also owes much to the extraordinary prowess of his campaign, whose organization is probably unmatched in American history. By combining old-fashioned grassroots community organizing, political rallies, and digital mobilization from the Internet to cell phones, in a seamless web of recruitment, networking and empowerment campaigns, volunteers and supporters, voter registration drives and fund raising, he and his managers built an electoral machinery of hope and audacity unprecedented in its innovation and reach. The results were astounding: they out-organized and out-fundraised the McCain campaign as they raked in more than $600 million from upwards of 3 million donors. In the closing weeks of the election, Obama flipped nine of the so-called Republican red-states: Colorado, Nevada, and New Mexico in the West; Iowa, Indiana, and Ohio in the Mid-West; and Virginia, North Carolina, and Florida in the South. It was a rout: McCain flipped no blue state.

The superior organization, steely discipline and strategic astuteness of the Obama campaign were complimented by his charismatic leadership, soaring eloquence, and unflappable temperament. As the electorate got to know him better, Obama eroded any doubt they might have had about his readiness to be Commander-in-Chief. Ironically, it was the more experienced and better known McCain who increasingly appeared indecisive and unreliable as the campaign unfolded. Obama's leadership qualities became particularly evident during the presidential debates and in the thoughtful manner in which he responded to the financial crisis on Wall Street. As McCain frantically shifted from one campaign gimmick to another and ratcheted up negative attacks on Obama, the latter stuck to his message of hope and his focus on the economy. Little of the mud thrown at him stuck.

Campaigns and candidates, however good they might be, are, in the end, only successful if they respond effectively to the times. Ultimately this explains Obama's victory. His campaign and candidacy captured and responded to the fierce urgency of a country in social transition and economic crisis. The rise of post-'baby boomer' and post-civil rights generations, including Obama's, which were impatient with or oblivious to the cultural wars of the 1960s; growing familiarity among high income whites with professional and highly successful blacks in many walks of life; and the development of less racially polarized social spaces and encounters, are why Obama won every demographic group except for whites aged 65 and older.

In short, the class restructuring of the African American community and society at large helped pluralize blackness and disentangle it from the homogenizing pathologizations of segregation. This is the context that made an Obama victory possible. But his election does not herald the end of racism, some aspects of which could even increase as the wider society prides itself in its achievement and abandons efforts to ameliorate the historic effects and contemporary manifestations of racial inequality. In electing Obama, America has indeed grown up but a postracial future remains a distant mirage. However, there is no denying that many whites and blacks will see themselves differently since Obama's election.

As I walked with the ebullient crowd from Grant Park back to my car parked a couple or so miles away, I thought of the two other occasions I had experienced similar euphoria. The first was in April 1994, when, like millions of people around the world, I sat glued to the television to watch South Africans cast the yoke of apartheid into the dustbin of history and inaugurate Nelson Mandela as the country's first democratically elected president. The second was also in 1994, in May, when I returned to my homeland, Malawi, after seventeen years of self-imposed exile from the Banda dictatorship, to witness the country's first post-independence democratic elections, which the opposition party proceeded to win.

On those two previous occasions as well as on this, the future seemed brighter than we had dared imagine only a few short years before. But the structural weight of the past soon casts its shadows on the future. The challenges ahead for President Obama are immense indeed: to rebuild the economy; repair the welfare state; heal the divided nation; rejoin the world without squandering this brief moment of global celebration of America's democratic self-renewal. But for that one night in Grant Park, one could be forgiven for basking in the glory of the moment: in Obama's incredible victory; in America's Mandela moment, which was unimaginable until it actually happened.

November 5, 2008.

Chapter 2

The Republicanization of America: An African's Observations on the 2004 US Elections

The US elections are over. President Bush has been re-elected with a decisive majority, while the Republican Party has increased its seats in both the Senate and the House of Representatives. Democrats are in a state of shock and much of the outside world is surprised by the results. Many had thought that the Bush administration would sink under the weight of disastrous policies abroad and at home, especially a foreign policy of misguided unilateralism and an economy skidding from anaemic job growth to exploding budget deficits and national debt. Instead, President Bush sailed to what by American standards was an impressive victory (fifty-one per cent of the popular vote). How does one explain this?

As an African watching the elections with its intransigent electoral patterns among the 'red' and 'blue' states, voting irregularities, and gerrymandering (the drawing of voting districts by the majority political party rather than by a nonpartisan body) I could not but be amused wondering what American commentators would say if this were an African election. I bet they would bemoan the regionalization of voting as a reflection of African incapacity to transcend primordial loyalties based on 'tribalism' and 'regionalism,' voting misdeeds would be ascribed to the propensity of African governments to rigging and the ignorance of 'illiterate' voters unaccustomed to democracy. The US elections clearly show that the notion of 'mature' democracies is a myth; democracy is always a work in progress around the world.

The popular mandate of the Bush administration is often attributed to the terrorist attacks of September 11, 2001, (9/11) which galvanized the nation behind its lacklustre president, and many have argued that in this election the nation was simply unwilling to change leaders in the midst of a war. The impact of 9/11 on the American national psyche is indeed critical to understanding current American politics, but it does not adequately explain the right-wing drift in American political culture, which has scaled new heights and dates back, in its current phase, at least three decades.

It seems to me that this drift – what I would call the republicanization of America – can be attributed to the complex and combustible politics of race, empire, and globalization. The triumph of the Republicans rests on their ability to manipulate the strains and stresses of civil rights struggles and uncertainties about America's place in a rapidly changing world. In short, the republicanization of America is rooted in efforts by conservative forces to roll back civil rights at home and project untrammelled imperial power abroad.

Many commentators note that the Republicans have succeeded in monopolizing and manipulating the discourse on cultural and moral 'values'. The issues concerning Iraq and the economy featured high in the election, indeed energized supporters of Senator John Kerry, the Democratic challenger, but they were trumped by the question of 'values' which mobilized an even larger number of supporters of the Republican Party. An administration that started as a fluke in 2000 from the hanging chads of Florida, and was propelled into office thanks to a controversial Supreme Court decision, received an extraordinary mandate in 2004.

However, the racial dynamics of the discourse on 'values' are often left unstated. Race is the bedrock of American society. It frames and explains a lot of the country's political, cultural, social, class, ideological, and intellectual dynamics. The cultural values trumpeted by the Republicans primarily tap into these racial codes of American life. They are driven by a desire to unravel the civil rights settlement of the 1960s which sought to enfranchise and empower African Americans and other racial minorities.

The enactment of civil rights laws by President Johnson's Democratic administration led to a crucial realignment in American politics, as Republicans adopted a strategy to capture supporters and states, especially in the South, alarmed by the dismantling of legal segregation. Many whites in the Southern states bolted from the Democratic Party to the Republican Party, which articulated its racist politics and policies in a variety of coded messages against 'quotas,' 'reverse discrimination,' and 'welfare' while standing for 'law and order' and 'traditional American values.'

The civil rights movement led by African Americans spawned other movements including the feminist movement and, more recently, the gay rights movement. These not only drew on the struggles and symbols of the original civil rights movement, they also inherited the opprobrium and opposition of conservative forces. Thus their respective signature issues – abortion and gay marriage – joined the litany of infamy allegedly undermining American values.

Collectively these movements reinforced each other and became central to the progressive agenda in American politics. They also became the target of radical conservatives who used every arsenal at their disposal, from radio to religion, from broadcasting studio to pulpit, to wage 'cultural war.' The politics of race ensured unity on the Republican side in this 'war' (the party remains predominantly white and in the 2004 election attracted no more than ten per cent of the black vote), but caused dissension on the Democratic side, as different identity and social projects competed for primacy (as can be seen in the heated debates about gay rights in the African American civil rights community).

Ethno-racial polarizations have bedevilled progressive politics in the United States for a long time and partly explain why leftist parties on the European model have never got anywhere here. Race and racism tend to override class solidarity and facilitate the framing of the national dialogue in cultural terms – especially as 'culture talk' has increasingly became synonymous with 'race talk.' This might illuminate the apparently strange spectacle of poor and working class whites (many prefer to call themselves middle class – a much beloved term in American popular discourse that serves to muddy class identities) voting with their cultural hearts *for* the republican capitalists rather than with their economic heads *against* them.

The politics of race is further fuelled by the country's changing demographic composition as the white percentage of the vote decreases and that of minorities' increases. Some welcome the prospect of a more multicultural and multiracial America, while others fear this will lead to 'national degeneration.' In a recent book, the influential policy wonk Samuel Huntington[1] (he of 'clash of civilizations' notoriety) is contemptuous of multiculturalism and alarmed by the recent waves of immigration and the failure of Hispanics (a rather amorphous minority) to integrate into America's supposedly Anglo-Protestant culture (where are the African Americans?). Huntington forecasts the emergence of a movement of white nativism.

Such a movement already exists – it is called white supremacy – and it has many institutional and political homes. To be sure, race has been appropriated by the different political parties at different times. African Americans identified with the Republicans (the party of Abraham Lincoln), even if most of them could not vote, until the era of President Roosevelt's New Deal when they began to gravitate to the Democrats – an affiliation consolidated during the civil rights movement in the 1960s. Since then the Republican Party has been concentrating its appeal to whites, notwithstanding periodic gestures to minorities in hotly contested districts. For its part, the Democratic Party is increasingly becoming the party of minorities.

The Republicans are better placed than the Democrats to promote both the project of white supremacy at home and imperial supremacy abroad. During the Cold War the Republicans portrayed themselves as the robust guardians of national security. The fact that the former Soviet Union collapsed when the United States was under a Republican administration could not but bolster this image; some ideologues even credit President Ronald Reagan's resolute anti-Communism and increased military expenditures for the fall of the Soviet Union.

The extinction of socialism and Communism in central and Eastern Europe and in parts of Africa and Asia in the 1990s was accompanied by two contradictory tendencies. On the one hand, the world witnessed a new wave of democratization, and on the other systemic options narrowed as political parties rushed to a centre that was drifting rightwards. Some even proclaimed the emergence of 'third way' politics. In effect, this represented the retreat of leftwing and social democratic parties to the right.

In the US, where ideological space has historically tended to be narrower than in Western Europe, the gap between the two major parties virtually disappeared – except on the question of 'values' as increasingly defined by the right. The administration of President Bill Clinton did not fundamentally challenge the rightward drift of American politics. Instead it appropriated Republican economic and social policies (notwith-standing populist rhetoric to the contrary) and Clinton's own personal popularity among various Democratic constituencies including African Americans. The ideological disarmament of the Democratic Party – its failure to articulate policies fundamentally different from the Republican Party – left America's politics open to appropriation by the true proprietors of the conservative agenda, the Republicans. Why purchase a copy when you can get the original at the price of the same vote?

From the 1990s, the United States became the lone and increasingly lonely Superpower. The restructuring of the world system was captured in the rather fuzzy concept of 'globalization'. The thinking was that a new era had emerged characterized by rapid flows of commodities and capital, ideas and individuals, and values and viruses. Above all, globalization was seen as an economic and technological phenomenon that threatened to erode the sovereignty of the state and the sanctity of local cultures and identities.

Much of what is said about globalization is 'globaloney'; more a projection of contemporary anxieties and aspirations than a descrip-tion of the actual processes of global interconnectedness. But there can be little doubt that a kind of global reflexivity has emerged, fanned by the media, international migrations, and the propensity of politicians to blame national problems on malicious or uncontrollable foreign forces.

The possibilities and perils of globalization have engendered trans-nationalisms and nationalisms everywhere. For the US globalization gave cause for celebration and concern; celebration in so far as its industries and institutions were among the major beneficiaries of globalization, and concern in that it promised to shift the measure of global power from military prowess to economic competitiveness. The burst of the dot.com bubble and the onset of recession at the turn of the new century reinforced these fears, and was articulated in the recent election in terms of 'outsourcing our jobs'.

Then there was 9/11. Much has been written about how the Bush Administration squandered the global goodwill expressed in the immediate aftermath of the attacks by embarking on a policy of haughty unilateralism that alienated many of its Western allies and provoked unprecedented hostility in many parts of the world. This imperial hubris[2] served the interests of an administration desperate for legitimacy after the botched elections of 2000, as well as of the neo-conservative cabal bent on recapturing the military glory of US imperialism buried in the killing fields of Vietnam.

It could also be said that terrorism became a substitute for Communism; a new enemy essential for a permanent war economy and necessary to produce nationalism and promote patriotism in this new era of 'globalization'. For a country that spends nearly half of the world's military expenditure, enemies are essential and the more ubiquitous they are the better. The post 9/11 association of terrorism with Islam rekindles deep-seated anti-Islamic memories in Western culture and the fact that the threat is largely seen as stateless reinforces the notion that this is indeed a clash of civilizations that antedate modern states.

This serves to particularize and primordialize global terrorism, depicting it as an upsurge of evil that has nothing to do with the policies of successive US governments, including those of the current Bush administration. It encourages Americans to ask the question: 'Why do they hate us?' and give the obvious self-serving answer: 'Because of our way of life, our freedoms, our wealth; in short because of who we are.' And so the despicable war in Iraq is portrayed as a heroic effort to bestow democracy upon a long-suffering people (forget the previous justification about weapons of mass destruction). Never mind that spreading democracy and freedom is a strange alibi for a country that has difficulty running its own elections and has historically not respected the democratic rights and civil liberties of its minorities.

It is hard for outsiders to understand how so many people in the world's most powerful nation with a massive media industry and intellectual resources can be so fooled. But perhaps it would not be if the monopolies of power in the US political economy were understood. There is less diversity of opinion in the American media than in many African countries, for example, because of concentrations of media ownership. The sycophancy of mainstream American hacks would shock many courageous African journalists who mercilessly attack their governments.

Imperial supremacy requires the constant production of the rhetoric of righteousness. The United States is a settler society with populations from around the world, and so such cruel fictions also serve to produce and police citizenship. The languages of empire abroad and race at home are interminably linked: Having domestic racial 'others' who have been abused for centuries – principally native Americans and African Americans – has provided the United States with the vocabulary of derision for foreigners, 'natives,' and non-whites. It is not a coincidence that the loudest supporters of white supremacy and imperial supremacy are to be found among Christian fundamentalists, a key voting bloc in the Republican Party. They would like to roll back many civil rights gains and any perceived threats to American global power.

President Bush's second administration will attempt to do both: through conservative appointments to the Supreme Court and other domestic policy initiatives (from tort and tax reforms to immigration and social security reforms – all intended to roll back the welfare state and establish a conservative 'New Deal'); and through a savage war in Iraq coupled with renewed threats against the so-called 'rogue states', principally Iran and North Korea. But the aggressive pursuit of these objectives offers the possibility of reversing the republicanization of America. Forces that have arisen in opposition to this decades-long process will be galvanized and strengthened in the coming years.

What does all this mean for Africa?

Predictably, most Africans were disappointed, indeed dismayed by Bush's re-election, although their leaders sent the customary congratulatory messages. The upshot is that Africa can expect more of the same: minimal attention where Africa's fundamental interests for development and democratization are concerned; and maximum manipulation in the service of US national interests where these involve the war on terror and securing 'safe' oil supplies. Security assistance will increase to fight 'terrorists', so will political and economic investments in the oil industry. Several African governments are already cynically using 'anti-terrorism,' much as 'anti-Communism' was used during the Cold War: to win favour with Washington and to erode hard won democratic freedoms. And Africa already supplies about a fifth of US oil imports, a figure that is expected to grow in the next decade.

Of course much more diplomatic noise will be made about American 'aid', especially about the developmental impact of the Africa Growth and Opportunity Act (AGOA), the $15 billion Emergency Plan for AIDS Relief, and the Millennium Challenge Account that promises up to $5 billion a year to African countries. But to date, the impact of AGOA remains quite limited, the disbursement of funds from the AIDS programme is painfully low and slow, and the Millennium Account has yet to distribute a single dollar. Not surprising for a country that remains the least generous among the industrialized nations in terms of development assistance, and for a global 'aid' industry high on rhetoric and short on substance, that always promises more than it delivers.

President Bush's second term, then, poses more challenges than opportunities for Africa, centred on the explosive marriage between terrorism and oil. This calls for vigilance by African governments and civil society organizations to guard against their countries becoming pawns in the US 'anti-terrorism' crusade, and for the oil producers to leverage a new relationship that promotes development and democracy rather than deepens dependency and authoritarianism. On a global scale, it calls for Africa to cultivate and strengthen relations with regions and countries that are poised to challenge, for all manner of objective and subjective factors and reasons, current US imperial hegemony. This includes 'old Europe' whose links and post-World War II subordination to the US are undergoing historic shifts, and the rising economic and political power of the global South led by China, India and Brazil.

At stake is the need to rid the world of US imperialist unilateralism, regardless of who is president; then to create a new world order governed by the age-old principles of progressive international and national politics: development, democracy, and self-determination. A world, in short, in which every region matters, African matters matter, and collective material and moral advancement matter.

November 4, 2004.

References

1   Samuel Huntington, *Who Are We: The Challenges to America's National Identity* (New York: Simon and Schuster, 2004).

2   Michael Sheuer uses this phrase in his book that sharply critiques the U.S.'s misguided policies in the so-called war on terror, *Imperial Hubris: Why the West is Losing the War on Terror* (Dulles, VA: Potomac Books, 2004).

Chapter 3

The Agony of Zimbabwe

For many of us from Southern Africa, Zimbabwe evokes conflicting memories and emotions: the heroism of the liberation struggle against settler colonialism; the hopes of reconstruction and social transformation in the early post-independence years; and the descent into tyranny and economic decline from the late 1990s. Today, Zimbabwe is in deep economic and political crisis, a once proud country held to ransom by a bankrupt and authoritarian regime whose revolutionary credentials look ever more tattered. Tens of thousands of Zimbabweans vote with their feet and leave for neighbouring countries or overseas, a development unimaginable in the early euphoric years of independence. What went wrong?

There are no shortages of explanations for Zimbabwe's current agonies. To the ideologues of the regime and its ardent external supporters, Zimbabwe is the victim of an orchestrated plot by Western countries – led by the devious Tony Blair, former British Prime Minister – bent on frustrating African progress. Charges of Western and British complicity and duplicity in the Zimbabwe crisis are not entirely without merit. Some have pointed out that the vitriol poured on Zimbabwe by the Western media has less to do with that country's state of governance than lingering Western empathies for settler colonialism. To its critics, the Zimbabwe government uses the rhetoric of nationalism, of an unfinished revolution, to cling to power, or as a mask to hide its political intolerance and economic incompetence. Again, there is a lot of truth in this indictment: the regime became more autocratic and adopted a more radical land reform programme as it faced a growing and credible political opposition, coalesced around the Movement for Democratic Change (MDC), and as its capacity to manage let alone rescue the economy declined.

A more comprehensive account of Zimbabwe's economic and political crises would have to consider Zimbabwe's transition from settler colonialism to a developing postcolonial state. The country's current crisis is rooted in the failures of that transition to-date. As any postcolonial state, the new Zimbabwe government in 1980 was confronted with the complex challenges of turning the triple dreams of Uhuru – nation building, development and democracy – into reality. And having waged a protracted war of liberation, which entailed the mobilization and politicization of the peasantry, these dreams went beyond the aspirations of the urban elites and working class. But unlike many countries that got their independence in the 1950s and 1960s, Zimbabwe attained its independence during a period characterized by global economic crisis and the ascendancy of neo-liberalism. The first severely limited primary commodity and export-driven economic growth, while the second entailed the 'rolling back' of the state and severely curtailed the developmentalist ambitions of the new government. To be sure, in the early post-independence years Zimbabwe's record of achievement in the provision of social services was very impressive. But it was unsustainable following the imposition of structural adjustment programmes, which, as in much of Africa, took a heavy toll on the economy, particularly social services and formal and public sector employment. In fact, the austerities of structural adjustment programmes (SAPs) galvanized the increasingly pauperized urban middle classes and the rural masses into the wave of protests and agitation that crystallized into struggles for democratization, for the 'second independence'.

If SAPs dented the revolutionary credentials and developmentalist capacities of the Zimbabwean state, the struggles SAPs engendered diluted the state's democratic claims and exposed its authoritarianism. The monopoly of power enjoyed by the liberation movement, notwithstanding its fierce internal conflicts, began to crack in the 1990s as the working and professional classes in the cities, the weakest link for the liberation movement, turned into a noisy civil society demanding the full rights of political citizenship to promote civil liberties and protect their declining economic fortunes. However, SAPs were not the source of all the problems for the political class and the state they had inherited from the Rhodesians.

The liberation movement had inherent spatial and social contradictions that became increasingly evident. The spatial divisions lay between the rural and urban areas as well as between the regions of Matabeleland and Mashonaland and within each region. The merger of Joshua Nkomo's ZAPU (Zimbabwe African People's Union) into Robert Mugabe's ruling ZANU-PF (Zimbabwe African National Union-Patriotic Front) in 1988, after a five-year violent campaign in Matabeleland, sought to defuse the regional tensions, although they did not disappear. In fact, they mutated into new forms. No less critical were the urban-rural divisions. It was the rural peasants who had largely fought in the liberation war, but the leadership and immediate beneficiaries of independence were the urban professional elites. It was in the latter's class interest to consolidate their power by promoting their own wealth accumulation, thus to fashion an economic base for the political power they had acquired.

The biggest opportunities for wealth accumulation were in land – real estate in the cities and farms in the countryside. Land was of course central to the peasantry, the backbone of the liberation struggle, and to the nationalist memories of violent dispossession by the forces of settler colonialism. But land resettlement for the peasantry, especially for the poor peasantry, was not pursued aggressively until the late 1990s. This has often been attributed to the constraints imposed by the constitutional safeguards of the Lancaster House Agreement, which favoured market-based land transactions and resettlement. Also, shortage of resources and the failure of the British government to honour its funding pledges have been blamed. It would seem that at stake were the accumulative interests of powerful segments of the political class. They wanted the land for themselves.

This balancing act – land for the masses and for the aspiring national bourgeoisie – found expression in the increasingly empty ideological language of socialism: a rhetoric that was not only out of touch with the realities in Zimbabwe and the interests of the political class itself but also with the intolerant demands of neo-liberalism, structural adjustment and the unfolding demise of global socialism. By the late 1990s the comrades in power could no longer fool their beloved masses in the rural areas, or the restive armies of unemployed educated youths in the cities, or the workers flexing their industrial muscles and discovering a new political voice through mushrooming civil society organizations and the MDC.

It was in this context that the government embarked on a radical land reform programme from 1998 and especially after it had lost the constitutional referendum in early 2000. Its aims were multiple and varied, but chiefly the government sought to resettle more peasants and thereby rekindle ZANU-PF's revolutionary credentials. It tried to do this both locally and regionally: locally with a new generation too young to be the war veterans in whose name the land seizures were originally unde-taken; and in a region now dominated by a reformist post-apartheid South Africa where the governing ANC coalition had abandoned any pretensions to revolutionary socioeconomic transformation. As well as bolstering the ruling ZANU-PF, the radical land reform programme also sought to weaken the MDC ideologically and operationally by under-mining its nationalist claims and character – still a compelling card in a post-settler society – and its mainly rural appeal.

These measures, augmented by violence, intimidation, and voting irregularities, enabled ZANU-PF to win the parliamentary elections of 2000 and 2005. Predictably, monitors from SADC pronounced the elections 'free and fair', whereas Western monitors cried foul. The elections of 2000 were more violent than those of 2005, an indication to some of the continued popularity of ZANU-PF. More likely, it reflected the effectiveness of ZANU-PF political terror and the ineffectiveness of the MDC, its inability to articulate a credible message of national transformation.

All this raises difficult questions as to the forces and strategies that can effectively bring Zimbabwe's nightmare to an end: that can facili-tate a transition from the command politics of the liberation movement to the democratic politics of a post-liberation society; from Mugabe to a new leader. Clearly, elections are not enough, but street action provokes violent retribution from the state. And concerted regional pressure seems unlikely. The regime's strength and Achilles heel is in rural areas, so the opposition must find ways of mobilizing the rural population; of bridging the rural-urban divide and linking urban and rural struggles. The generalized economic crisis that has become more severe since the most recent elections might offer a new opening.

A little remarked aspect of the farm invasions is that they led to the displacement of tens of thousands of workers from neighbouring countries, especially Malawi and Mozambique, some of whom had been in Zimbabwe for more than a generation. In effect, the rural areas were being emptied of both European *and* African settlers. The urban areas also boast large populations who can trace their origins to neighbouring countries, which may partly drive the government's attempts to disenfranchise urban residents, who constitute the backbone of the MDC. A new form of Zimbabwean citizenship is being constructed based on autochthonous rather than residential claims. This underscores what is at the heart of the Zimbabwean conundrum: how to restructure, develop, and democratize a former settler colony that relied on migrant labour from within and without; which necessitated massive land alienation and left behind legacies of high structural unemployment, racial disenfranchisement and dispossession, and militarism and the use of political violence as weapons of both control and liberation. In short: how to construct an inclusive citizenship which subjects state power and the political class to democratic accountability.

As a former settler colony in search of a viable future, Zimbabwe causes intense political emotions. It does so also for the mirror it holds to South Africa. Both countries illustrate most painfully the highly racialized, exploitative and abusive modern encounter between Europe and Africa, spawned by European imperialism and colonialism. It is not surprising that both the foes and friends of the Mugabe regime look to South Africa to provide international leadership on the Zimbabwe 'question'. To some in South Africa the Zimbabwe crisis serves as a warning of the dangers of African nationalist demagoguery; to others it is an impetus for the country to undertake extensive land reforms and socio-economic transformation if it wants to avoid Zimbabwe's fate.

It is arguable what motivates President Mbeki's 'quiet diplomacy' – Zimbabwe as an ally in the post-colonial liberation wars of the region or as an alibi for accelerated reform in South Africa? What is clear is that the agony of Zimbabwe continues to deepen and profoundly affect the entire Southern African region. South Africa, the SADC countries, and the rest of Africa have a responsibility to help the country chart a more productive future. Solidarity need not entail collaboration with the corrupt and self-serving autocrats in Harare who have obviously outlived their historical usefulness. Rather, it requires principled support for the ordinary people of Zimbabwe struggling for a democratic and developmental state; for a society worthy of their protracted fight against settler colonialism and postcolonial misrule.

May 9, 2005.

Chapter 4

The Political Wrath of Hurricane Katrina

Like most people in the United States, I was transfixed by the horrific images of the death and destruction wrought by Hurricane Katrina on the US Gulf coast. The proud city of New Orleans, birthplace of jazz and so much of what is original in American popular culture, lay before us deluged in a combustible slew of devastation, despair, and fury. Americans were shocked by the criminal incompetence of their government, which blamed the wrath of nature, and not its own ineptitude and indifference. Those of us from Africa are familiar with this script: how drought is used as an alibi for famine. At least African governments can plead poverty, however self-serving and misleading that plea is. Not so for the world's wealthiest country. The rest of the world watched with surprise, sympathy, and scorn. Many have offered assistance – to America's obvious embarrassment, rather than gratitude. Katrina has sunk New Orleans's and America's sense of greatness; the world's lone superpower has become ordinary.

Katrina is the antidote to 9/11, which stunned the United States into patriotic fervour at home and imperial rage abroad. Katrina has stoked deep national divisions and widespread international derision. Disasters, whether natural or manmade (and Katrina was both) are revelatory mirrors that expose a society's subterranean fissures; its existing socioeconomic inequalities and political pathologies. Katrina has provided a giant and agonizing mirror for America, in full view of the world it normally despises, forcing it to look squarely in the face, to its profound shock and shame, all those marginalized people it silences with its strange but seductive myths of equal opportunity and the American Dream. Race and class, the enduring systemic and symbolic deformities that mark and mock the fantasies of American exceptionalism, have betrayed their simmering presence in the teeming masses huddled in

35

biotoxic sports arenas, under the sweltering patches of broken bridges, or waving desperately from the rooftops of submerged buildings. Many more remained trapped or buried in their flooded homes, while bloated bodies floated in the rivers that overtook the streets of tourist revelry.

The immediate victims of Katrina's wrath, then, were all those invisible people normally hidden in the sewers of a service economy that has grown with the growing de-industrialization of America. They are mostly poor and black, a grim testimony to the limits of the civil rights movement that ended legal racial segregation but left the seclusions of economic class intact. In fact, the gap between the rich and poor in America has never been wider than it is now: the ranks of those living below the poverty line have swelled, and downward mobility for the beleaguered middle classes is more likely than upward mobility. Clearly, the ferocious storms of Katrina ripped open the fault lines of American society in a way that the furious fires of 9/11 did not and could not. 9/11 was an act of terror that could be blamed on evil foreigners; Katrina as an environmental disaster could not. With no external enemy on which to focus the nation's anguish and rage, attention turned inward to the social identities of the victims and the ineffectiveness of state intervention.

9/11 was an assault on the financial and military citadels of America, which provoked swift state response as its victims were not marked in terms of colour and class because many were white and well-off. Racial and class markers are often reserved for the poor and racial minorities. I have been struck, although not surprised, by the derogatory and racist language used in the media to describe the victims of Katrina: the obsession with violence and the different descriptions of whites 'helping' themselves and blacks 'looting' from deserted shops; and the unflattering, indeed, contemptuous comparisons with the Developing World and Africa – the implication being that conditions in New Orleans are more befitting those benighted places than America.

This is the rhetoric of denial and dismissal; denial that poverty and the exploitation and marginalization of blacks have always been an integral part of the US, indeed fundamental to its growth and development; and dismissal of the African American poor as failed citizens who rightly belong to their underdeveloped ancestral homeland. Indeed, African Americans as a whole seem to suffer from double disenfranchisement: they have yet to be perceived by the larger white society as fellow citizens and fellow human beings. Katrina has shown how deeply embedded both poverty and blacks are in America's social ecology, which no amount of rhetoric about the United States being the wealthiest country in the world or the statistical myth that blacks are no longer America's largest minority – a status supposedly usurped by Hispanics who, however, can be of any race – can hide.

The social dynamics of race and class, and the differences in the nature of the two disasters, might explain the relatively slow and chaotic response of the American government to Hurricane Katrina compared to the terrorist attacks of 9/11. But there are two other powerful forces at work: one is Iraq, the costly and disastrous military adventure that links 9/11 to the government's failure to respond properly to Katrina; and the other is neo-liberal ideology, that connects the muddle of the relief effort to the innate incompetence of the public sector. 9/11 facilitated the American invasion of Iraq, but the stalemate in Iraq has fostered America's impotence before Katrina. If Iraq has weakened America's capacity to manage a domestic disaster of the magnitude of Katrina, the latter will most likely weaken America's capacity to prevail in the war in Iraq, given the scale of the resistance. The reason for this lies both in the sheer material costs of managing the two disasters, and also the crucial link that, I think, Americans may finally be making between the Iraq war and domestic well-being. America's enemies are likely to draw their own connections as well: already under-awed by America's military prowess in Iraq they are unlikely to be impressed by its ability to manage large scale disasters at home, both of which might increase America's vulnerability to terrorism.

While it is foolhardy to underestimate the country's economic capacity, let alone the popular will to rebuild shattered infrastructures and communities, the United States does not have infinite resources. The levels of its budget deficits and national debt are unsustainable in the long term. China and cheap energy have helped keep the economic bubble afloat. Oil prices were already rising steeply before Katrina and spiked sharply afterwards because of damages to the region's important oil production and refining industry. If they remain high the effects will ripple throughout the economy, especially the already troubled airline and automobile industries. This was already turning to be the summer when support for the Iraq war finally tipped and stayed in negative territory, and most of the displaced people – uncharitably and incorrectly called refugees – who were interviewed in the peripatetic media made the link between military commitments in Iraq and the incompetence and disarray of the relief effort. Interestingly, in both gulfs – the Middle East Gulf region and the stricken US Gulf coast – salvation is seen to lie in the hands of the military. Indeed, some of the troops being deployed in the areas shattered by Katrina are veterans of the Afghanistan and Iraq wars.

The spectacle of the military as a hurricane relief force raises troubling questions about the capacities of civilian agencies. 9/11 reinforced the militarization of homeland security; Katrina has exposed the impoverishment of human security in an important but vulnerable region. Listening to the befuddled director of the Federal Emergency Management Agency (FEMA) make the rounds of TV interviews I was stunned by his mendacity and fecklessness and of many other officials from the vast Department of Homeland Security to which FEMA belongs. They pleaded that they could not foresee the full impact of Katrina; or that the levees keeping New Orleans a habitable city below sea level would break. Never mind that FEMA itself and numerous agencies and studies had long predicted New Orleans would be devastated by any major hurricane landing on its shores. In fact, as recently as 2001 FEMA warned that New Orleans presented one of the country's top three most likely catastrophic disasters. I was reminded of those African leaders who feign surprise when drought strikes resulting in crop failures and food shortages.

Neither the ignorance of state officials nor the lethal power and capricious unpredictability of Katrina are wholly responsible for the destruction of the levees. Rather, as the world has since learned, it was their terrible state of disrepair thanks to massive budget cuts by the Bush administration – almost halved since 2001. Also, there were no adequate plans to evacuate the poor and vulnerable who had no means to leave as Katrina roared to the Gulf Coast. Blacks and whites with resources – from cars and money to the social capital of relations and friends in unaffected cities and states – were able to flee. Thus Katrina was essentially a crisis of public policy, of the provision of public goods and pursuit of collective action: building and maintaining the public infrastructure in normal times and providing public assistance for vulnerable people in times of disaster.

The effects of this public policy crisis have been seen in the gruesome television images of public disorder and desolation; of people in a major American city stripped of their dignity, and sometimes civility, scavenging for food and water, without shelter and toilets; of distraught children too tired to cry; of gaunt old people dying in their wheel chairs; and patients in dimly lit hospitals hanging by the thread of empty tubes and the heroic efforts of distressed doctors and nurses. The chickens of neo-liberalism – the dangerous fiction that the state at best is irrelevant, at worst is a source of problems – have come home to roost. Since the world economic crisis of the 1970s, neo-liberalism has been the dominant ideology of economic policy and management, its ascendancy buttressed by the collapse of actually existing socialism and American post-Cold War triumphalism. Africa and other parts of the global South have two 'lost decades' to show for the perilous inanities of neo-liberalism imposed with religious zeal by the international financial institutions with all their global capitalist might, cheered on by successive US governments.

Since the Reagan administration in 1980, the United States has been under the regime of what we in Africa call structural adjustment programmes (SAPs). Since then the Republican mantra, to which Democrats have largely acquiesced, has been getting the government off people's backs: that is, reducing government expenditures and cutting taxes. For the developing countries, including many in Africa, SAPs have led to the erosion of developmental advances achieved in the pre-SAP days; resulting in growing indebtedness, deepening social inequalities and insecurities, and rising poverty. Under this ruthless regime of individual wealth accumulation the relative exploitation and repression of the working class and racial minorities in the United States has increased – as can be seen in the growing income gaps between workers and executives and the backlash against civil rights.

But given its global power, the US has been able to deflect and 'hide' some of the costs of SAPs by importing vast quantities of capital through both direct investments and debt – the US is the world's largest debtor nation. Iraq has dented the facade of superpower military invincibility while Katrina has exposed the underbelly of neo-liberalism in America. Since this is a highly racialized country, the class dynamics of neo-liberalism are interpenetrated with the unyielding hierarchies of race. Hence, the iconic images of the victims of Katrina are the black poor.

9/11 elevated a lacklustre president into a national leader; Katrina severely weakened the recently re-elected president's leadership. It shattered the aura of a 'can do leader' and government competence, and the administration's mask of unflappable confidence often hiding uninformed complacency and ideological fanaticism that does not even countenance the scientific consensus about global warming, which many believe is responsible for the growing strength and frequency of hurricanes. It is easier to lie about the anarchy in far away Iraq than the mayhem within the United States itself; to control the flow of images of the American dead and wounded from Baghdad than the flood of images of the desperate and dying in the Big Easy.

It is tempting to lay the blame for the tragedy of Katrina entirely on the shoulders of the Bush administration. After all, it brought the imbroglio of Iraq upon America against the wise counsel of history, and anti-war activists, and diverted much-needed resources that could have facilitated a quicker and better response to Katrina. Large amounts of equipment and numbers of the National Guard – one third of Louisiana's and even more from Mississippi – who are often used in state and national emergences were in Iraq when Hurricane Katrina struck.

President Bush was not known for his eloquence or sympathies for the poor or blacks, notwithstanding an Ivy-League education and pretensions to 'compassionate conservatism'. His approval ratings were already plummeting before the calamity of Katrina, which became his biggest domestic political crisis ever. His initial ineffectual handling of the hurricane reinforced an already widespread perception that he fancied himself more as a 'war' president than an engaged leader, more interested in beefing up military security than social security, pursuing policies that demand sacrifices from the poor but not the rich. But Bush did not invent Reaganomics and previous administrations largely neglected the levees following the New Orleans floods of 1965.

What happened under the Bush Administration was that racial neo-liberalism at home, and the imperialist adventurism of the neo-cons abroad, reached their apogee in massive tax cuts favouring the richest Americans. Hurricane Katrina brought home to Americans the dangers, to their own security and self-image, of this explosive brew. One senses a growing loss of confidence in the ability of the political class and institutions to safeguard the things that matter in the daily lives of most ordinary people. Out of the floodwaters of New Orleans and the Gulf Coast as a whole, Katrina's political wrath has started something. The doctrinaire argument for small government may have lost its seductions. At stake is the future political direction of this powerful country, home to many people in the African Diaspora, that has yet to fulfil promises to its marginalized peoples, or the rest of the world, seeking peace and human security, development and democracy, rather than militarism and imperial bullying.

September 4, 2005.

Chapter 5

The Postcolonial Uprising in France

For more than two weeks in November 2005, fires raged across France, burning public buildings and private businesses, torching schools and police stations, incinerating cars and the conceits of this proud post-imperial country. They have exposed the contradictions and conflicts hidden deep in French suburbs – its *banlieues* – and in the national psyche of racial and religious intolerance. The state is shaken; so is the society, and both are desperately seeking to explain and contain the crisis, shifting from one characterization to another, one strategy to another. It is not just the *banlieues* that are in flames, but the very idea, the cherished ideal, of French republicanism. Memories of May 1968 are mined for illuminating parallels. But this civil unrest appears different. It is more widespread and more destructive than the student revolt of '68, with an unfamiliar cast of actors. The social crisis triggered by the riots evokes another history; the history of empire and anti-colonial struggle. This was a postcolonial uprising: Africa striking back.

The flames were sparked by the deaths of two youths of Tunisian and Mauritanian descent on October 27 – electrocuted in a power substation while fleeing the police. From the shabby, segregated suburbs of the Paris visitors and the smart classes never see, the explosion quickly spread to hundreds of cities and towns. By the end of the first two weeks more than 7,000 vehicles and dozens of buildings had been destroyed, more than 2,500 people had been arrested, thousands of police patrolled the restive streets, and a state of emergency had been declared. Not even elegant, tourist Paris could escape as police ringed the Eiffel Tower and Champs-Élysées, nervous Western governments issued travel warnings. Already reeling from losing both the referendum on the EU constitution and the Paris bid for the 2012 Olympic Games, the French establishment panicked. President Jacques Chirac disappeared from public view leaving the stage to his two aspiring successors: the second generation immigrant interior minister, Nicolas Sarkozy, with his inflammatory disdainful rhetoric and vague noises about 'positive discrimination', and the unelected aristocratic prime minister, Dominique de Villepin, with his more diplomatic utterances and promises of more jobs and services.

The street battles, or riots as the media prefers to call them, have helped frame the uprising as a duel between the repressive police and rampaging youths. The French police are notorious for their harsh treatment of youths of African descent, which grew even harsher after the current rightwing government launched its so-called zero-tolerance anti-crime campaign as it lurched further to the right in an effort to appeal to an electorate increasingly frightened by globalization, 'Islamic' terrorism, and 'foreigners.' The political class had been alarmed by the 2002 presidential elections. In the first round, and for the first time in the forty-four-year history of the Fifth Republic, a neo-fascist party came second by winning nearly one-fifth of the votes cast and beating the socialists. The National Front's leader, Jean-Marie Le Pen, proceeded to run against Chirac in the runoff elections. This is the political context in which the uprising took place – a country that had been drifting steadily more rightwards since the 1990s.

It should not be surprising that the lead in the uprising has been taken by the youth because it is they who have borne the brunt of social and economic marginalization. Children of African immigrants have been trapped in a vortex of high unemployment, impoverishment, discrimination, disaffection, hopelessness, and isolation. They are an alienated Diaspora for whom the dualities of culture and citizenship are particularly agonizing in a society that refuses to recognize difference in principle or uphold equality in practice for its minorities. Their weapons of struggle are as characteristically French as they are reminiscent of anti-colonial protest – streets are their theatres of demonstration; violent demonstrations. And they resort to the old technologies of firebombs for attack and the new technologies of mobile phones and the Internet to organize.

Quite predictable attempts have been made by ideologues of the regime and other frightened observers to dismiss the riots as rampages orchestrated by criminal gangs, or to see behind them the sinister hand of Islamic extremism. It is a fact, of course, that a large proportion of the

African population in France, the largest in Europe, is Muslim, but this is not a religious rebellion. Indeed, the Islamic Organization of France, an umbrella group that was only allowed to form as late as 2003, issued a fatwa prohibiting Muslims from taking part in the riots, and many Muslims have participated in multireligious and multicultural marches against the violence. Nor is the uprising simply a youth rebellion, against rigid social immobility and righteous secular indifference. It is about the failure of the French model of citizenship and integration rooted in the history of French colonialism and its unresolved aftermath.

The uprising of 2005 is the latest in a cycle of postcolonial revolts in France. Riots broke out at regular intervals in the 1990s in various French cities, among them the riots in Lyon in 1991 and 1996, in Paris in 1997 and 2000, and in Toulouse in 1998. The summer of 1983 was also rocked by riots in minority neighbourhoods in several cities. But 2005 saw the most widespread civil unrest in recent French history. The declaration of a state of emergency shows the gravity of the crisis confronting the French state and society. It is instructive to note that the law used to proclaim curfews was originally drawn up in 1955 to suppress unrest in Algeria during its liberation war, and was last used in 1984 to quell turmoil in the French Pacific Ocean territory of New Caledonia. The archives of colonial repression have been reopened. It is a poignant, tragic irony that African youths seeking freedom in postcolonial France are being suppressed with the same law used to fight their grandparents or parents who sought freedom in colonial Africa.

France has always prided itself on its revolutionary and republican traditions that gave the world the slogans of liberté, égalité, fraternité (freedom, equality, brotherhood). Missing was the idea of diversity. National myths tell us much about both the virtues and the vices that are embedded in a country's collective consciousness. French republicanism claims to recognize individuals, not groups; it promotes an integration model of common citizenship unmarked by ethnic, racial or religious differences. It allows no room for identity politics. For immigrants it means that their cultural origin, religious orientation, and racial classification is ignored at best and actively suppressed at worst. There is no place for multiculturalism in this model, nor for affirmative action for historically oppressed groups. There are no institutional or ideological mechanisms to acknowledge and address social inequality that more often than not is based on group identities, however tenuous or stereotypical, imagined or real, rather than on the content of an individual's character. Denying the social existence of races and racism in a multicultural society is a foolish fetish at best and a dangerous dogma at worst.

In a country where it is even illegal to collect or keep statistics on race or religion (so that the population of 'blacks' or Muslims in France is based on educated guesses rather than official census data), there can be no systematic attempt to rescue ethnic minorities from their economic and political ghettoes. Not surprisingly, despite having the largest non-European immigrant population in Europe; outside of sports and entertainment, the number of minorities in senior positions in the public and private sectors is miniscule even by the abysmal standards of much of Europe. Minorities are largely invisible on television and are virtually invisible in parliament, but they make up more than half of the prison population. An integration model that claims colour-blindness in a society where overt racism is rampant offers a recipe for institutionalized racism. Denied recognition and redress through the law or state institutions, Muslims, for example, are forced to focus their energies on such highly symbolic issues as the right for girls to wear the *hijāb* in public schools. Predictably, Diasporan Africans vent their frustration and anger in periodic riots. The 2005 uprising only came as a surprise to those whose heads are buried deep in the fantasies of French republicanism.

According to France's patriotic defenders, the French tradition of racial tolerance was born during the Enlightenment, articulated in the work of the celebrated eighteenth-century thinkers – the *philosophes* – then sanctified by the revolution that ended the *ancien régime* and paved the way for democracy and republicanism. This, the story goes, marked the rise of the free citizen. Yet revolutionary France was no less beholden to African slavery than its Western European rivals, and later no less imperialist and colonialist. The *philosophes* were advancing doctrines of biological racism while at the same time proclaiming human equality. In short, negative attitudes towards Africans are as firmly embedded in French culture as elsewhere in Europe. France may be different only in the degree to which it refuses to recognize that it has a racial problem deeply rooted in its modern history.

Colonialism reinforced the contradiction at the heart of twentieth-century France and imperial Europe as a whole: the self-aggrandizing conceits of civilization wrapped in the silenced or sanitized barbarities of colonialism. Despite self-serving claims to the contrary, French colonialism was no less racist than that of the other European powers. Assimilation, the official French policy of colonial governance, was not a doctrine of racial equality, but of African inferiority; it was based on the arrogance that only those Africans who whitewashed themselves into Frenchness could be accorded full human rights and social recognition. But French colonialism was not a humanist project, so assimilation always remained confined to a tiny elite: the bulk of the masses in the colonies were 'subjects' prey to the abuses of forced labour and summary justice. But even the *evolues* – the assimilated elites – discovered the cruel fiction of assimilation when they went to France, where they were recast as despised natives, or mimic men from an inferior race. They channelled their anger and angst into negritude, the poetry and philosophy of African self-affirmation.

Assimilation failed in colonial Africa; the uprising shows it has failed in postcolonial France. French colonialism denied separate identities to the colonies claiming they were an indissoluble part of France; postcolonial France denies multicultural identities to its citizens from the former colonies claiming they are individuals. Such are the depths of denial that a law was recently passed making it mandatory for school textbooks to put a positive spin on French colonialism, to extol its benevolence and the benefits it bestowed on Africa, including North Africa – a blatant attempt to wish away the Algerian war (which was not officially called a 'war' until 1999), the bloodiest war of African liberation. That war killed more than a million people and tore France itself apart and ushered in the Fourth Republic.

It was colonialism that gave France its African Diaspora that it has had so much difficulty in integrating and whose uprising we have been witnessing. The first African migrants in modern times to arrive in France came following the conquest of Algeria in 1830. The African presence grew during the First World War when tens of thousands of workers and troops were recruited from the French African Empire, some of whom remained in France after the war. African migration increased during and after the Second World War as more workers were recruited. After the war some demobilized soldiers settled as France sought to marshal cheap labour from its colonies for economic reconstruction and the postwar economic boom, which lasted until the early 1970s. In the 1960s there was widespread confidence in the country's capacity to absorb and integrate the newcomers.

But the consensus for an open immigration regime crumbled as both the postwar boom and the self-assured Gaullist era came to an end at the turn of the 1970s. Ironically, as immigration restrictions were imposed African migrants in France increasingly took citizenship and brought their families, thereby not only swelling their numbers but also turning themselves from temporary immigrants into a permanent Diaspora. Immigration played an important role in the rise of the right-wing National Front whose electoral victories, in turn, facilitated the drift towards conservatism in French politics even during Francois Mitterrand's ostensibly socialist era in the 1980s and early 1990s. Immigration became embroiled in concerns about French national identity being decomposed and reconfigured by the forces of European integration and globalization at a time of slow economic growth and massive cultural transformation.

In the 1980s and 1990s African migrations continued, indeed accelerated, when African economies suffered the consequences of structural adjustment programmes and several Francophone countries such as Algeria and Côte d'Ivoire erupted into bloody civil wars, especially since, like in the other industrialized countries, it reflected important shifts in the composition of previous flows dominated by fellow Europeans and Christians. These ensured that African immigrants would be at the centre of painful debates about French identity and citizenship. The imposition of tighter immigration controls was accompanied by increased regulation of labour markets; regulation which limited the rights of established immigrants.

Clearly, this latest uprising, led by the African Diaspora, is rooted in the complex and combustible mix of French colonial history and rampant racism which has diluted the promise of citizenship for the African French and exposed them to discriminatory policing, harassment and violence. A collapsing economy caused high rates of unemployment among especially black male youths and the rigid model of integration fails to recognize that France is no longer a monolithic country, if it ever was, but a multicultural country which is home to millions of Africans.

It is easy to see the uprising as a reflection of the peculiar failings of French state and society, as chauvinistic commentators have been wont to. For some it is payback time, for French commentators are often quick to point fingers when other Western countries get into trouble with their restive minorities. But the problem goes beyond the special rigidities of the French republican model of integration. Other models have been no less fraught with problems and eruptions of racial violence and social conflict – not the multicultural model of Britain and the United States, nor the discredited guest-worker model of Germany. At heart is the fundamental inability of Euro-American societies to accept racial difference without stigmatizing it, without marginalizing, alienating, and criminalizing racial or religious minority populations. Neither colour-blind equality nor lip-service multiculturalism can succeed as long as each retains the stubborn virus of social and spatial apartheid. What is needed is genuine equality.

There can be little doubt that the economic and social alienation of minorities would diminish and integration would accelerate with full employment, and the provision of better housing, social services and community policing. But the rioters who have been burning French cities and perhaps burying the cherished myths of the French nation are seeking more than access to jobs and less harassment from the police. They are demanding mutual respect, social recognition, and the full rights of citizenship based on equality of opportunity and power. If the Europe of African and Asian Diasporas remains separate, unequal, and unhappy the other Europe will pay high material, political, social, and moral costs.

The French uprising is not only a wakeup call to France but to the whole of Europe. Notwithstanding periodic fluctuations in the labour market, Europe's aging and diminishing population needs workers from the global South. For their part, African countries will continue to export their labour and cultures to the global North, including Europe. This is not new. Africans have been exporting their labour and cultures since the grim days of the Atlantic Slave Trade. What is new is that Africans in Europe are demanding recognition as Europeans, African Europeans. It is a moment made possible by the conjunctures of postcolonialism and globalization. If the underlying fury behind the fires is not addressed, sooner or later there will be other uprisings in France and in other

European countries as well. This is the opportunity France must seize from the flames of rage sweeping across the country from the *banlieues* of Paris.

November 15, 2005.

Chapter 6

Madam President: The Changing Gender Dynamics of African Politics

At last, in January 2006, postcolonial Africa got its first democratically elected female president. Ms Ellen Johnson-Sirleaf was inaugurated at a colourful and moving open-air ceremony to the pounding of drums instead of the traditional twenty-one gun salute. The war-torn capital of Monrovia had been vigorously spruced up for the historic occasion that was attended by several African leaders, foreign dignitaries and thousands of women from across the continent. This was an extraordinary moment for the troubled beacon of liberty, Liberia, founded by African Americans in 1847 and Africa's oldest modern republic. It was also significant for Africa at large, long ruled and ruined by men, as well as for women everywhere who are still largely invisible in the corridors and councils of power. Ms Johnson-Sirleaf triumphed in a fraught election that pitted her against twenty-one other candidates in the initial round of voting, then against a popular international soccer star in the final round; a contest in which gender, generation, class, and rural-urban interests jostled for primacy. She joins an exclusive masculine club of global political leaders as one of only six female presidents (the others are in Finland, Ireland, Latvia, the Philippines, and Chile). Thus her inauguration is an occasion for celebration but also censure: it is a milestone memorable for its rarity; a testimony to the limited advances women have made in rising to the highest levels of national and international politics.

The global record of women's political representation among heads of state and government is dismal. During the twentieth century there were only forty-six female presidents and prime ministers worldwide, many of whom served for short periods, sometimes less than a year. Three were from Africa: Elizabeth Domitien (1975-76) of the Central African

Republic; Sylvie Kinigi of Burundi; and Agathe Uwilingiyimana of Rwanda. The last two served as prime ministers in 1993-94. The former was ousted in a coup and the latter murdered in the genocide of 1994. There are still countries that have never had a woman as cabinet minister (e.g. Saudi Arabia), or have had only one (e.g. Burma), or have only had deputy ministers (e.g. Laos).

But even in those countries with more than a handful of female ministers, the latter tend to serve in stereotypical 'social welfare' type departments, such as education, health, or women's and youth affairs, rather than in such prestigious and powerful ministries as finance, defence, and foreign affairs. In this regard, South Africa is one of the few admirable exceptions. At the time of writing, its cabinet is one of the most representative in the world. There are thirteen female and fifteen male ministers and ten female and eleven male deputy ministers. Many of the female ministers are in crucial ministries including foreign affairs, agriculture, home affairs, minerals and energy, and public service and administration. Only Sweden can claim a better record in terms of gender parity: at the time of writing, there are eleven ministers of each gender.

Clearly, political representation for women remains dreadful over much of the world. It is nearly three decades since the United Nations General Assembly adopted the Convention on the Elimination of All forms of Discrimination Against Women. The UN has sponsored four World Conferences on Women (Mexico in 1975, Copenhagen in 1980, Nairobi in 1985, and Beijing in 1995), not to mention the numerous regional and international conventions attended by governments with great fanfare.

While from a global perspective women's access to public office is very disappointing, we should not lose sight of the progress that has been made in some countries in recent years, largely in response to the growth of the women's movement and intensified struggles for democratization. How do African countries fare and compare with the rest of the world? Is the resounding victory of Ms Johnson-Sirleaf (she won about three-fifths of the vote) and her election as President of Liberia an isolated incident or indicative of larger shifts in the gender dynamics and culture of African politics?

It is, of course, dangerous to generalize about Africa, a continent of astonishing diversity. It is more prudent to argue that women's participation in politics and public life among Africa's fifty-four countries has made uneven progress. It is also quite evident that the African region as a whole compares favourably with other world regions. This is amply borne out in a comprehensive research report, *Gender Equality: Striving for Justice in an Unequal World*, published last year by the United Nations Research Institute for Social Development and which assesses progress in gender equality across the globe since the Beijing Conference.[1] In the interests of full disclosure, let me point out that I was one of nine members of the advisory group for the project, which commissioned dozens of background papers by researchers all over the world. The report focuses on four major themes: first, macroeconomics, well-being and gender equality; second, women, work and social policy; third, women in politics and public life; and fourth, gender, armed conflict and the search for peace. It needs to be read by all those interested in the question of women's rights and gender equality, one of humanity's most enduring dilemmas and, in my view, one of the central challenges of our age.

The economic policies of neo-liberalism and the political pressures of democratization have influenced the complex and sometimes contra-dictory changes in the position and participation of women in various spheres of social life since the 1990s. The data shows that since Beijing there have been notable increases in female participation rates in primary and to a smaller extent in secondary and tertiary education, in the paid labour force and migration flows, and in public institutions including elected assemblies. Also, fertility rates have fallen and awareness of women's sexual and reproductive rights has risen.

But statistical increases have not necessarily been translated into social improvements, nor has awareness entailed redress. In many parts of the world, including Africa, female enrolments have risen as public funding for, and the quality of, education have declined; the 'feminization' of the labour force has been accompanied by deteriorating terms and conditions of work; and advances in fertility and reproductive health have spawned sex ratio imbalances through 'son preference' that have led to millions of 'missing women' – estimated in 2005 at 101.3 million or 5.7 per cent of the women's population worldwide (80 per cent of these 'missing women' are accounted for by China and India; Africa accounts for an estimated 7 per cent). There is overwhelming evidence that the costs of the privatization of services caused by economic liberalization and deregulation have been disproportionately borne by women. The case for addressing the gender implications of macroeconomic policy and incorporating gender in any national project of sustainable development is imperative, indeed.

The needs and interests of women will remain peripheral until there is a critical mass of women in leadership positions and decision-making processes. African women have a long and proud history of involvement in politics and public life. There are numerous examples of powerful women and illustrious leaders going back to Pharaonic times. Historians have conclusively established that during colonial times, women were centrally involved in anti-colonial struggles from demonstrations to riots and armed combat, as protestors, agitators, organizers, and guerrillas. In fact, in the societies that waged protracted armed liberation struggles and adopted radical programmes of socialist transformation, there were great expectations for gender equality and women's emancipation and empowerment after independence. The extent to which attempts were made by the post-independence states to realize these expectations of course varied. However, the record was, on the whole, quite unsatisfactory.

In the 1970s and 1980s African women's movements crystallized around the rather confined ideological parameters of the women-in-development projects (later renamed women-and-development and gender-and-development) and what some have called state feminism— state sponsored women's organizations including the notorious 'First Ladies' Clubs. As the struggles for democracy—the second independence— gathered momentum from the late 1980s and early 1990s, women's movements redirected their energies and sought to recapture their autonomy, attract new adherents and allies, and adopt new agendas. They became integral to Africa's reinvigorated civil society, central to the social movements spearheading the pro-democracy struggles that shook Africa's 'big men' from their delusions of grandeur. Through their own activities and strategic alliances with other social movements, both old and new, women activists pushed for constitutional and electoral changes (such as the '50/50' campaign). These movements were part of a growing transnational feminist networking and activism, bolstered by globalization and the new information and communication technologies, which helped establish a new global normative and discursive architecture for women's rights and human rights.

President Johnson-Sirleaf is a product of this historic wave. By 2005, there were only sixteen countries worldwide whose proportion of women in their national assemblies had reached 30 per cent, often regarded as the benchmark for 'critical mass'. The world average was 16 per cent, up from 9 per cent in 1995. Three of the sixteen countries were from Africa, led by Rwanda (48.8 per cent), Mozambique (30 per cent), and South Africa (30 per cent). Rwanda boasted the highest level of women's national assembly representation in the world, followed by Sweden (45.3 per cent). No Asian country made it onto the list.

The differences in numbers of women in elected assemblies do not seem to correlate with levels of economic or educational development or national income, as shown by the fact that female representation is quite low in the wealthy and 'Western' United States – in fact much lower than in many poor and 'traditional' African countries.

Quite intriguing is the fact that most of the African countries with relatively high levels of women's participation in national politics have emerged from protracted wars of liberation or civil wars or both. The explanation might lie in the propensity of war to destroy not only physical assets but also pre-existing social relations including patriarchal structures, even if only for the duration of the conflict. They may also mobilize the political consciences of women who during the conflict may have been perpetrators and victims of violence, or peacemakers. Moreover, many conflagrations, such as the Rwanda genocide, decimate a disproportionate number of men, thereby reinforcing the transformations in gender relations engendered by the conflict in the first place. As is well known, the horrendous destruction of the Second World War, including the removal of millions of men from the civilian economy into the military machine that pulverized them, played a major role in transforming women's roles in society and galvanizing the women's movement in North America and Western Europe.

More difficult to decipher is the role of culture, especially ethnicity and religion, both of which have acquired a new political salience since the 1990s. Ethnic and faith-based movements have demonstrated a powerful ability to challenge authoritarian states and misguided modernization, thereby helping to open up political space. Often armed with ample material and moral resources they have been able to mobilize women, to provide them with the comforts of cultural respect and belonging and the possibilities of security, support and even leadership. But more often than not these movements promote chauvinisms and fundamentalisms that militate against the advancement of women's rights. Not surprisingly, in much of the world including Africa, women's representation in politics and public life has been relatively low in countries or regions under the sway of radical religious movements such as political Islam, Christian fundamentalism, or Hindu nationalism.

Less contentious is the role played by the nature of the electoral system and the commitment of the political class, which in turn reflects the social weight of the women's movement. Countries with electoral systems based on proportional representation rather than plurality/majority systems, often combined with affirmative action based on quotas or reserved seats and constituencies for women candidates, tend to enjoy the highest levels of women's representation. South Africa boasts one of the world's most vibrant women's movements and civil societies. At the continental level, the African Union appears determined to advance gender equality through affirmative action: two out of five members from national parliaments seconded to the Pan-African Parliament have to be women, and half of the members of the ten-person African Union Commission are women. This is the first regional organization in the world to undertake such affirmative action gender policies as part of a comprehensive programme to promote democracy, good governance, and human rights.

There is no guarantee of course that high levels of women's representation leads to legislative policies favourable to women's concerns, for female politicians are no less susceptible than their male counterparts to the divisive pressures of party affiliation, class, ethnicity, religion, and ideology – but without it the possibilities are considerably diminished. Some evidence from countries with a critical mass of women's representation indicates that women legislators do indeed tend to promote bills and policies favourable to women's rights and interests. The prospects for this are heightened if the ideological climate and the institutional capacity for introducing and implementing gender equity legislation are conducive and where women politicians and their political parties enjoy close links with the women's movements, and especially if feminist groups within these movements are strong.

Above all, narrowing the gender gap in political representation is, in itself, fundamental to expanding democracy. In this regards, the world's two 'largest democracies', India and the United States, exhibit serious democratic deficits in so far as both have some of the lowest levels of women's representation in national public office. The same can be said of Africa's most populous country, Nigeria, where women comprise less than six per cent of the national assembly. On this account, President Johnson-Sirleaf's election represents a limited victory for women in Liberia, only eight of whom (12.5 per cent) were elected to the sixty-four member House of Representatives and five (16.7 per cent) to the Senate.

From a gender perspective, then, in terms of women's presence and performance in national politics and public office, the road to democracy in Africa and much of the world has a long way to go. The fact that President Johnson-Sirleaf will be the lone woman among her fellow presidents at African summits of heads of state is not a cause for celebration, even as we salute her achievement as a trail blazer. For the sake of African democracy and development we can only hope 'Mama Ellen', as Liberians fondly call her, will not remain the sole elected woman president for long.

January 16, 2006.

Reference

1   United Nations Research Institute for Social development. *Gender Equality: Striving for Justice in an Unequal World.* Geneva: UNRISD, 2005.

Chapter 7

Cartoons as Weapons of Mass Provocation

In September 2005 an international crisis erupted when cartoons caricaturing the Prophet Muhammad as a terrorist were published in the Danish newspaper *Jyllands Posten*, and subsequently reprinted in some Western countries. There were mass demonstrations in several countries around the world, trade boycotts, withdrawals of ambassadors, travel advisories, dismissals and resignations of journalists, and sporadic outbreaks of violence. These resulted in several deaths, the burning of Danish flags and embassies, and soured the already strained communal relations within Europe and between the West and the Muslim world more generally. To some this is a harbinger of the much-trumpeted clash of civilizations, a sign of the deep chasm between the West and Islam, between tolerant modernity and fanatical medievalism, or between a malicious secular culture and a maligned spiritual community. The outrage and controversy over the cartoons do point to widespread anger and anguish in the Muslim world and intolerance and indifference in the Western world. But this was not a clash of civilizations, rather a clash of fundamentalisms.

The religious dimensions of the conflict have encouraged many to see it as a contest of implacably opposed values, a battle of rights: the right to freedom of expression and the right to freedom of religion; the right to offend and the obligation to tolerate offence – with moral equivalence for both provocation and response. This forced discourse of binaries is false. Publishers of the notorious, and to Muslims sacrilegious, cartoons and their rightwing defenders invoke freedom of speech as their unassailable defence. They treat it as an absolute value, the bedrock of Western democracy, under threat from 'radical Islamists' and other purveyors of the backward and bankrupt ideologies of political correctness. Even some of their liberal and leftwing critics concede the sanctity of this value, and only blame the publishers for their poor judgement and bad taste. In reality, the issue is neither about freedom of speech nor indiscretion. It is about political provocation, the assertion of the supremacy of white Europe at home and abroad. It is an attempt to put Europe's numerous 'others' in their place, especially Muslims, historically so close to Europe and now so intimate a part of Europe, whose growing presence challenges European fantasies of cultural purity and whose ancestral lands continue to be ravaged by Euro-American imperialism.

Freedom of speech is an important value, but in this crisis its value is largely ideological, deliberately deployed as a weapon of cultural aggression. There can be little question that by attacking the Prophet Muhammad the cartoons were intended to inflict the most egregious hurt to Muslims, to inflame not to inform. Claims that caricatures of the sacred are normal and even healthy in a secular society ignore the fact that there are secular taboos for journalists in the Western mainstream which the media dare not cross for fear of breaking the law or popular conventions. Indeed, we are told the Danish newspaper that published these scurrilous anti-Islamic cartoons turned down cartoons lampooning Jesus Christ because readers would find them offensive. And the embattled editor of the paper was sent on indefinite leave when he announced his intention, in a gratuitous effort to test Western commitment to freedom of speech, to republish Holocaust-denying cartoons provided by the rightwing Iranian newspaper, *Hamshari*.

In many cases the discourse tends to suspend the rights concerned from the historical, material and institutional contexts in which they are enjoyed. No less important to remember is the fact that the Western mainstream media is a business – a huge business – subject more to the imperatives of profit-making than advancing informed public discourse; and more attuned to the interests of the powerful and pandering to popular prejudices than to the voices of the disenfranchised and disaffected who tend to be concentrated among racial, ethnic or religious minorities and the poor. Freedom of expression in the West would indeed be a good thing if it actually existed for all regardless of corporate status, class position, national location, ethnic or racial identity, or ideological orientation.

Nowhere in the Western world is the right to the freedom of expression absolute in principle, let alone in practice. It is a relative right contingent on other rights, circumscribed by context. Rights entail responsibilities: the two are interwoven with threads of mutuality that are neither eternal nor universal but constantly negotiated in ongoing and often painful conversations within and between societies. The mainstream Western media routinely avoids publishing or showing overtly racist, anti-Semitic, or pornographic materials. In fact, in many of these countries there are laws against hate speech, anti-Semitism, and child pornography, as well as libel and defamation. The laws and conventions that seek to protect such groups are reactions to the sordid past of racism and genocide, the barbarities of slavery, colonization, and the holocaust that are as much a part of Western heritage as all the positive values the West claims exclusively for itself.

Given these realities, the publication of such obnoxious Orientalist cartoons appears to most Muslims as hypocritical at best, at worst threatening. It is a reflection of the rising tide of racism and xenophobia in Europe. It is the face of a new anti-Semitism, this time directed not against Jews, but against Muslims, who in the European imaginary are often racialized as Arabs. The cartoons draw on a long and hideous history of anti-Jewish cartoons that facilitated the dehumanization of Jews before the Holocaust. This connection between the old and new breed of European anti-Semitism is usually not drawn by defenders of the newspaper's right to publish the Islamophobic cartoons. Nor do those who seek to respond by recycling fascist cartoons against Jews and the Holocaust seem to appreciate their collusion in a new form of European anti-Semitism. There can be little doubt that the publication and republication of the cartoons has occurred in a context of growing anti-Muslim religious and racial bigotry in Denmark and across Europe.

It started as a localized crisis in a country becoming increasingly unsure of its national identity and intolerant of its minorities. The decision by the rightwing *Jyllands-Posten* to publish the cartoons was in character with the increasingly conservative political climate in which a strongly anti-immigrant and anti-Islamic party, the Danish People's Party, had become part of the parliamentary coalition. In a cruel expose of the national myth of Nordic tolerance and egalitarian-ism, Prime Minister Anders Fogh Rasmussen passed draconian laws relating to the marriage, citizenship, religious and language rights of immigrants. In Denmark, the initial reaction to the anger caused by the cartoons was quite revealing. The Prime Minister refused to meet the European Committee for Honouring the Prophet, or a group of diplomats from eleven Islamic countries protesting the publication of the cartoons, and, as Danish Muslims took to the streets, many Danes expressed incomprehension at what the fuss was all about. It is only when the furore of protests broke out in the Middle East and elsewhere that the gravity of the crisis hit the Danish government. Suddenly, Denmark was faced with its worst post-war crisis, its image in the Muslim world in tatters. The Prime Minister and the newspaper offered belated apologies for causing offense but not for the original decision to publish.

By then, the cartoons had appeared in several mostly rightwing papers in various European countries, ostensibly in solidarity with the Danish paper and the Danish people in their efforts to protect freedom of expression and European values under assault from 'Islamic radicalism'. Interestingly, the mainstream British media largely refrained from joining the jingoist chorus, as did the mainstream American media, perhaps reflecting their greater multicultural sensitivities, as some commentators claimed, or for fear of bearing the brunt of Arab and Muslim fury already inflamed by their wanton invasion of Iraq.

Solidarity in the escalating crisis cut both ways. Many Muslims in Europe and in other parts of the world found common cause: the cartoons seemed to reinforce the collective vilification of their religion that had been escalating since the end of the Cold War, and particularly following the terrorist attacks of 9/11. In effect, the cartoon controversy brought together two crises: the profound feelings of fear and insecurity among marginalized European Muslims; and the simmering anger and vulnerability felt by Muslims in the Middle East who had witnessed the invasion of Afghanistan and Iraq, and were hearing ominous threats against Iran. In fact, memories of Western aggression in the Middle East went much deeper and concerned the humiliation of colonial invasion, occupation and pillage, and in recent decades the enduring tragedy of the Palestinians. It is not surprising, therefore, that the epicentre of Muslim outrage over the cartoons was in the Middle East, a region historically at the receiving end of Western terror.

Networks of transnational communication, both old and new, facilitated the fusion of these two crises. When the Danish Muslim groups were refused audience by the Danish Prime Minister they began lobbying, first through diplomats from Arab governments, then, after these were also snubbed, directly to governments and organizations in the Muslim world. Danish Muslims made the rounds of North African and Middle Eastern capitals with a forty-three-page dossier of the cartoons and other documents, and before long the outrage began to build steam, fanned by the region's new and spirited media, and sanctified by key bodies such as the Organization of the Islamic Conference and the Islamic Educational, Scientific and Cultural Organization. The turning point came when Saudi Arabia withdrew its ambassador from Denmark, a move that was soon followed by Libya and Iran.

The besieged Muslim Diaspora in Denmark and Europe was reaching out to Islamic homelands in search of support and solace. This is of course not new – Diasporas have always sought the protective mantle of homelands. But historically it is the European Diasporas that could rely on their homelands to send gunboats to protect them from restive natives. In fact, the annals of colonization in Asia and Africa are replete with wars of salvation for beleaguered settlers, although they were often characterized as crusades to save benighted 'primitive' souls, and spread civilization. Now, Diasporas from the global South can more easily summon support from their homelands, although conventional military support remains inconceivable. Clearly, the revolution in telecommunications and travel offers these Diasporas new opportunities to be transnational, to connect with each other across countries and continents, and to maintain links between their old and new homelands in ways that were unimaginable a generation ago. This is what accounts for the rapidity and intensity of many global protests today, including the outbreak of the demonstrations over the cartoons. Cyberspace is the new medium of mass mobilization, a powerful mechanism to organize and express protest. The waves of demonstrations over the cartoons were driven as much by emails, blogs, cell phones and text messages as they were by satellite television, radio, coffeehouse talk, and street rumours.

As in all such conflicts, the manipulative machinations of governments are not hard to find. All governments whose populations are involved have sought to cynically exploit the conflict to their own immediate advantage, to appear resolute in the face of foreign agitation, to defend the values that their societies supposedly cherish. Authoritarian and unpopular Middle Eastern governments sought to burnish their Islamic credentials while containing the spread of political Islam and pressure to democratize. Militarist and hypocritical Western governments have tried to use the crisis to reinforce the case for the 'War on Terror' and to isolate radical Islamic states and movements in the region that have put up the most resistance to their imperial project. This suggests that the forces most invested in the conflict over the cartoons are militants on both sides, the unrepentant ideologues of Western imperialism and political Islam. Both should be seen as political fundamentalists. Both are committed to a clash of civilizations that the vast majority of Westerners, many of whom are Muslim, and Muslims, many of whom are Westerners, are fundamentally opposed to.

In so far as Islam and the West are not mutually exclusive cultural and historical entities, but social spaces where various peoples and cultures mix together, the conflict over the cartoons cannot be seen in grand civilizational or purely religious terms. Even if protagonists on both sides might prefer to talk in the calcified language of ancient hatreds, this is a quintessentially contemporary protest over specifically current conditions – the challenges of forging common citizenship and fostering cosmopolitan values in an increasingly transnational world. It is about how European Muslims and non-Muslims can live together in peace and equality, and by extension how the Western world and the Muslim world can co-exist amicably. The two worlds have more that binds than separates them, going all the way back to their very foundations. Modern Europe is inconceivable without the contributions of Islam, and the modern Muslim world is inconceivable without the West, for better or worse. The webs of mutuality are so deep that even the fundamentalisms on both sides reproduce each other. Lest we forget, contemporary political Islam is an utterly modern phenomenon, created out of forces constituted and reproduced by the historic and ongoing intersections of the mixed worlds of the West and Islam. Western imperialism bred political Islam, and political Islam provides a convenient scapegoat for contemporary Western imperialism. In short, the histories of the two phenomena are tragically interconnected.

It is encouraging that the vast majority of Muslim leaders and organizations encouraged peaceful and dignified protests, although the sensationalist Western media has focused on the few violent incidents in order to justify their loud denunciations of that violence. The challenge for Muslims when confronted with the cultural assaults represented by the cartoons is to find ways of defending their religious faith and their political rights, both in the West and in the Muslim world, that advance the cause of human freedom and decency as well as open-ended intercultural and interreligious conversation and civility based on the fact that ultimately we all share a common humanity in all our splendid diversities. For people in the West committed to similar values, they must resist the temptation to support aggression, wherever it may lurk, including in their own countries, by hiding behind the veil of freedom of speech.

February 11, 2006.

Chapter 8

Angelina Jolie Discovers Africa

After spending a long day visiting a couple of towns several hours drive from Caracas, Venezuela, I settled into my hotel room and switched on the TV to catch up on the day`s news. I would have loved to watch the local channels but my Spanish is virtually non-existent, so I opted for the venerable BBC, whose pronouncements on the day`s events are always delivered with the self-assured authority of a country that until recently ruled an empire. It was the usual litany of carnage in Iraq: the American victims, as always, were named – this time two soldiers – the Iraqis remained faceless numbers, characterized as mindlessly violent terrorists sometimes grudgingly called insurgents, but never dignified as nationalists fighting against foreign occupation. Also depressingly familiar was the story of an Israeli missile that apparently missed its intended target and killed Palestinian children playing on a street in Gaza; one more incitement in the endless conflagration in that unfortunate land of competing nationalisms and victimhood and international cynicism. Only the story about Charles Taylor, the notorious former Liberian president, arriving in Holland, his face downcast with humiliation, represented a fresh script; well, almost, for the commentary soon reverted to style about Africa`s proverbial genius for producing dictators. The original triumph of Taylor`s arrest several months ago was, in my view, now tarnished by Africa`s inability to try one of its most murderous dictators somewhere on the continent where his heinous crimes were committed. But this is to digress. It was Angelina Jolie who really caught my attention.

It is not that I am enamoured by Ms Jolie as such, whose beauty and acting talents I cannot vouch for – having a different persuasion of female beauty as defined by my wife, of course, and having only seen one of her movies in which she acted with the inimitable Denzel Washington. But she graces so many gossip magazines that she is hard to ignore. So I knew she had snatched Brad Pitt from another reportedly beautiful and talented but less vivacious actress, Jennifer Aniston. I also knew Ms Jolie had given birth to her daughter with Mr Pitt in Namibia, or rather Africa, as the geographically challenged media kept repeating. Individual nationhood is apparently an attribute reserved for those living in the blessed parts of the world, sometimes referred to, in bigoted company, as the 'civilized' countries, or less offensively as 'Western', or as the 'global North' in the polite bureaucratic language beloved by the United Nations and politically correct cosmopolitans. It is certainly not for the benighted masses of the 'Third World', or the 'global South', or let's just say Africa, the sorriest place of them all. This is also to digress. It was what Angelina Jolie said that got me riled up.

Predictably, she said it on CNN, to which I had switched for a little comparative sampling of the day's news coverage. I gave up on CNN for its unabashed jingoism during the first Gulf war and hardly watch it unless I am travelling and there are no alternatives, or I want to catch some 'breaking news'. In the United States itself, the CNN that people see is different from CNN International beamed to foreigners abroad, some see it as 'liberal'; and it might be, in comparison to the proudly rightwing Fox News, but that only confirms how narrow the political space occupied by the mainstream American media is. But this is another digression.

Asked by a fawning Anderson Cooper, who made his fame for his emotional coverage of Hurricane Katrina, to explain why Africa had so many refugees – the interview was to mark world refugee day – why so many conflicts, problems, the great actress opined: 'They are a tribal people, you know,' and added for good measure that they had just recently emerged from 'our' colonial rule, but they were trying, really trying; there were pockets of good news in Africa.

Tribes, tribal, tribalism: harsh, contemptuous, condemnatory words that evoke nothing but primitivism, savagery, backwardness; primeval communities and conflicts. Words that are reserved for Africans and those 'indigenous' peoples of Asia and South America that are periodically discovered in remote jungles by National Geographic or featured on Discovery Channel. But supposedly modern Africa still has tribes everywhere; a whole continent is held to ransom by the primordial pathologies of ancient tribal life. Africans are stamped with tribal marks from birth to death. Tribes are beyond history, they have always existed in Africa, and they explain everything: the poverty, the civil conflicts, the corruption, and the dictatorships. European colonialism failed to stamp out the tribe, postcolonial modernization withers in its glare and contemporary democratization has no chance in its suffocating shadows.

Whereas in other parts of the world issues and conflicts may be named as political, economic, social, environmental, class, gender, religious, or cultural, in Africa they are almost invariably about tribes and tribalism. Nobody of course talks of tribes in Europe, except in reference to the remote past; of contemporary tribal conflicts in the Balkans, or Northern Ireland, or Spain. European groupings are defined as 'nations' and their conflicts accorded specific characteristics, combatants, causes, closures, and consequences. In Asia people are often divided into ethnic or communal groups and their conflicts termed ethnic or communal. Nations for Europe, ethnicities for Asia, tribes for Africa – a sliding scale of civilizational status and possibilities.

So Ms Jolie was in good company despite her limited education and obvious ignorance of African histories, cultures, societies, polities, and economies. She was merely repeating received Western wisdom on Africa. Tribes may have been banished from Africanist academic discourse, but they are alive and well in the Western mass media. Yet even in Academia the term sneaks in from time to time, as I discovered at a party when I first arrived at Pennsylvania State University. The head of a certain otherwise progressive department, who had done a little comparative research in Africa, asked me: 'What tribe are you from?' My shocked gasp said it all, but just to make sure that she got the message, I sent her an email explaining the politics of the term 'tribe' to which she responded with a grovelling apology. But many a Western journalist assigned to the African beat defends the use of the term 'tribe', on the grounds that Africans themselves use it. One student of mine returned from a four week study in Kenya feeling empowered to use the term and challenged my allegedly Western liberal antipathy to it. There was a time when African 'groupings' were called 'nations', before the rise of colonial racism and academic anthropology, and in my language the term used for African and European groupings is the same, '*mtundu*'. 'Tribe' is an acquired term of colonial self-denigration, not self-definition, let alone self-empowerment.

Western reporting of Africa rests on four well-tested mantras: selectivity, sensationalism, stereotyping and special vocabulary. The media has to select the stories deemed worth reporting from the innumerable events that occur across the world every day. This is particularly so for television where in between advertising there is not much time for in-depth coverage of news. It is even more imperative when covering foreign lands. The more sensational a story the more likely it is to be selected – the man bites dog syndrome; bad stories make good news. To hold the attention span of the notoriously fickle audience it is important to present foreign news in an easily digestible form. That is where stereotypes come in, they aid consumption of the news, and they become the news. They obviate the need for context, for complexity, for thinking. When it comes to Africa everyone knows that it is very hot there, and the animals are great but the people are poor and always dying from endless wars, incurable diseases, biblical famines, and bad governments. In short, they are a tribal people, you know. Tribe is the magical, special word that captures everything that happens in Africa and that American audiences need to know about Africa.

At heart, Euroamerican reporting of Africa is less about Africa itself than the Euroamerican imaginary of global hegemony and white racial supremacy. Negative stories of Africa were historically manufactured and deployed as weapons to beat the African Diaspora into submission during slavery and after emancipation and integration, to remind them of the primitive ancestral home from which they had been blissfully liberated. As racism, or rather racial rhetoric, gradually lost respectability in the civil rights and post-civil rights era, Africa bashing became a safe substitute for America's obsessive denigration of black people. It often works: some African Americans are ashamed of Africa, and many American conservatives admonish those who complain about American racism to go back to Africa.

Angelina Jolie's ill-conceived comments were only extraordinary in their ordinariness. Anderson Cooper beamed in agreement and proceeded to praise her role as a goodwill ambassador for the UNHCR, for caring so much for these people, the wretched of the earth. How did she do it, he wondered, how did she feel? Jolie's self-indulgent but carefully modulated answers were interspersed with Cooper's own empathy for African suffering: his discovery of Africa during the recent famine in Niger. In both their cases these African 'awakenings' were duly sanctified by a dying child; for Anderson in a makeshift hospital in Niger and for Jolie in a refugee camp in Sierra Leone. Each of them was horribly, indelibly, marked by these deaths. The two of them commiserated on the burden of owning these children's memories, for they possessed the only available pictures of these unfortunate children, a still photograph for Jolie and video footage for Anderson. These technical reproductions trumped any memories the children's own poverty-stricken parents might have, and I was struck by this appropriation of memory to Africans' inability to own their own past.

Africa has had an incredible capacity to attract saviours from Euroamerica, since the time of the Atlantic slave trade. Missionaries came in droves at the dawn of colonialism; indeed they blessed colonial conquest as a civilizing mission, an opportunity to Christianize these pagan peoples, notwithstanding the fact that Christianity has an older history in some parts of Africa than in Europe. The most conscientious of them would occasionally attack colonial excesses but not the infinite virtues of the colonial project itself. Africa's modern missionaries come in all shapes and sizes: some come in impeccable business suits with attaché cases full of policy advice for development; others are self-styled statesmen who delight in shoring up their humanitarian credentials even as they wage brutal wars elsewhere; and then there are the assortment of stars and would-be stars from the world of entertainment – music, cinema, television, and even sports. Why do they come like vultures in search of misery, of death?

It is of course difficult to fathom the motivations for such a motley crew. Some undoubtedly find solace in philanthropy, in giving away some of their wealth. In the United States especially philanthropy is a vast enterprise involving individuals, corporations, and all types of institutions giving America's ruthless capitalism a benevolent face. Others may be looking to revive stalled careers: Bob Geldof achieved more fame with his 'band aid' initiatives than any records he may have released; or to add a gloss of humanitarian gravitas to a successful career as an entertainer in the manner of U2's Bono. God, gold, glory, gratification, all these are powerful motivations that obviously inspire different stars differently.

The rules for the discoverers of Africa have not changed much since the days of the Scottish missionary, David Livingstone and the American adventurer and accomplice of King Leopold of Belgium, the murderous plunderer of the Congo – they of the famous encounter in darkest Africa: `Dr. Livingstone, I presume`. The only difference now is that there is television. Television rules, it is insatiable for images; powerful images that can be beamed out on prime time news or infomercials, giving audio-visual proof that the star was actually there, that she really saw those people, even touched them, felt their pain. Great care is therefore made to frame the photo-op. Contemporary discoverers of Africa need to follow ten simple, but crucial, rules.

First, always show that the benighted place is forbiddingly remote, that the roads are bad if they can be called roads at all. Feign a breakdown of your otherwise hardy four-by-four to add authenticity to your strenuous efforts to reach these hapless people. Second, *en route* to and from the site, usually a camp, show wild animals galloping or resting in the distance so that the audience back home know for sure that you were truly in Africa. Third, when being interviewed, assume that nobody, least of all the natives themselves, really knew or understood before you arrived the gravity of whatever crisis or tragedy is the flavour of the moment. Fourth, at all costs avoid interviewing local experts and relief workers, but if you must have locals, it is recommended that it be some pot-bellied government official who denies there is a crisis and mumbles in such a thick accent that captions are required for the audience back home. Fifth, always appear in front of scrawny, pot-bellied children with running noses and flies licking their famished faces, hug one if possible or at the very least hold their bony hands.

Sixth, avoid being pictured in the presence of African men, the source of all these troubles and scourges, but include a few white men from any relief agency, and of course lots of listless African women squatting under leafless trees and staring emptily into the air, or chewing some stick waiting patiently for something to happen. Seventh, choose the landscape carefully; avoid lush vegetation, or anything that looks like fresh water; dry, dusty and arid areas make the best background for they add ecological drama to Africa's eternal woes. Eighth, dress modestly, no bling, preferably in safari garb adorned with a hat, it could be a helmet even, especially for those of delicate Caucasian skin for protection from the sweltering tropical sun. Ninth, never, ever show the five-star hotel to which you happily return after the cameras are shut off now immensely enriched by your hard earned humanitarian credentials.

Tenth, when you get back home try to get on Oprah, or if that fails one of the TV magazine shows that love stars with a heart, or you could go on David Letterman or Jay Leno and show that you still have a sense of humour despite all the agony you have seen; audiences want humanitarian stars with a light touch, not priestly agony and admonition written all over their faces – they want to feel good about themselves, not guilty about the tribulations of tribes and tribal tragedies in far away Africa.

You know you have really arrived as a global African humanitarian when you can talk to President Bush and Prime Minister Blair, the champions of democracy, development and peace (don't believe those malicious stories about Iraq and Afghanistan and Guantanamo) in the same week or in the same venue, say, the G8 Summit, and if you can call yourself, or better still you can be called by your admiring fans, Mr Africa and Ms Africa without blushing. And yes, the ability to organize a global event, a rock concert is best for the depoliticized youth who love music and dancing, without the hapless Africans themselves, is the ultimate accolade; it's godly in its intoxicating possibilities to liberate Africa from itself.

Rumour has it that other fading celebrities are considering giving birth in Namibia, er, Africa. If true, Ms Jolie has carried the discovery of Africa to a whole new level. Hollywood has found a new script. Forget Tarzan. Star reality TV is so much better. The academic in me only wishes these stars would hire African tutors to teach them a thing or two about Africa's complexities before they open their mouths. But that would spoil the Discover Africa Show, which is primarily about entertainment not education, exoticism not enlightenment.

June 21, 2006.

Chapter 9

The Arab-Israeli Conflict Revisited: Back to the Madness of War

In 1976, for one of my final year undergraduate research papers at the University of Malawi, I wrote on the Arab-Israeli conflict. I found the subject challenging, complicated, and contentious: there was no agreement in the literature as to the causes, courses, or consequences of the conflict. There still isn't, as rockets and bombs rain regularly on innocent civilians in Gaza, Lebanon, and northern Israel in the latest cycle of war and violence which has tormented and scarred the region since the Second World War. Commentators compete to apportion blame and offer solutions, cynical Western governments connive with Israel as ineffectual UN diplomats scramble for ceasefires, and the streets of the Arab world seethe with mounting rage as their emasculated and autocratic regimes dither shamelessly. Meanwhile, the rest of the world watches with horror and dismay the destructive barbarism that constantly refills the reservoirs of hatred, creating new memories of vengeance, and nurturing new generations of enemies eager for the fire next time, for a replay of the convulsion, whatever the immediate spark.

What is striking thirty years on is how much the world has changed but how little the Arab-Israeli conflict has changed. That is the tragedy: every so often the world is forced to confront the same violence and carnage with renewed outrage. Yet nothing is done to address the fundamental causes of the conflict and so it returns like a nightmare with predictable regularity. Thirty years ago when I wrote my undergraduate paper, a month away from my twenty-first birthday and a couple of months from my graduation, the Cold War seemed eternal and Apartheid intractable (the Soweto Uprising was two months away and Nelson Mandela in the twelfth of his twenty-seven years of incarceration). Both have since disappeared, but the

Arab-Israeli conflict remains, a cruel mockery of the ideals of freedom and democracy, human rights and social justice, civility and moral decency the so-called international community claims to cherish so much.

In April 1976, the second G7 Summit was two months away. Most of the seven leaders who attended it are now dead. China was under Mao Zedong, India under Indira Gandhi, Iran under the Shah, and Saddam Hussein had not yet assumed power in Iraq. In popular culture, Elvis was still rocking, the first hip hop music recordings had not yet been released, and the Montreal Summer Olympics, which were boycotted by African countries over the organizers' refusal to bar New Zealand for its rugby team's tour of Apartheid South Africa, were around the corner. Microsoft was a year old but personal computers had not yet been invented, and the birth of the Internet was nearly a decade away, as were cellular networks for mobile phones. In academia, Marxism was still popular and terms like neo-liberalism, structural adjustment, globalization, postmodernism and postcoloniality were largely unknown; it would be two years before Edward Said's canonical book *Orientalism* appeared. The world population was a little over four billion, two billion less than today, the 'population bomb' struck environmental terror as global warming currently does, and the number of sovereign states was far less than the present figure of 202.

To be sure the Middle East, an explosive region of complex and shifting alliances and interests, has seen leaders and movements come and go over the same period. Israel was then under Yitzhak Rabin, who had taken over from Golda Meir in 1974, and the PLO led by Yasser Arafat, expelled from Jordan and now based in Lebanon, was admitted that year to full membership of the Arab League. The Lebanese Civil War had started the year before and would drag on for another fourteen years, with all its multifarious influences on the disputed region, including Israeli aggression and occupation, and the birth of both Hezbollah and, later, Hamas. Hezbollah was incubated in the brutal aftermath of the 1982 Israeli invasion of Lebanon primarily to resist the subsequent eighteen-year Israeli occupation of southern Lebanon, while Hamas was eleven years away from its creation during the First Intifadah engendered by the traumas of the Israeli occupation of the Palestinian territories, and Al-Qaeda had yet to emerge from the American-supported mujahideen cobbled together to fight the Soviet Invasion of Afghanistan in the 1980s.

But little else has changed, not the bitter Palestinian-Israeli contestation over land, the imbalance of power between the two nations, the apparent intractability of the conflict that has defied numerous UN resolutions including the very resolution that created Israel in 1948. Today, Israel holds the record for breaching and ignoring UN resolutions. Between 1953 and 1995 more than eighty UN resolutions were passed against Israel's actions in the occupied territories and the neighbouring countries, especially Lebanon, notwithstanding US vetoes, 34 of them between 1972 and 2001. Clearly, in the eyes of the international community, as reflected in the UN, Israel is the aggressor, the occupying power, the serial invader. Of course, to Israel's supporters this is evidence of the UN's irredeemable anti-Israeli bias; yet the same people eagerly invoke and demand the implementation of the UN resolution calling for the disbandment of militias – read Hezbollah – in Lebanon.

More is at stake than empty UN resolutions. Almost invariably when the simmering conflict erupts into open warfare, it is the Palestinians, Lebanese and other Arabs who pay a much higher price than the Israelis in the destruction of lives and property. There is no equivalence, in Israel, of the 17,000 civilians slaughtered by Israeli artillery and aerial bombardments of Lebanon in 1982, or of the Second Intifada of 2000-2004 that killed an estimated 3,223 Palestinians and pulverized an entire country's infrastructure – airports, roads, bridges, power stations, and communication towers, not to mention housing, offices, factories and schools – as we have witnessed in recent days in Lebanon and Gaza. The tide of misery and anger is horrific. Human rights activists accuse Israel of war crimes, of violating international humanitarian law.

To Israel and its backers in the international community – read Euroamerica – this asymmetry is essential for Israel's very survival in a sea of enemies committed to its destruction. To its antagonists, it is the very cause of Israel's insecurity, the inspiration for its opponents, especially the occupied victims, to resort to the age-old tactics of asymmetrical war – guerrilla warfare. Certainly, after more than sixty years of conflict and military victories the region is no closer to peace. Indeed, the more massive and lethal Israel's military rage and retribution, the more its opponents have resorted to guerrilla warfare and mass resistance. These have sapped the Israeli army and dented its reputation for invincibility, forcing it to withdraw from some of the occupied territories – South

Lebanon in 2000 and Gaza in 2005 – and further emboldening new generations of resistance, which in turn prompt Israel to return to an escalating spiral of cataclysmic violence. Already this war has lasted longer than Israeli generals thought it would and proved more deadly for Israel as Hezbollah has proved a more ferocious foe.

The current war is instructive in this regard: it is not a conventional war between Israel and the Arab states as in 1948, 1956, 1967 and 1973, but a war between the Israeli state and two nationalist and social movements—Hamas and Hezbollah—that retain relative autonomy from the apparatuses of their nation's fragile states. Each movement that Israel has tried to destroy, the leaders it has assassinated, have been replaced, in due course, by more implacable foes, more widespread resistance, and less international support outside Euroamerica. Even some of its defenders are troubled by Israel's lack of restraint, comparing it unfavourably to Spain's handling of the Basque nationalists, Britain and the IRA, and India's response to the most recent terrorist attack that killed more than 200 people. As several commentators sympathetic to Israel recognize, Hezbollah can't be wiped out because the 40 per cent Lebanese Shiites it represents can't be wiped out. Indeed, a failed Lebanon would turn the country into Israel's Iraq, as Lebanon was Israel's Vietnam in the 1980s and 1990s. The long history of the Arab-Israeli conflict underscores the dangers of simplistic attribution of provocation or prescriptions for its ultimate resolution. The outbreak of the current war is often blamed on the capture of Israeli soldiers, one by Hamas and two by Hezbollah. But how about Israeli seizures of Palestinian and Lebanese prisoners, rocket attacks and assassinations in the days, weeks, months, years prior to that? It is also said that Hamas and Hezbollah are merely puppets fighting proxy wars for Syria and Iran to distract attention from their regional and nuclear ambitions. Ignored is the fact that these movements are braided into the tapestry of their nation's politics and rooted in the history of anti-Israeli resistance. On the other hand, US and European support for Israel is seen as based on higher principles. And where once the Arab-Israeli conflict was embroiled in the ideological rivalries of the Cold War, now it is reframed in the rhetoric of the war on terror. It is pitted as a struggle between the forces of democracy and darkness, never mind the attempted destruction of the only genuinely democratically elected governments in the Arab world, in Gaza and Lebanon.

There can be little doubt that the current war reflects interlocking local, regional, and international factors and dynamics and both sides have much to prove to their constituencies, the new Israel civilian leaders to demonstrate their military mettle, and Hamas and Hezbollah to burnish their revolutionary credentials. The hypocrisies and double standards in the current war are glaring indeed in their mendacity: even the right to self-defence is accorded unequally between the combatants and the humanity of the victims is given different values. The US Secretary of State, Condoleezza Rice, talks glibly of this as the 'birth pangs of a new Middle East' and refuses to countenance an immediate ceasefire before a 'sustainable ceasefire' has been imposed on the vanquished, until the 'terrorists' that threaten Israel have been rooted out, until the region's political map has been redrawn in the image of a Pax-Americana that has failed spectacularly in Iraq.

The rhetoric eerily echoes what I used to hear in the Malawi of my undergraduate days. After the 1973 Arab-Israeli war Malawi was one of only a handful of African countries that refused to break diplomatic relations with Israel. President Banda, a ruthless dictator, self-styled church elder and an avowed enemy of Arabs and Islam, used many of the arguments presented in the American media today, especially among neo-conservative and Christian fundamentalists. My undergraduate essay was written under this cloud of pro-Israeli and anti-Arab sentiment. Banda may have been a self-declared dictator and George W. Bush a self-proclaimed champion of democracy, but their stance on the Arab-Israeli conflict was remarkably similar. Banda was, of course, leader of a small, impoverished nation with no capacity to influence the course of the Arab-Israeli conflict, while Bush was the leader of the world's remaining superpower whose actions and inactions, sins of commission and omission, have enormous consequences. Even by the dismal standards of US foreign policy the nature of Bush's intervention after years of diplomatic neglect was staggering in its short-sightedness.

The Bush administration did not invent the Arab-Israeli conflict, but it has shaped the trajectory of the conflict. In a fundamental sense, Europe created the Middle East conflict and the United States has sustained it. Euroamerican support has been critical both to Israel's survival and its insecurity. Euroamerica facilitated the establishment of Israel and ensures its isolation in the Middle East. Israel is a creation of Euroamerica in two crucial ways: the Jewish 'Question' and anti-Semitism, the pervasive racism that engendered centuries of Jewish persecution culminating in the Holocaust that was an invention of Christian Europe. Through the founding of the state of Israel Europe tried to atone for its historic crimes against European Jews and to export the Jewish 'problem' outside Europe. During the early twentieth century Britain seriously discussed establishing a Jewish homeland in Uganda or Argentina. The Zionist movement preferred Biblical Palestine, which was already attracting waves of Jewish immigrants fleeing Europe's deepening anti-Semitism and looming holocaust.

The Arab-Israeli conflict is clearly not rooted in ancient hatreds between Jews and Arabs, as religious fundamentalists and ideologues prefer to cast it, nor is it part of centuries-old problems in the Middle East, as some observers contend. Rather, it is a very modern conflict spawned by European imperialism. Israel was a product of the colonial project that founded European settler states in the Americas, Australia and parts of Africa. The crucial difference is that it was the last settler colonial state to be established in the twentieth century, at the very time that decolonization was gathering momentum. Thus, Israel enjoyed neither the demographic nor ideological advantages of the much older settler societies of the Americas and Australia, where the indigenous peoples were decimated into inconsequence. Instead, Israel resembled the eventually doomed settler states of colonial Africa. Apartheid South Africa understood this and sought common cause with Israel, and in the African political imaginary the two were tied together.

The sordid histories of anti-Semitism and imperial racism colluded in the creation of Israel at the very time that both had been discredited by the Second World War and were threatened by the rising tide of anti-colonial nationalism poised to triumph in the post-war era. This is to suggest that Arab opposition to the creation of the state of Israel was no less fortuitous or foolish than Euroamerican support for Israel. Both are products of imperial racism and anti-colonial nationalism. It is not simply European guilt over the Holocaust or the fabled prowess of the Jewish lobby in the United States,[1] the most successful and powerful settler society of the modern era, that explains unflinching Western support for Israel, but the imperatives of imperial racism that implicitly dehumanize and devalue 'natives', denying them equal claims with settlers to nationhood and dignity.

Intimidation, indifference, denigration and humiliation are indispensable to the arsenal of imperial racism, whose ideological superstructure has to be bolstered by an infrastructure of overwhelming physical force. Similarly, popular Arab support for the Palestinians and Lebanese cannot be attributed solely to the gullibility of the masses and their susceptibility to the Islamic fundamentalists and so-called terrorists. Euroamerica and its outposts have great difficulty in understanding that they have no monopoly on nationalism, that the poor and the weak love themselves and their lands, histories and identities as much as the wealthy and the powerful.

That is why decolonization in Africa and Asia happened despite overwhelming odds and the imperial fantasies of interminable regimes duly backed by military might and terror. Africa has vast graveyards of settler colonialism to show: Algeria, Angola, Kenya, Mozambique, Namibia, South Africa, and Zimbabwe. Asia has its killings fields that hobbled and humbled the world's largest military machines: Vietnam, Iraq, and Afghanistan. Imperial racism might triumph for a while, even for generations, but in the end modern history is on the side of the nationalism of the dispossessed – unless the latter were decimated beyond recovery right at the beginning of the colonial settler project. There is a lesson in all this for Israel.

In the clash of nationalisms in the Middle East, the history of Apartheid South Africa might hold salutary lessons. Historical parallels are of course never exact. South Africa, to-date one of Africa's most successful post-settler states (for a disastrous case see Zimbabwe), offers the closest model for resolving the Arab-Israeli conflict. Apartheid South Africa was not militarily vanquished but became increasingly incapacitated both militarily and politically – an isolated 'skunk of the world' as President Mandela put it in his inaugural address, notwithstanding the racist support of its Western allies based on the delusion that it was an outpost of Western civilization in darkest Africa.

The Afrikaner architects of Apartheid had tried a two-state solution, the division of the country into a wealthy white South Africa and a patchwork of dependent poverty-stricken Bantustans. It didn't work. By the late 1980s, the forces of settler and indigenous nationalisms were, after generations of combat, in a stalemate and forced into a historic compromise which was neither inevitable nor miraculous, but willed by vision and statesmanship, embodied most poignantly in the dignified and defiant humanity of Nelson Mandela. Here were two peoples at a critical juncture daring to think big, dream peace, and transcend the righteousness of both victor and victim, to reconcile and rebuild the rainbow nation bequeathed them by settler colonialism and its protracted resistance.

Perhaps the solution for Palestine and Israel, then, is not a two-state solution, but a one-state solution: the creation of a secular, democratic, non-racial nation. At the very least the peoples of the region have no choice but to coexist, they cannot bomb each other into oblivion. A negotiated settlement is a historical necessity – unilateralism has no future. Whatever solution is eventually devised, it is essential to recognize that at heart the Palestinian-Israeli conundrum represents the crisis of settler colonialism. Failure to do so will ensure repeated outbreaks of destructive wars, which will continue to universalize Europe's anti-Semitism and engender more desperate and retrogressive forms of Arab nationalism. That cannot be in the long-term interests of either the Israelis or Palestinians, let alone regional or global peace and security.

This blood-drenched land that has given the world so much, from religion to scholarship to oil, deserves principled support from the rest of the world for a truly comprehensive peace settlement. To bring closure to one of the saddest legacies of European imperialism and geopolitical miscalculations of the postwar era the cycle of addictive hate and violence must be broken. An immediate and long-lasting ceasefire is the crucial first step.

July 27, 2006.

Reference

1   See the controversial book by John J. Mearsheimer and Stephen M. Walt, *The Israel Loby and US Foreign Policy* (New York: Farrar, Straus, and Giroux, 2007). For a history of the heated controversy over the book and the original essay published in the *London Review of Books* (March 23, 2006) on which it was based see Wikipedia at http://en.wikipedia.org/wiki/The_Israel_Lobby_and_U.S._Foreign_Policy. Mahmood Mamdani further develops the thesis of settler solidarity in US imperial policies in the Middle East in *Good Muslim, Bad Muslim: America, the Cold War, and the Roots of Terror* (New York: Three Leaves Press, 2005).

Chapter 10

Clouds Over the Rainbow Nation:
South Africa and the Zuma Saga

Coming from a Southern African country, South Africa has always held a special fascination for me. I grew up listening to its music, reading its magazines, and hearing of relatives who had gone to work in its mines, factories and farms, some of whom never returned. I read and listened to harrowing tales of the racist brutalities of the Apartheid regime as well as exhilarating accounts of heroic liberation struggles. I came of age at the very moment of the Soweto student uprising in 1976, an event that marked a critical watershed in the struggle for Black liberation. Since 1994, when the skunks of segregation and Apartheid, and the inhuman cruelty of the minority racist government, were defeated, I have been visiting South Africa regularly. Within the last ten months I have gone there four times to attend conferences, give lectures, and for a holiday. And over the past two and a half decades, I have intermittently taught South African history, on its own or as part of Southern African history or African history in general.

The Zuma saga started when he was implicated and later charged in a corruption case involving an arms deal. Last June President Mbeki relieved him of his duties as the country's deputy president – although he retained his position as deputy president of the ruling African National Congress – when his financial adviser, businessman Schabir Shaik, was found guilty and sentenced to fifteen years in prison and the presiding judge described the relationship between the two as 'generally corrupt'. As if that was not enough, towards the end of last year, Mr Zuma was accused of rape by a 31-year-old HIV-positive family friend. This incendiary mix of political and moral corruption seemed lethal and some began writing his political obituary. In reality, whatever might be the eventual fate of Mr Zuma's legal troubles and presidential ambitions, the drama over his rape and corruption trials opened the simmering tensions underlying South Africa's seemingly successful transition from Apartheid to a new democracy. Beneath the surface lay the unfinished business of the historic struggles for social transformation.

There is much to admire about the new South Africa. Over the years following the demise of Apartheid its economy has been growing more rapidly than it had done in the previous three or four decades, fuelling the explosive growth of a black middle class that now numbers more than two million, or 10 per cent of the adult black population, which is rising by 50 per cent a year. Its politics are played out within an admirable constitutional framework characterized by vibrant freedoms, separation of powers, official levels of gender representation almost unmatched anywhere in the world, and a civil society noisily protective of its struggle for autonomy. South Africa's diverse society is becoming more educated, more multicultural, more secure in its Africanness, and more confident of the future as it looks forward to the World Cup in 2010 - the first African country to host the world's greatest sporting spectacle. Moreover, post-Apartheid South Africa has staked out, if not established, its leadership not only within Africa but in the larger global South as well. But the structural scars of the past linger: three centuries of unrelenting racist violence and racial capitalism have left enduring legacies that manifest themselves in some of the sharpest socioeconomic inequalities in the world: relatively high rates of crime and sexual violence; persistent rural poverty and squalor for the urban poor; palpable racial and ethnic tensions; rising xenophobia against African immigrants; growing impatience with the rate of change; and the cruel ravages of the scourge of our times – HIV/AIDS.

Much of Africa has traversed this road before, the early exhilaration of independence, the immediate post-independence years of relatively rapid economic growth, the expansion of the middle classes, followed by creeping disillusionment with the fruits of Uhuru by the once beloved but increasingly neglected masses. Of course the two moments – the decolonization and independence of many African countries in the 1950s and 1960s and the demise of Apartheid and construction of the new South Africa in the 1990s and 2000s – vary in their historical legacies and possible trajectories. But the myth of South African exceptionalism must be resisted; it is a conceit fuelled by the fantasies of racist and Apartheid South Africa – that it was an extension of 'Western civilization' on the 'dark continent' – and encouraged by European imperialists who saw it as a European outpost in need of their material, moral and political protection.

This is to suggest that South Africa has much to learn, more in fact from the rest of Africa than from Euroamerica, as far as its future may be concerned. And these lessons are quite sobering. We have all witnessed the destructive power of populist demagoguery. The Zuma phenomenon smacks of a desperate populist search for a more workable future. The frenzied support Mr Zuma has received reflects the creeping disaffection by important social constituencies with the post-Apartheid dispensation, and a struggle not only for the soul of the ANC but the country as a whole. It is a conjuncture pregnant with pitfalls and possibilities, as South Africa struggles to settle into the normalcy of ordinary politics. The transition from the revered President Nelson Mandela to President Thabo Mbeki will prove less momentous for South Africa's future than the transition to Mbeki's successor.

To most outside observers, and for many South Africans, the possibility of an alleged rapist ascending to the nation's highest office is frightful in its implications. To be sure, Mr Zuma was cleared of the rape charges, although he admitted to having unprotected sex with the daughter of a comrade who had grown up regarding him as an uncle. His defence was staggering in its mendacity: the distorted and sexist invocation of Zulu culture; the infamous shower as protection from HIV coming from the mouth of a former head of the National AIDs Council; the martial masquerades outside the courtroom by his supporters; and their gratuitous attacks on the accuser.

Why would such a deeply flawed politician, one so tainted by moral decrepitude and accused of corruption, be seen by his supporters as worthy of the leadership of Africa's major power? The answers surely go beyond Mr Zuma's own personal ambition, although he has rejected entreaties from some of South Africa's most renowned figures, including the Emeritus Archbishop Desmond Tutu, to withdraw voluntarily from national politics and save the country the supreme agony and embarrassment of a possible Zuma presidency. Why is he able to garner such fierce support from so many different constituencies within South Africa?

Why is Zuma is greeted with rapturous welcome at various forums especially in parts of his regional homeland, KwaZulu Natal, and among the militant wings of the ANC alliance including the ANC Youth League, the South African Communist Party, and the labour federation, COSATU?

The Zuma saga is embedded in and reflects at least four interrelated dynamics in South Africa's contemporary political economy and sociocultural terrain: fractures within the ANC alliance, and, the centrifugal forces of class, ethnicity, and gender. The cracks within the ANC coalition are born out of the overwhelming dominance of the ANC, the difficult transition from the commandist politics of a liberation movement, the accumulative imperatives of the new black bourgeoisie, and the challenges of transformation. The ANC increased its electoral standing from 62.6 per cent in 1994 to 66.4 per cent in 1999 and to 69.7 per cent in 2004. The leading opposition parties, the Inkatha Freedom Party and the Democratic Alliance, pose little credible challenge to ANC hegemony: one is circumscribed by its ethnicity and the other by its whiteness. Under such circumstances it is not surprising that political contestation within the ANC alliance assumes such salience.

The growing dissension within the ANC over the presidential succession reflects pressures for political transparency, for the open contestation of the ANC's top leadership position. And yet, the apparent current beneficiary of that drive is the very person whose rise to prominence is owed largely to his appointment as deputy president in 1999. Much is made of the different personal predispositions of Mbeki, often seen as intellectual and technocratic, standing aloof from the masses, and Zuma, who is notable for his populist touch and mass appeal, but there is little indication of concrete policy differences between them. The speculation that a Zuma presidency would adopt more radical, leftist economic policies remains just that.

The dynamics of class politics have shifted as the rigid boundaries enforced by Apartheid have eroded and social differentiation among the black population has accelerated. Not only is the black middle class growing rapidly as noted earlier, so is the black bourgeoisie through the Black Economic Empowerment (BEE), a project elsewhere called Africanization or indigenization, that was central to nationalist movements and the postcolonial state across the continent. Indeed, in

South Africa's own history, the Apartheid state was critical to the expansion of the Afrikaner bourgeoisie and the middle class. As the class dimensions of black identity and politics have become more pronounced, ideological fault lines within the ANC, both old and new, are rekindled and reframed.

One of the main lines of contestation is between those enamoured by the reformist policies of neo-liberalism and African accumulation and those still wedded to the old radical dreams of structural transformation and the empowerment of working people. The latter are concentrated in the South African Communist Party and COSATU, and increasingly also in the ANC Youth League. But their electoral prowess is uncertain were they to break into a separate party and so they invest their hopes in Mr Zuma, one of the architects of ANC government policies and whose expensive lifestyle brought him the grief of corruption charges. Thus, as Mr Zuma lost his credibility among the elites and middle classes, his leftist credentials were burnished and his political star rose among those anxious for a new political direction in the post-Mbeki era. Such cynicism is the stuff that populism is made of; it is a telling commentary on the ideological impasse facing the South African left.

The Zuma saga also has an ethnic dimension. During the days of the liberation struggle many progressive South Africans were inclined to believe that a post-Apartheid South Africa would be saved from 'tribalism', a spectre duly discredited by Apartheid, diluted by urbanization, and dented by nationalism. But the seductive power of ethnicity was wished away too soon. As the sun set over white political power, the inclusive blackness forged by Black Consciousness began to fracture for 'Coloureds', 'Indians', and 'Africans'. For the latter, 'moral' ethnicity, i.e. ethnicity as complex web of social obligations and belonging became increasingly tinged with 'political' ethnicity – 'tribalism' – the competitive mobilization of 'ethnic contenders' for access to the material and social resources controlled and mediated by the state.

Xhosa domination in the ANC – presidents Mandela and Mbeki are both Xhosas – is an issue of contention in parts of the country, however reluctant the party might be to talk about it openly. In fact, Mr Zuma owed his rise to ethnic brokerage, to the crucial role he played, as a provincial Zulu ANC leader, in ending political violence in KwaZulu Natal between the ANC and Inkatha and promoting the fortunes of the

ANC in the region. In his recent political and legal misfortunes, many of Mr Zuma's loudest supporters have come from KwaZulu Natal and articulate their support in Zulu cultural idioms. Zuma's accession also shows a troubling African political tendency for incumbent presidents to choose lacklustre deputies in the mistaken belief that they will not pose an immediate threat to their own position. A classic example is President Jomo Kenyatta choosing Mr Daniel arap Moi, an ill-educated politician who proceeded to misrule Kenya for twenty-four years.

No less glaring are the gender dimensions of the Zuma saga. For a country that boasts some of the most progressive policies on gender equality in the world, Mr Zuma's rape trial was a disheartening display of the enduring perils of misogyny in a nation that has one of the world's highest rates of sexual violence. As many South African women activists noted during the course of the trial and after the verdict, the grotesque abuses hurled at the complainant by Mr Zuma's supporters, including women, represented a serious setback for women's rights and empowerment. The fact that the ANC Youth League and COSATU held a pro-Zuma demonstration during the trial and vilified members of the People Opposing Women Abuse was a troubling sign of masculinist antagonism to women's progress in ostensibly radical movements. The reportedly lukewarm reception the then deputy president, Ms Phumuzile Mlambo-Ngcuka, reportedly received at these organizations' forums, as compared to the ecstatic reception accorded to Mr Zuma, cannot be unrelated to gender politics. Although the apparent failure of most of the leading lights in the women's movement – including the ANC Women's League – to manifest loud and visible support for her is equally troubling.

There is little doubt the presidential succession will aggravate the increasingly fractious politics of the ruling party and its underpinning class, ethnic, and gender contestations. In such a context, in the absence of clear ideological choices given the current hegemony of the ANC, personalities loom unusually large and populism becomes a substitute for principled leadership. The emotionally charged politics of populism, the hunger for a charismatic leader, the cynical appeal to the working and poor masses accompanied by stifling webs of clientism, have been damaging features of many a postcolonial state in Africa. Mr Zuma bears all the hallmarks of Africa's notorious 'Big Men', the patriarchal, 'charismatic', populist leaders that have ruled with impunity and done so much damage to Africa's prospects. The last fifty years have taught us the harsh lessons of bad leadership; quality of leadership is fundamental to our nations' prospects for development, democracy, and self-determination, the age-old goals of African nationalism for which so many people sacrificed their lives.

When Mr Zuma was dismissed as deputy president much of Africa and the world were impressed that South Africa was serious about stemming the scourge of corruption. When he was acquitted of the rape charges, and his corruption case struck off the roll, it confirmed that the legal rights of an accused leader could be respected. But at stake is not legality; it is leadership. South Africa has a vibrant civil society and democratic culture, born out of decades of struggle against Apartheid, and embodied in vigorous associational life, independent institutions, and the media that may yet ensure political reason will prevail, or that might even limit the damage of a Zuma presidency.

Some of the very forces that facilitate populism may undermine it: the power of business; the search for alternatives by labour; the dynamism of the women's movement. And the ANC itself has a long and distinguished history of rising to new challenges.

One can only hope that all these players will save their beloved country from a discredited populist leader. Otherwise they will go down a well-trodden path in Africa's postcolonial history: the spectre of morally bankrupt and bad leadership. But this time they will not be able to claim they did not know what they were getting themselves into.

September 19, 2006.

Chapter 11

The Power, Possibilities and Perils
of African Nationalisms

Recently, I attended an important conference at Cornell University on 'Power and Nationalism in Modern Africa' where I gave a keynote address[1]. I sought to reflect on the history of African nationalism over the last two centuries, a period in which nationalism has been one of the world's most important ideas and instruments of political leverage and legitimacy. It is clear nationalism has had a chequered career. Once valorized for its emancipatory possibilities, nationalism is now often vilified among many scholars, especially in the global North, for its alleged primordial pathologies. In the delirious discourses of globalization and the antifoundationalist anxieties of the 'posts' – post-structuralism, postmodernism and postcolonialism – both the ideology of nationalism and its institutional anchor, the nation-state, are thought to be historically outdated, relics of discredited geographies and histories, incapable of shaping the trajectory of contemporary politics, economy, and culture. How true is this for Africa?

I would like to argue against the indiscriminate dismissal of nationalism, and for the need to distinguish between the repressive nationalisms of imperialism and the progressive nationalisms of anticolonial resistance. There is a huge difference between the nationalisms that led to colonial conquest and genocide and those that sought decolonization and liberation for oppressed nations and communities; between struggles for domination and struggles for freedom; between the reactionary, reformist, or revolutionary goals of various nationalisms. Socially, nationalism has diverse ethnic and civic dynamics; spatially, territorial and transnational dimensions. Its ideological and intellectual referents and representations also vary. Nationalism is, indeed, a house of many mansions. The nation-state remains a crucial site of organization of social life, a meaningful and coherent space of struggle for empowerment for billions of people across the world who live outside the imagined freedoms of transnational flows and identities that are often celebrated by so-called cosmopolitan intellectuals.

The fashionable repudiation of nationalism, and in the case of the Afropessimists of its proudest moment for Africa – decolonization, is ultimately a disavowal of history, an act of wilful amnesia against the past and the future. Against the past because it forgets, in the case of Africa, that the progressive nationalist project, which is far from over, has always had many dimensions in terms of its composition, objectives, and tendencies. Some postcolonial critics dismiss nationalism because of its alleged mimicry and elitism; that it is derived from the master-narrative of European nationalism and colonial discourse. This echoes the charges by colonial ideologues at the height of empire that Africa had no history outside Europe, that the misguided nationalists were misleading the innocent masses, as if the masses had no material interests and imagination for a social order different from the colonial one and were not invested in elements of the nationalist project led or articulated by the elites. But it is simply self-saving mystification, if not anti-intellectualist, to claim that as intellectuals we can never understand what the subalterns say, think or desire.

The widespread notion that nationalism was invented in Europe and exported to the rest of the world is rooted in Eurocentric historiography; the teleological assumption that Europe is the original site of all modern phenomena that the rest of the world is doomed to follow, to repeat, without variation. It is a narrative that universalizes the 'West' and provincializes the 'Rest'; a historical fiction that needs to be discarded. There can be little doubt that nationalism in the colonial and postcolonial world has its own distinctive moments, motivations and meanings; its specific projects, possibilities, perils and even perversions rooted in each country's own history. Certainly, African nationalism could never be a mere replica of European nationalisms given Africa's unique historical experiences of the Atlantic Slave Trade. In any case, nationalism was not an *idea* taught to the hapless 'natives' by the colonizers, but an insurgent initiative by the colonized to recover their history and humanity. This is to caution against the tired practice of writing African history by analogy and subsuming it into European history; of confining African nationalism to the historical path already trodden by Europe.

Clearly, nationalism has never simply been an idea, or the ideological pastime of elites. It has also entailed conditions of material dispensation: concrete struggles over resources and livelihoods that are of utmost concern to the so-called masses. And it encompasses other less tangible, but no less important moral and psychic dimensions: the striving for a sense of collective wellbeing, dignity, and integrity. Thus, there are political, economic, and cultural articulations of nationalism, although it is often difficult to separate them from each other, and nationalism is often aimed as much at existential empowerment as epistemic emancipation. In short, nationalism represents a constellation of ideas, activities, movements, and organizations, in which collective consciousness and action are mobilized to construct and promote national identity, historical agency, and cultural difference for the imagined community. It may, and often does, entail acquiring and defending state power. Clearly, the vocabularies and manifestations of nationalism exhibit enormous variations from one place to another and one period to another.

African nationalism was marked by such diversity that it is difficult to define its parameters. Part of the challenge concerns the fact that African colonial states were an imperial cartographic invention that brought together disparate groups: to paraphrase Ali Mazrui in the film documentary series, *The Africans: A Triple Heritage*, colonialism separated people who had been together and brought together people who had been separate. Colonial states in Africa were, and their postcolonial successors are, almost invariably multiethnic, multilingual, and multicultural; they are often multireligious, and sometimes multiracial. Under such circumstances, what is, or what can be the basis of nationalism? The pluralism of African countries has sometimes been used to point to the artificiality of African states and to the impossibility of creating coherent nations, and is used to discredit the legitimacy or integrity of African nationalism. This charge presumes that there are some 'natural countries' with 'natural boundaries'. Such countries hardly exist anywhere in the modern world. Which nations today have existed as unchanging entities for centuries and enjoy cultural or ethnic homogeneity?

The search for nationalism in the singular is obviously unhelpful not only for Africa but for much of the world. All nationalisms are not only constructions, but they are often multiple in their manifestations. The more useful question then might be: what are the main forms of nationalism and what are their connections, contradictions, and conflicts? For African nationalism the tendency has been to conceptualize and classify nationalisms in terms of period, social composition, spatial scope, and objectives. In the first instance, distinctions are often made between colonial and postcolonial nationalisms. Second, elite and mass nationalisms are sometimes distinguished from each other. Third, differentiations are usually made between ethnic, national, regional, and Pan-African expressions of nationalism. Finally, ideological distinctions can be drawn between different secular or religious, liberal or socialist nationalisms, and so on.

To be sure, these categorizations are not mutually exclusive. It is often said, for example, that early nationalist movements were elitist before mass nationalism developed in the aftermath of the Great Depression and the Second World War. In this case, the social constructs of nationalism are given a temporal framing. In fact, I am inclined to argue that while classifications cannot be avoided because of their heuristic value, our analyses of nationalism, as of other historical phenomena, must always be attentive to the sheer messiness of social reality, the dangers of forcing complex social movements into sealed boxes. In particular we need to beware of dichotomous models. For this reason, I would propose more varied periodizations for the different nationalisms and their intersections in different parts of Africa. This is to suggest that we need to resist the temptation to homogenize developments across Africa.

Nevertheless, it is possible to argue that with all its internal complexities and diversities, African Nationalism – with a capital N – was a project that sought to achieve what Thandika Mkandawire[2] has insightfully called five historic and humanistic tasks: decolonization, nation-building, development, democracy, and regional integration. In other words, in spatial terms African nationalism was territorial, regional, as well as transnational; in social terms it was democratic and developmentalist. Even a cursory glance at the archive of African nationalism shows that since the nineteenth century African nationalists were as concerned with their specific societies as they were about Pan-Africanism and other internationalist movements and ideologies. The reasons for this lie in the experiences of imperialism and colonialism which were simultaneously localizing, regionalizing, and internationalizing. The fact that the dreams of African nationalism have yet to be fully achieved is not an argument for their irrelevance. In fact, I would submit, much of the anguish in Africa and the angst of its intelligentsia are engendered by the unfulfilled promises of Uhuru.

African nationalism was born and bred in the tumultuous maelstrom of European imperialism that began with the Atlantic Slave Trade and culminated in the continent's colonization. Both these destructive projects relied upon the dangerous fictions of civilizational difference between Africa and Europe and the negative realities of mass exploitation and oppression. From its inception, then, African nationalism had a dual face: it was a struggle *against* European rule and a struggle *for* African autonomy and reconstruction; a drive to substitute European suzerainty with African sovereignty; to recapture Africa's historical and humanistic agency. Thus African nationalism was both a revolt against Europe and a reaffirmation of Africa. It was woven out of many strands. Ignited and refuelled by local and specific grievances against colonial oppression and exploitation, it drew ideological inspiration from diverse sources, including those from Africa itself, the African Diaspora, Europe, and the colonial and ex-colonial worlds of Asia and Latin America. If the nationalist movement constituted the primary institutional vehicle for nationalist expression and struggle, decolonization was the immediate objective. Clearly, the African nationalism that was championed by the nationalist movements and intelligentsia was forward-looking, notwithstanding appeals to tradition and the African past. It sought to build new societies, to refashion precolonial and colonial cultures into a new African modernity or rather modernities.

It cannot be overemphasized how exceedingly complex were the nature and dynamics of African nationalism. To begin with, the spatial and social locus of the 'nation' imagined by the nationalists was fluid. It could entail expansive visions of Pan-African liberation and integration, territorial nation building, or the invocation of ethnic identities. Secular and religious visions also competed for ascendancy. Some nationalists wanted the future political kingdom to follow the edicts of Islam, others preferred capitalism stripped of its colonial associations, and yet others professed various socialisms – Marxist, African or Arab. These visions were often inspired as much by internal discourses as by the need to make gestures to foreign ideological friends. The 1950s and 1960s were a period of great intellectual ferment, which saw a flowering of African thought and creativity in literature, the arts, and political philosophy. Thus decolonization was also a literary movement, a cognitive protest against the imperial epistemic order and its erasures, distortions and fabrications of Africa.

Articulated and fought on many fronts, nationalism embodied self-conscious struggles by African peoples to protect and promote their interests and identities through the assumption of colonial state power. The development of nationalism of course varied from colony to colony, even in colonies under the same imperial power, depending on such factors as the way the colony had been acquired and was administered, the presence or absence of European settlers, the traditions of resistance, the social composition of the nationalist movement and its type of leadership. Anti-colonialism was expressed through political and civic organizations, including professional parties, youth organizations, welfare associations, ethnic movements, and trade unions, as well as cultural and religious organizations, such as independent churches, and peasant movements.

Each of these movements had its own spaces and strategies of struggle. Almost invariably the political and civic organizations were led by urban based elites, although their members were drawn from both urban and rural areas especially as mass political parties developed. The membership of the cultural and religious organizations was similarly broad. The peasant movements were largely confined to the rural areas, although some of their leaders and ideas might be drawn from urban elites and workers. Campaigns, petitions, demonstrations and boycotts were the weapons of choice by the political parties and civic associations. In addition to using some of these tactics, trade unions wielded the strike weapon, while the independent churches encouraged their members to disobey colonial laws, boycott colonial institutions, and sabotage colonial infrastructure. Rural peasants engaged in both individual and collective acts of protest, including flight, evasion of taxes, agricultural regulations and official markets, harassment and attacks on chiefs and their minions, and they undertook episodic holdups and rebellions to protect their land, livestock, and livelihoods.

It was often assumed in old histories of African nationalism that women were not as involved as men. Research conducted since the 1970s shows that this was clearly not the case, although women's participation varied among the movements identified above, depending on their gender dynamics. The nationalist movements contained many illustrious women leaders and activists. Women were to be found in the political parties, trade unions, independent churches, welfare associations, peasant movements, and as combatants in the liberation struggles of Algeria, Kenya, Angola, Mozambique, Guinea-Bissau, Namibia, Zimbabwe, and South Africa. There were also protests organized entirely by women. Renowned examples include the Aba Women's War of 1929 in Nigeria; the Anlu Women's Uprising in the Cameroons, and the spontaneous uprisings of South African women in the 1950s. But as might be expected given the under representation of women in the wage labour force during the colonial period, women's presence and activism was more evident in peasant than in labour movements. Similarly, as women's access to colonial education was limited, the likelihood of women being leaders in cultural and religious movements was higher than in political and civic ones.

African nationalism in the nineteenth and twentieth centuries underwent at least four phases. The first phase consisted of the varied resistances against colonial conquest itself. These were struggles to *retain* existing African sovereignties. The second phase was marked by struggles to *reform* colonialism in the immediate aftermath of the defeat of what used to be called 'primary resistance'. The third phase was characterized by the drive to *remove* colonialism. The fourth phase sought to *recreate* independence. To use the colonial-postcolonial typology: the first three were characteristic of colonial nationalisms; and the last of postcolonial nationalisms – the gruelling challenges of trying to create viable nation-states in the face of turbulent transformations of domestic social forces, including in some cases the crumbling of the nationalist coalition into its constituent ethnic, class, cultural, and gender separatisms, as well as the recurrent interventions of outside powers and the cruel sanctions of the global political economy.

It stands to reason that the timing, trajectories, and facilitating factors of these phases differed from colony to colony and country to country, as did the identities of the main actors, their strategies, and the languages and weapons of combat over time. The differences are quite evident if we look at the time span of decolonization. If we take the restoration of the monarchy in Egypt in 1922 as the beginning and the demise of Apartheid in South Africa in 1994 as its end, then decolonization lasted seventy-two years, although the bulk of African states got their independence in the two decades between the mid-1950s and the mid-1970s. The winds of political change were initially concentrated in North and West Africa before they started blowing across the settler laagers of Southern Africa. The process of decolonization involved both peaceful transitions and liberation wars, with local accommodations and international conflicts. Almost invariably, the later the decolonization, the more violent it was.

As on many topics in African history, decolonization is a subject that has generated spirited debate. Some argue that African nationalism was primarily responsible for the dismantling of the colonial empires. Others contend it was a product of imperial policy and planning. And there are those who seek to place decolonization in the context of changes in the world system. It would seem to me that a process as complex as decolonization was undoubtedly a product of many factors. It involved an interplay of the prevailing international situation, the policies of the colonial powers, and the nature and strength of the nationalist movements, which in turn reflected internal conditions both in the metropoles and the colonies and the ideologies and visions of the postcolonial world. There were clearly variations in the patterns of decolonization among regions and colonies conditioned by the way in which these factors coalesced and manifested themselves. Decolonization was also affected by the relative presence and power of European settlers and each colony's perceived strategic importance.

Decolonization was undoubtedly the great achievement for colonized peoples, of anti-colonial nationalism, and one of the monumental events of the twentieth century. With the demise of Apartheid African nationalism could claim to have achieved the first historic and humanistic goal on its agenda. What about the other four goals: nation building, development, democracy, and regional integration? It is of course not possible here to provide a full stocktaking of the last half-century of African history. Suffice it to say, the record of performance is extremely complex and uneven across postcolonial periods, countries and regions, social classes, economic sectors, genders and age groups, which fit neither into the unrelenting gloom of the Afro-pessimists or the unyielding hopes of the Afro-optimists.

What can be said with certainty is that postcolonial Africa has undergone profound transformations in some areas and not in others. Nation building exhibits palpable contradictions: both state and ethnic nationalisms are probably both stronger now than at independence. National and ethnic identities and the struggles over them eclipse Pan-African nationalisms within the continent and with the Diaspora. Thus, the dreams of regional integration have been compromised for the sake of nation building, although as a result of regional mobility, integration schemes, transnational migrations and the emergence of new African Diasporas, they are stirring more vigorously than before.

Development remains elusive. The rapid growth of the early post-independence era was followed by the debilitating recessions of the structural adjustment decades, and the tentative recoveries of more recent years. But the African population is much bigger than at independence, currently stampeding towards a billion despite all the calamities of war, disease, and natural disasters; and this population is more educated, more socially differentiated, and more youthful than ever. And democracy is cautiously emerging on the backs of expanding and energized civil societies and popular struggles for the 'second independence', from the suffocating tentacles of one party states and military authoritarianisms, notwithstanding the blockages, reversals, and chicaneries of Africa's wily dictators.

Clearly, nationalism is one of the great intellectual and ideological forces of modern African history. Contemporary Africa is simply inconceivable without understanding the role and impact played by nationalism. Trying to unpack the historical dynamics of African nationalism – its causes, constructions, compositions, contexts, courses, and consequences – is immensely complicated but critical to mapping more productive futures for Africa. We should begin by separating the retrogressive nationalisms of ethnicity and religion that have wrecked some parts of postcolonial Africa from the progressive civic, regional and Pan-African nationalisms that are indispensable for Africa's historic and humanistic reconstruction.

October 6, 2006.

References

1   The address is published in, 'The Historic and Humanistic Agendas of African Nationalism: A Reassessment' in Toyin Falola and Salah Hassan, eds., *Power and Nationalism in Modern Africa* (Durham, NC: Carolina Academic Press, 2008): 37–53.
2   Thandika Mkandawire, "Globalization and Africa's Unfinished Agenda," *Macalester International* 7 (1997): 71–107.

Chapter 12

Barack Obama and African Diasporas: Dialogues and Dissensions

During the Democrat Party's leadership selection process, I received numerous phone calls from friends and colleagues in various African countries who were bewildered by charges that Senator Barack Obama was not seen as 'black enough' by some African Americans. I often point out that at one level this was a controversy manufactured by the white-dominated media, with its incurably racist and patronizing attitudes towards African Americans, now peddling the notion that they are incapable of judging a 'black' candidate on his or her merits. Historically, it has of course been European Americans who have displayed such blinding racial loyalty – until Obama's election, a person of colour has never been president in America's 231-year history as a republic.

The controversy got mileage when an early poll after Obama had declared his candidacy showed that his support in the African American community trailed behind that of Senator Hillary Rodham Clinton, and that prominent civil rights leaders such as the Reverend Jesse Jackson and the Reverend Al Sharpton, themselves previous presidential contenders, had not rushed to endorse him. A later poll showed Obama overtaking Clinton and several civil rights leaders formally endorsed him including the Reverend Jackson. But this did not stop the debate about Obama's blackness, both among whites eager to proclaim their colour-blind anti-racism and blacks anxious about the new racism of colour blindness.

The language of colour blindness is the new rhetoric of racism in the United States, as several perceptive observers of what my colleague the philosopher Charles Mills[1] calls the 'racial contract' have noted. This new racial ideology is what the sociologist Tyrone Foreman[2] calls 'racial apathy', or what Mills[3] describes as 'white ignorance': a wilful, culpable, strategic ignorance, indifference or antipathy towards race and the effects of racism that results in the delegitimization of racial minorities and public policies that might ameliorate their structural and symbolic subordination. Hurricane Katrina showed the world the depths of racial and class marginalization for African Americans in the United States.

The discourse about Obama's blackness is fuelled by America's continued obsession and silence about race. Race is everywhere in everyday life but largely disregarded in public life. It remains the bedrock of American identity and citizenship and has defined the hierarchies of belonging and the scales of human worthiness, in which the memories and lives of African Americans remain outside the seductive and sanctimonious but spurious national narrative – the US as the land of immigrants, opportunity, and democracy. To be sure, white America periodically embraces black figures – from the icons of popular culture to potential political leaders (remember the courtship of the Colin Powell of the first Gulf War and the canonization of the assassinated Martin Luther King) – in a desperate bid to escape its sordid past of slavery and segregation and the continuing marginalization of people of African descent. But among many African Americans such gestures often do little to dull the lingering pain and anger of centuries of racial abuse and exploitation that has yet to be fully atoned for. An official apology for slavery has yet to be given, reparations remain inconceivable, and the limited restitution of affirmative action is withering away.

There are other dynamics at play. The United States is becoming more diverse thanks to new waves of immigrants, especially from Asia and Latin America, and to a smaller extent Africa. New minorities have emerged who reaffirm the narrative of the American dream, against which the African American story stands as a permanent indictment: the Asians are praised as a model minority, notwithstanding the poverty and marginalization of many Asian American communities, and the Hispanics are often pilloried as illegal immigrants despite evidence to the contrary. Soon after the elections of 2000, it was declared that Hispanics had overtaken African Americans to become the country's largest minority. The eagerness with which this was proclaimed by the media and political establishment seemed to betray a deep-seated longing for African Americans to disappear into political irrelevance. Forgotten in all this was the simple fact that Hispanics can be of any 'race' – white, black, native American, etc – and many of the Hispanic immigrants are black; after all, about a quarter of Latin America is black, almost twice the percentage of African Americans in the US population.

The African Diaspora in the US has itself become more diverse, partly because of increased migrations from Africa and South America and continuing migration from the Caribbean, and partly because of post civil rights social and class cleavages within African American communities. And the age-old collective black identity based on the one-drop rule began to fracture following the emergence of the biracial and multiracial movement as a political and cultural force, whose power was sanctified in the 2000 Census that allowed respondents to choose more than one racial category. (The Hispanic category was introduced in the Census of 1970 – an indication of the power of social movements and the state to create new 'races'). It has been suggested that the rise of this movement reflected changes in the racial and gender dynamics of biracial parentage. More white women were marrying black men and giving birth to mixed race children, while historically it had been black women who gave birth to such children, often in the context of coercive sexual relations with white men. The difference between a biracial and a black person is not, therefore, always detectable in terms of phenotype or skin colour: there are many African Americans who look like the actress Halle Berry or President Obama but who are not biracial in the sense that these two might be considered so.

At issue then are the changing constructions of blackness in the United States, in which the racial classifications are increasingly becoming Latin Americanized and Africanized. A three-tier or multiple racial system common in Latin America and parts of Africa is being increasingly adopted in place of the historic white-black binary racial system. Ironically, as the US becomes more Latin Americanized in its racial discourse and dynamics, parts of Latin America seem to become more Americanized, with the resurgence of black racial struggles for recognition beyond the myths of racial mixing or what used to be called in Brazil, 'racial democracy'. In the land of his biological father, Kenya, President Obama would be considered 'mixed race' because his mother was white; in South Africa he would be 'coloured'. Thus, the case of Obama's racial identity should be familiar to many in Africa where mixed race populations were, and often still are, placed in a distinctive social category. This is not to say he would not be elected or could not aspire to high political office: Jerry Rawlings, Ghana's president for twenty years is biracial, and so is Ian Khama the current Vice-President of Botswana who will take over the presidency of Botswana after the term of the current president expires next year. Ironically, it is in the 'new' multiracial South Africa that it is often said a 'coloured' person, such as the highly regarded Finance Minister Trevor Manuel, has little chance of becoming president in the near future.

Underlying the debates about Obama's racial identity, then, are the changing demographics and constructions of race in the wider society and of blackness itself, in which the black category seems destined to remain at the bottom of the racial and socioeconomic hierarchy. It is this persistent reality and fears of continued black subordination that structure discourses about Obama in sections of the African American community. Ambivalent attitudes might also reflect both suspicion and worry, historic suspicions about the ability of black leaders popular among whites to advance black interests, and future worries that Obama is being artificially propped up by the white media for an inevitable fall and humiliation of the 'race'.

Increased migration of people from Africa and the African Diaspora also raises complex questions about African American identity and the struggles for restitution for the long centuries of slavery and segregation. Those who say Obama is not 'black enough' often mean that his family does not have a history of subordination under slavery and Jim Crow segregation. They are not referring to his race, but to his history. In this sense, the debate over 'blackness' represents a struggle over historical memory and meaning of the African American experience. The news that there were slave owners on Obama's mother's side only reinforced the apparent gulf between Obama and many African Americans, but it also underscored the ubiquity, the quintessential Americanness of his story: that those with long family histories in the US are likely descended from slave owners and slaves, or both as is indeed the case among many African Americans who are 'mixed' to varying degrees. Certainly, many African Americans are shocked to be called 'mixed' or 'coloured' when they visit parts of Africa.

These debates and struggles are likely to intensify as immigrant populations considered 'black' in the US grow, and differentiation and polarization within the historic African American community deepen. I say 'black' because there are African immigrants who do not fit into this category. There are at least four waves of African Diasporas in the US and other parts of the Atlantic world: first, the historic communities of African Americans, themselves formed out of complex internal and external migrations over several hundred years; second, recent immigrant communities from other Diasporic locations, such as the Caribbean, who invoke when necessary or convenient national identities as Jamaicans, Puerto Ricans, Cubans, Dominicans, Haitians, and so on; third, the recent immigrants from the indigenous communities of Africa some of whom share racialized affinity with the first two groups; and finally, African migrants who are themselves Diasporas from Asia or Europe, such as the East African Asians or South African whites.

Each of these Diasporas, broadly speaking, has its own connections and commitments to Africa, its own memories and imaginations of Africa, and its own conceptions of the Diasporic condition and identity. The third group is sometimes divided by the racialized codifications of whiteness and blackness, sanctified in the colonial cartographies of North Africa and Sub-Saharan Africa, and by US immigration law under which North Africans are classified as white. Given the complexity and diversity of the African Diasporas in the US, it stands to reason that relations between the various groups are exceedingly difficult to map out. There is a growing body of literature focusing on different aspects of the complicated relationship between the new and old African Diasporas in the country.

I would like to suggest a possible analytical schema to better comprehend relations between these waves of immigration and the complex overlapping layers of Diasporization. Three elements seem to structure these relations. What I would call, first, the contexts of engagement, second, the constructs of engagement, and third, the character of the engagements. By context I refer to the social arenas in which the different Diasporas interact; by constructs I mean the dynamics that mediate their interactions; and by character I mean the content and processes of interactions.

The contexts in which the historic and contemporary Diasporas interact with each other are both private and public. The private or privatized spheres include family and interpersonal relations. In the case of families we can think of inter-Diasporan marriages and partnerships as well as intra-family generations of Diasporization. Marriages and partnerships between African migrants and African Americans have been growing, although there are important differentiations of gender, class, religion and what can be called settlement geographies. For example, some studies seem to suggest that more African men marry African American women than African American men marry African women, which can be attributed to the gender imbalances in the composition of college graduates and professionals in the African American community, as well as to constructions of beauty.

But even in families in which the parents are from the same African country, culture, or community, challenges of intra-generational Diasporan relations arise between the parents and their American-born children and their grandchildren who are progressively acculturated into not only American society, but African American society. All of us who are parents have experienced this – I know I have: the constant nego-tiations over socialization that are framed in the idioms of age and Diasporization in which the cultural and cognitive authority of parent-hood and the original homeland are pitted against the new host country and the increasingly Americanized children. There is a class dimension to these dynamics: the fears, real and imagined, of professional class reproduction in so far as most African immigrants are middle class, while African Americans are routinely pathologized in America's racial imaginary, although the majority, too, are middle class.

The public contexts of intra-Diasporan engagements are obviously even more multidimensional. I have identified seven in terms of their social weight and explanatory possibilities. They are: (1) educational institutions (composition of students and faculty in K-12 and tertiary institutions, curricula representations of Africa and African America, and membership of sororities and fraternities); (2) labour market (access to employment, workplace culture, and workers' organization); (3) religious practices (Christianity, Islam, and the African-derived religions); (4) leisure activities (sports, entertainment, media, and festivals); (5) business enterprises (size, location, ownership and employment patterns); (6) political process (citizenship, voting patterns, leadership roles, lobbying activities, and involvement in public protests); and (7) community life (neighbourhoods, activities and organizations).

There can be little doubt that the encounters within each and across the various social domains are complex, contradictory, and always changing. For example, there are challenges of political coalition building among the new Diaspora and the historic Diaspora over on the one hand, US foreign policy towards African countries and, on the other, public policy in the US towards black communities, in which each group makes proprietary claims. And academics such as myself are all aware of the tensions between African and African American students and faculty in schools and universities, engendered by struggles over identity in America's highly racialized imaginary, access to resources, and the limited social capital of affirmative action. This last was originally intended to mitigate the centuries' long deprivations of slavery and segregation that the historic African American Diaspora experienced, but which has greatly benefited recent professional African immigrants and their children, as well as other racial and ethnic minorities and white women. Witness the debate about the overrepresentation of Africans and Afro Caribbeans in the Ivy League universities that has been widely reported by the media. It is no secret that sometimes universities prefer to admit African immigrants to serve affirmative action mandates thereby saving themselves from combative race relations with African Americans, some of whose memories of racial terror and bigotry are deeply ingrained.

The connections and disconnections among the different Diasporas are conditioned by four sets of dynamics, namely: institutional, ideological, identity, and individual. Different sectors and organizations have specific institutional cultures that set the broad parameters of intra-Diasporan interactions, as do the push and pull of ideological affiliations – left wing or right wing, conservative or liberal, Afrocentric or Euro-centric, nationalist or internationalist, sexist or feminist. All these affect the tenor and possibilities of cooperation, accommodation, or conflict within specific or between different Diaspora groups. The nature and formation of collective identity and individual subjectivity, which are constructed through the prevailing practices of socialization, spatialization, and representation, also help structure these dynamics. In so far as all communities have multiple identities, inter-group relations are partly affected by the intersections of some of these identities and interests.

The social and historical geography of new immigrant and Diasporic identities involve fluid and sometimes competing claims constructed around ethnic, national, subregional, linguistic, Pan-African, and transnational identities. Some of these intersect with the identities of the historic Diasporas, while others do not, which can provide the basis for cooperation or conflict. A person who prizes his or her ethnic identity may find it hard to forge a Pan-African identity. This is to suggest that first-generation African immigrants who already have trouble dealing with people from other ethnic groups in their own countries of origin may have difficulties dealing with African Americans.

How can we conceptualize the content and character of the intra-Diasporan engagements? Five dimensions can be identified that may or may not denote cumulative phases of acculturation mediated by the length of stay in the US for the new Diasporas: their social and spatial locations; their respective connections to Africa and America; and the attitudes – hospitality or hostility – of the historic Diasporas. On the whole, the contemporary Diasporas, unlike the historic Diasporas, enjoy unprecedented opportunities offered by modern information, communication and transport technologies to be transnational and transcultural, to be people of multiple worlds and foci, to exhibit cosmopolitan commitments and loyalties, and to straddle simultaneously several countries or several continents. They are able to maintain connections to Africa in ways that were not possible to the historic Diaspora.

Relations between the old and new Diasporas can be characterized by antagonism, ambivalence, acceptance, adaptation, and assimilation. Antagonism is engendered by stereotypes and poor communication on both sides. Several studies have recorded the negative stereotypes the two groups hold about each other. African American stereotypes of Africans evoke negative bodily images, whereas African stereotypes of African Americans evoke negative behavioural images. The bodies of African blacks are despised for their colour and alleged ugliness, while African Americans are detested for their alleged propensity to violence and criminality. African Americans blame Africans for having sold them into slavery and see them as embodiments of cultural and economic backwardness, while Africans accuse African Americans of laziness and not taking advantage of their country's enormous resources. And both groups sometimes see each other as arrogant.

These stereotypes are rooted in the sensational media representations of both groups, as well as selective experiences with each other both in the United States and in Africa. However, antagonism is only one facet of the relationship. We need to investigate more systematically the other dimensions, the dynamics that tilt the relationship towards assimilation. Historically, this is what has happened as successive waves of new arrivals have been integrated, over time, into the African American community. Our challenge as researchers in the field of African Diaspora Studies and as Pan-Africanists is to map out these processes and promote mutual understanding through education and communication, to encourage strategic solidarity among our communities that will come from respect for each other's histories and struggles, from a clear understanding of the ties that bind us as we seek to recover from the ravages of the past and build new futures. Indeed, the connections between Africa and its Diasporas – both old and new – have been far deeper, more diverse and more beneficial for African peoples on both sides of the Atlantic than is generally acknowledged.

April 4, 2007.

References

1   Charles Mills, *The Racial Contract*. Ithaca, NY: Cornell University Press, 1997.
2   Tyrone, Foreman, 'Colour-blind Racism and Racial Indifference: The Role of Racial Apathy in Facilitating Enduring Inequalities.' In Maria Krysan and Amanda Lewis, eds. *The Changing Terrain of Race and Ethnicity*. New York, NY: Russell Sage, 2004: 43-66.
3   Mills, Charles. 'White Ignorance.' In Shannon Sullivan and Nancy Tuana, eds., *Race and Epistemologies of Ignorance*. Albany, NY: SUNY Press, 2007: 13-38.

Chapter 13

In Defence of the New Diasporas and Brain Mobility

Africa has had a troubled relationship with global migrations rooted in the horrific memories of the Atlantic Slave Trade, which set the foundations of the asymmetrical relations between the continent and Euroamerica subsequently reproduced and reinforced by colonialism and neo-colonialism. Today, many worry about the brain drain, how Africa is apparently losing its best and brightest to the global North, a phenomenon that has accelerated since the lost developmental decades of the 1980s and 1990s. As we mark the bicentennial of the abolition of the Atlantic Slave Trade this year by Britain, the world's leading slave trading nation of the eighteenth century, and next year by the United States, the world's lone and lonely superpower, Africa's transnational migrations raise fundamental questions about the continent's position in the world, and the perils and possibilities for Africa and its historic and new Diasporas.

The late twentieth century has been characterized as the age of globalization marked by the rapid movements of capital, commodities and cultures, across communities, countries, and continents. To what extent can it also be seen as 'the age of migration'? Going by the hysterical pronouncements of politicians and the media, especially in the global North, and the inflated rhetoric of the academic seers of globalization, one would think the world is undergoing massive and unprecedented waves of international migration. In much of the current literature there is a tendency to ignore earlier waves of global migrations, which were as large as or even larger than contemporary migration flows.

The available evidence on contemporary global migrations – since 1960 – points to two broad conclusions. First, while the number of international migrants has grown significantly in absolute numbers since the 1960s, the percentage of people who have left and remained outside their countries of origin has remained remarkably steady and small. Second, there have been significant changes in the character and direction of international migration. The flow of people at the global level has lagged behind the flows of capital and commodities. Available estimates indicate that the number of foreign-born persons worldwide, including migrants, refugees, and asylum-seekers, increased from 75.5 million in 1960 to 190.6 million in 2005, but this represented a rate of growth far below the rate of international tourist arrivals, or the phenomenal growth in world trade and capital flows. Equally revealing, the change in the proportion of migrants in the world population was slight, from 2.5 per cent in 1960 to 3 per cent in 2005. It was 2 per cent in 1910 and 2.1 per cent in 1930.

During the 1960-2005 period Europe overtook Asia as the region with the largest number of migrants. Its migrant population more than quadrupled from 14.2 million to 64.1 million, compared to Asia's which rose from 28.5 to 53.3 million. Also experiencing fast growth was North America whose migrant population more than trebled from 12.5 million to 44.5 million, while that of Oceania more than doubled from 2.1 million to 5 million. Latin America and the Caribbean's migrant population experienced the slowest growth, from 6 million to 6.6 million. But several regions experienced declines in their percentage of the global stock of migrants including Africa, Asia, Latin America and the Caribbean, and Oceania, while they rose for Northern America. Similarly, there was a decline in the share of migrants in the population of Africa, Asia and Latin America and the Caribbean, with sizeable increases in Northern America and Europe, and a slight increase for Oceania. As might be expected, there were sub-regional variations within each region.

While the quantitative magnitude of international migration is not as extensive as is often assumed in the hyperbolic literature of globalization and the populist media –ninety-seven per cent of the world's population still lives in the country of its birth – changes in the composition and direction of international migration have been quite profound. We can isolate three critical developments. First, there has been growing diversification of sending and receiving countries. Second, despite the growth of international migration over long distances – across regions and continents – the majority of migrants reside within their respective regions. Third, skilled migration has assumed greater importance, both in terms of the actual flows and in the formulation of migration policies at national, regional, and international levels.

It is evident that the flows of international migration have shifted from the global South to the global North. But the bulk of migrants from the developing countries still go to other developing countries – 47 per cent compared to 40 per cent who reside in the high-income OECD countries. The same is true among the high-income countries, in which 84.4 per cent of the migrants reside in high-income OECD countries and 3.2 per cent in high-income non-OECD countries.

As elsewhere, Africa's migrant population increased, nearly doubling from 9.1 million to 17.1 million, but like other regions in the global South, Africa's share of the world's migrant stock declined from 12.1 per cent in 1960 to 9 per cent in 2005. There was also a decline in the share of migrants in the African population, from 3.2 per cent to 1.9 per cent. Also similar to other world regions, has been the growing feminization of African migrants, as more women migrate independently through legal and occasionally irregular channels to seek better lives for themselves and their families. Moreover, as in the global North, in many African countries immigrants are victims of ambivalent or even hostile public attitudes and restrictive policies, official harassment, and punitive repatriations.

Clearly, there are many similarities between migration trends in Africa and other world regions. But there are also differences of magnitude. First, an unusually high proportion of the continent's migrants go to other African countries. Second, a large percentage of the migrants are made up of refugees. While the world average of refugees among migrants in 2005 was 7.1 per cent, for Africa it was 17.7 per cent. Third, Africa's transcontinental migrants largely flock to the global North rather than to regions in the global South. There are of course some notable exceptions: large numbers of migrants from parts of north-eastern Africa have migrated to the Gulf States. In fact, Saudi Arabia was second only to France in the numbers of African immigrants it hosted in 2005 (1.5 million), followed by the United States (1.25 million representing a mere 3.5 per cent of the total foreign-born population), Spain, the United Kingdom and Italy.

Also, African migrants to the global North enjoy high levels of education, so that even if their numbers are comparatively small, they represent a much higher proportion of the regional skilled labour than elsewhere. In 2000, while the continent's share of skilled workers was only 4 per cent, 30.9 per cent of all immigrants from the continent were skilled workers. In other words, the 'brain drain' is exceptionally severe for Africa. For example, the African born population in the US currently claims the highest levels of education of any group in the country, foreign born or native born. In 2000, among the African-born residents aged 25 and above, 49.3 per cent had a bachelor's degree or more as compared to 25.6 per cent for the native born population and 25.8 per cent for the foreign born population as a whole. The irony of people from the least educated continent in the world having the highest levels of education in the world's richest country is quite striking.

The migration of skilled African workers is a product of conditions in both Africa and the North. Economic, social, political, and educational developments in Africa have conspired to generate emigration pressures, while the skill-selective and wealth-selective immigration policies of the Northern countries have offered opportunities for highly skilled Africans to migrate. The migration flows have been sustained by the intricate and intense educational networks that link universities in Africa with those in the global North, the recruitment drives and inducements of various institutions and organizations, and the cumulative traditions of migration that have emerged as skilled migration has expanded. Like skilled international migrants from other regions, African migrants have increasingly become part of transitional communities involved directly and indirectly in both home and host countries.

It is easy to see African international migrations, especially to the global North, as an unmitigated economic, political, and cultural disaster for the continent. Remittances from the migrants, while important for migrants' families and local communities and for some countries in their national balance of payments, do not seem to compensate for the net losses of the migrants' productivity and potential contributions to national development. It has also been argued that the skilled emigrations deprive civil society of the organizational political skills of middle-class professionals. All this may be true, but in recent years there has been a sea of change in the attitudes of researchers, governments, and multilateral agencies towards migration and development, prompted in large measure by the 'discovery' that migrant remittances to the developing countries exceed several times over official development assistance and net private capital flows. In 2004 Africa's total remittance receipts had shot to $19.2 billion (representing 8.5 per cent of the world total), accounting for 2.4 per cent of GDP, compared to the world average of 0.6 per cent and 1.7 per cent for the less and more developed countries, respectively.

But this new euphoria about the potential contributions of migration to development is as problematic as the old fears about the perils of migration for development. In fact, the development industry seems to be particularly prone to historical amnesia and paradigm shifts, the recycling of development mantras as its discourse swings from one extreme to another, between pessimism and optimism, in a desperate search for the magic bullet. Since 2001, there has been an explosion in remittance flows and migration studies, accompanied by a resurgence of more positive views and policies on the developmental possibilities of migration. The language has shifted accordingly from 'brain drain' and 'brain waste' to 'brain gain' and 'brain circulation'.

It is naïve, indeed dangerous, to put migrants on a pedestal, to see them either as perpetrators of underdevelopment or agents of development for their countries. The pitfalls of the 'brain drain' are real, but so are the possibilities of 'brain mobility'. International migrants, especially the skilled ones among them, represent both developmental liabilities and assets for the developing countries. What is at stake is how to convert migration drains into gains, which depends on the congruence of interests of the principal stakeholders, namely: the Diasporas themselves, governments, and multilateral agencies. At stake for the Diasporas is their ability to mobilize, their motivation, and the enabling environment in both their host and home countries that, in turn, are greatly affected by the policies and actions of governments and multilateral agencies, which set the broad structural parameters for development. This is simply to suggest that Diasporas, however mobilized and motivated, cannot by themselves effectively tackle the developmental challenges facing their home countries. Governments are primarily responsible for establishing the infrastructures for development through which migrant remittances can be turned into either meaningful consumptive and productive assets or cash flows of little material and social consequence.

Government policies towards migrants and Diasporas have been characterized by three main tendencies: the permissive, restrictive, and Diaspora options. Up to the early 1970s, international migration was either welcomed by governments in both the sending and receiving countries or it occurred in a permissive policy environment in which migration policies were poorly developed. The adoption of restrictive policies from the early 1970s reflected a growing concern with migration management. Governments in the global North sought to limit further immigration and focused on integration of previous immigrants, while those in the global South sought to curtail more emigration and encourage the return of emigrants. Both sought to create disincentives for migration, although their emphases varied: the developed countries were particularly concerned about unskilled migration; while the developing countries were troubled by skilled migration. Policy prescriptions included taxation and return programmes. More recently, the restrictive option has taken the form of bilateral or multilateral agreements limiting or regulating the immigration of skilled professionals. None of these policies have succeeded in stemming migration flows.

The Diaspora option is based on the recognition that migrants become Diasporas, people with multiple identities, firmly tied to their countries of origin and residence, who are willing and able to contribute simultaneously to both. Unfortunately, the Diaspora option tends to be seen by governments and development agencies largely in economic terms, as an economic resource, a remittance pipeline. There can of course be little doubt the new African Diasporas constitute a strategic economic asset, that they are already the continent's biggest donor, with remittances exceeding foreign direct investment and official development assistance. These Diasporas also possess an enormous stock of social capital – skills, knowledge, networks, civic awareness, cultural experience and cosmopolitanism – that can provide not only access to global markets and investment and stimulate technological innovation, but also invigorate democracy, strengthen civil society and encourage the growth of new philanthropic cultures. Moreover, Diasporas can be crucial intermediaries between Africa and foreign governments and international development agencies.

Clearly, engagements with the Diaspora need to go beyond capturing their remittances. There is need to advance to Diaspora networking and

Diaspora integration. Diaspora networking entails brain mobility, supporting and facilitating the freer movement and circulation of Diaspora knowledges and skills. Several programmes have been created over the years including the Transfer of Knowledge Through Expatriate Networks (TOKTEN) established by the UNDP in 1977, Migration for Development in Africa established in 2001 by the International Organization for Migration with the support of the Organization of African Unity, the predecessor of the African Union (AU), and AfricaRecruit established by the New Partnership for Africa's Development (NEPAD) in 2002, which maintains an extensive database with more than 150,000 entries, and seeks to promote Diaspora skills transfer and investment.

In addition, various international organizations have established research programmes and organized conferences where intellectual and policy support for Diaspora networking is increasingly articulated. Examples include the World Bank's Research Programme on International Migration and Development, the European Investment Bank's Facility of Euro-Mediterranean Investment and Partnership, the United Nation's Global Commission on International Organization for Migration and Development and the UN's High Level Dialogue on Migration and Development held in September 2006. Even the European Union has recognized the potential of migration and development and has embraced the concept of 'co-development'. In September 2005 it issued a policy document setting out proposals for facilitating and enhancing the developmental impact of remittances, promoting Diasporas as actors in their home countries' development, encouraging circular migration and brain circulation, and mitigating the effects of the brain drain.

For Diaspora networking to be effective, policy changes by governments in countries of origin and residence are of course vital, but not adequate if the Diaspora itself is not well organized. The formation of Diaspora associations and networks has been immeasurably improved through the explosion of information technologies especially the Internet, leading to the unprecedented process of digital Diasporization. But Diaspora mobilization is only as effective as motivation is strong, which requires activism, confidence, and coordination. Since the 1990s the formation of Diaspora knowledge networks has skyrocketed, jumping from a handful in the early 1990s, to 41 in the late 1990s tied to 30 different countries, and 155 by March 2005, of which 51 were African and covered 10 countries. Several of the African networks tend to be continental, more than is the case in other regions, a lingering tribute to Pan-Africanism.

In addition to the knowledge networks, numerous Diaspora advocacy organizations have emerged that play an increasingly important role in promoting African development. Examples include the Migrations et Développement (M&D) which was created by Moroccan migrants in France in 1986 and has since become one of the world's leading development-oriented Diaspora organizations. Another is the African Foundation for Development (AFFORD), formed in 1994 by Africans in the UK as a charity organization to promote African input in mainstream British development policy and facilitate direct developmental linkages between the African Diaspora and Africa. AFFORD has engaged in numerous educational and advocacy activities and launched a campaign for remittance tax relief. Increasingly European governments and development agencies see Diaspora organizations as important developmental actors; although for such relationships to work most effectively they need to be based on genuine partnership rather than paternalism.

Diaspora integration involves a lot more than tapping Diasporas for remittances or building knowledge exchange networks between Diaspora communities and institutions and their countries or regions of origin. It involves recognition of the Diaspora as part of the political community by conferring on it dual citizenship and all the rights that this might entail, including voting rights and political representation in state parliaments, as well as preferential investment options and other economic and social privileges accorded to resident national citizens. Only a few African countries currently allow dual citizenship. They include Egypt, South Africa and Ghana. If African countries are serious about their Diasporas, more of them need to pass the necessary legislation permitting their Diasporas to retain their citizenship. A larger question concerns dual citizenship for the historic Diasporas who have no known connections with Africa's contemporary nation-states, created towards the end of the nineteenth century. The African Union has expressed the need to recognize the historic Diaspora, going so far as recognizing the Diaspora as the AU's sixth region and including it, for the time being, in the AU's Economic, Social and Cultural Council. Extending and concretizing this promise will be the ultimate test of Africa's seriousness about the integration of the Diaspora as a force for the continent's transformation in all its dimensions – economic, social, cultural and political.

Africa and its Diaspora have not always effectively mobilized to serve and advance each other's interests as has been the case, for example, between the Jewish Diaspora and Israel, or increasingly the Chinese Diaspora and China and the Indian Diaspora and India. Israel's clout in Washington has less to do with the economic importance of Israel to the United States than with the political clout of the Jewish lobby, which others such as TransAfrica have sought to replicate for Africa and the Caribbean, although not always reciprocated from the African side. Similarly, China's and India's rapid economic development in recent years have been fuelled to a large extent by investments of finance and technological skills from their respective Diasporas. But it has to be remembered that the increase in Diaspora investments and knowledge exchanges followed implementation of enabling policies and massive infrastructural investments by the governments of the two countries.

The new African Diaspora and their offspring can help re-awaken interest in Africa among the historic African Diasporas. They can serve as cultural mediators, as trans-oceanic bridges, in the case of the Atlantic, between Africa and African America, whose communication and knowledge of each other have largely been through the distorted lenses of imperialist and racist media. Immigrant Africans have an important and specific role to play in brokering relations between Africa and the global North, in blackening the Atlantic and the Mediterranean. They must resist the seductions of their new homelands to become native ventriloquists; complicit authentic others who validate narratives that seek to marginalize Africa. Nor should they let themselves be manipulated as a fifth column in Euroamerica's eternal racial wars by disavowing the protracted struggles of historic African Diaspora communities for full citizenship. Sometimes immigrants from Africa tend to forget that the roads they ride on to their jobs in industry or the academy were paved by all those brave men and women who fought so gallantly for civil rights. Solidarity requires respect for each other's struggles and recognition of our splendid diversities. It should be anchored on a strategic commitment to our collective liberation, in so far as it is our collective identity that has provided the historical basis for our racialization, exploitation and the debasement of our humanity, whether in Africa or in the global North.

If the contemporary Diasporas are to be useful for African development, there must be a clear understanding that they constitute a strategic asset possessing enormous social, financial, and intellectual capital. In the case of the new Diaspora, it is already the continent's biggest foreign investor, and the only constituency in the global North that has a profound emotive and cognitive commitment to Africa, or the capacity to play a progressive role in Africa's social transformation. In the case of the historic Diaspora, it has the political potential and propensity, which it has demonstrated in struggles against colonial rule and Apartheid, to mobilize in support of a new civilizational compact between Euroamerica and Africa.

It must also be recognized that many in the Diaspora may not be able or wish to return permanently to their native countries. Still, like most migrants, they are often highly motivated to contribute to development back home whether by altruism, self-interest, the need to repay the family and social debts of their upbringing, for co-insurance purposes against future risks, or out of plain abandonment guilt which they seek to assuage by maintaining connections. In days gone by, global migration often entailed permanent relocation or long separation and infrequent encounters with one's native home through mail and the occasional visit. The contemporary revolution in telecommunications and travel has compressed the distances between home and abroad, thus offering these new Diasporas, unlike the historic Diasporas, unprecedented opportunities to be transnational, to be people of two worlds, perpetually translocated, physically and culturally, between several countries or several continents. Globalization is not simply facilitating the rapid flows of capital and commodities, but also revitalizing old cultural and community networks, thus strengthening transnational ethnic, racial, and national identities, interests, and interventions.

In this context it makes sense to abandon restrictive, punitive and ineffectual policies that demonize and even criminalize international migrants. In fact, such policies have had the ironic effect of encouraging permanent settlement by discouraging migrants from making periodic visits home for fear of being refused re-entry into their new host countries. This means, I contend, providing dual citizenship to those among the new and historic Diasporas who wish for such formal and empowering citizenship rights. Indeed, taking up citizenship in their countries of residence is critical if the new Diasporas are to influence relations between their host and home countries, or to effectively broker relations with the huge but often self-serving development industry in the global North.

It is not enough for African countries to court the Diaspora economically but shun them politically. And the Diaspora should not decry the alleged pathologies of Africa while reproducing those same perversions, including the cancers of tribalism and corruption, in the Diaspora, or fuelling them at home by supporting dictators and warlords and sponsoring conflicts and wars. African countries should improve the investment climate for the Diaspora beyond developing better and cheaper instruments for remittance flows. The Diaspora option requires devising creative strategies for knowledge and skill circulation, the formation of national, regional, and continental knowledge networks that facilitate brain mobility, from academic exchanges to consultancies and temporary return migrations, to the transmission of information and the vigorous defence of Africa, which is routinely defamed in Euroamerica with little social cost.

In short, the Diaspora constitutes Africa's eyes and ears in the world, the interpreter of the world to Africa and Africa to the world. It is indispensable to the globalization of Africa and the Africanization of globalization. It is in this intermediation that the Diaspora's true power and potential lies.

April 20, 2007.

Chapter 14

Love, Lies, Wolfowitz, and the World Bank

The corruption scandal of former World Bank president, Paul D. Wolfowitz, was an intriguing and entangled tale of love: the personal love life of Mr Wolfowitz himself; the current love affair between neo-conservatism and neo-liberalism; and the long-standing marriages of capitalism and corruption, the development industry and the military-industrial complex, and the Northern-dominated international financial institutions and the institutionalization of dependency and poverty in the global South. The scandal derives its significance not simply from the salacious details of a powerful man's peccadilloes, but as a morality tale of the free market, the unsavoury strands woven into the fabric of contemporary global capitalism.

The World Bank is more than a multilateral development agency committed to the eradication of world poverty, as it likes to portray itself in its glossy publications. It is one of the principal gendarmes of global capitalism, set up in 1944 together with the other Bretton Woods institutions: the International Monetary Fund and the World Trade Organization (then called the General Agreement on Tariffs and Trade), to make the world safe for capitalism after the Second World War. This was in the aftermath of the destabilizations of the Great Depression, the devastations of the war itself, and in a period of fierce ideological rivalries between the capitalist world and the then expanding socialist bloc which would culminate in the Cold War between the superpowers and their proxy hot wars in the global South, including Africa. Clearly, more was at stake in this saga than Mr Wolfowitz's personal corruption. The larger issue is the World Bank's own corruption, its structural corruption if you will: the way it has corrupted development in the global South; how it has systematically undermined prospects for sustainable development, self-determination, and democracy in these countries, sacrificing them to the almighty altar of Euroamerican global economic hegemony.

Mr Wolfowitz is an easy man to dislike, as a neo-con hawk, one of the key architects of the indefensible and disastrous American invasion of Iraq, although you would not know it looking at his official biography that used to be on the World Bank website. Of his tenure at the Pentagon the site noted: 'As Deputy Secretary of Defence under President George W. Bush from 2001-2005, Mr Wolfowitz's responsibilities included oversight of the budget process as well as development of policy to respond to the terrorist attacks of September 11, 2001.' It is stated so blandly, so cleanly, so innocently; it is so eerie in its silences.

The details of the scandal are well known. He helped arrange a generous package for his girlfriend, the Libyan born Ms Shaha Ali Riza, who was transferred from her job at the World Bank as the senior gender and civil society coordinator in the Middle East and North Africa Social and Economic Group to the State Department (although she is not a US citizen and it's not clear how she got clearance) when Mr Wolfowitz became president in order to avoid conflict of interest. Her pay rose from $132,660 to $193,590 – higher than the then secretary of state, Ms Condoleeza Rice. Furthermore, upon Mr Wolfowitz's retirement from the Bank in 2010 or 2015, Ms Riza was promised return to the Bank at higher rank – as director or senior advisor if she returned in 2010 and vice-president if she returned in 2015.

But Ms Riza was not the only beneficiary of Mr Wolfowitz's generosity. So were the two lieutenants he brought from the Pentagon to shield himself from the professional Bank staff – Kevin Kellems and Robin Cleveland. Both were given hefty salaries of about $250,000 each, equivalent to the salaries of long-serving World Bank vice-presidents. And there were reports that some of the top officials he appointed were from western countries that supported America's misguided Iraq war policy. The World Bank board of directors was forced to extend its inquiry into Mr Wolfowitz beyond the allegations of favouritism to Ms Riza.

Predictably, as the storm gathered momentum Mr Wolfowitz sought to stem it by offering an apology:[1] 'In hindsight, I wish I had trusted my original instincts and kept myself out of the negotiations ... I made a mistake, for which I am sorry.' He pleaded for 'some understanding' of the 'painful personal dilemma' he faced when he joined the Bank as he 'was trying to navigate in uncharted waters'. He had of course shown little understanding of the dilemma of others, not least when he was Deputy Defence Secretary for the Iraqis whose country's invasion he helped orchestrate, and as World Bank President Mr. Wolfowitz when he suspended aid to several countries from India to Chad, Kenya to Uzbekistan on charges of corruption, both real and some imagined; Uzbekistan's crime was to oust American troops in 2005, while lending to Iraq's puppet government was resumed!

We are all titillated by the unmasking of the intimate connections between the personal and the professional, the private and the public; the exposure of lies at the very heart of global finance, by a man who embodies most poignantly the ties that bind neo-conservatism and neo-liberalism in a union that has brought so much grief and misery to the rest of the world. There was a kind of poetic justice in the tale of a man who launched an anti-corruption crusade against poor nations only to be trumped by his own corruption; the preacher caught committing the very sin he rails against.

It is a spectacle that embarrasses the regulators of international financial institutions, the overseers of the global order, and even staff at the Bank, many of whom were vehemently opposed to his original appointment when it was mooted by the Bush Administration. The World Bank Staff Association demanded Mr Wolfowitz's resignation, so did thirty-two top Bank officials in a group letter , and a Wolfowitz Must Resign website was created with the following slogan: 'Wolfowitz's reign of sleaze and corruption at the World Bank must end. Demand that the Board of Directors act to restore the World Bank's credibility.' Apparently some took to calling Ms Riza, with uncharitable and sexist irony, his 'neo-concubine'.[2]

The chorus calling for Mr Wolfowitz's resignation soon included important financial newspapers and the establishment media. The European media was particularly vociferous, from *The Financial Times* and *The Economist* , to *The Times* of London and *Le Monde* of Paris, and the assorted columnists of *The Guardian* in the UK. Several influential papers in the United States joined the bandwagon from *The New York Times* to the *Wall Street Journal,* although he garnered support in papers like *The Wall Street Journal* and *The Washington Post.*[3]

All these groups and commentators wanted the embattled Mr Wolfowitz out for losing his 'credibility', for harming the 'image' and 'moral authority' of the World Bank. Never mind that he had little credibility to begin with when he was imposed on the Bank by the arrogant Bush administration and other governments – who kept any misgivings to themselves and were shamelessly cowed into submission when he was unanimously approved to become the Bank's tenth president. What did they expect? Moral probity from one of the chief architects of an unprovoked war? Some may be using the scandal as an excuse to backslide on their pledges to the Bank. More importantly, the World Bank already has a poor image in much of the global South and enjoys little moral authority. Those who believe it has ever had unimpeachable ethical credentials live in fantasy land.

But living in their cocoons of self-righteousness, in which material wealth is equated with moral worth, the transgressions of Mr Wolfowitz matter a lot. They find him guilty of hypocrisy, so that he can no longer serve as an effective ambassador for the Bank; his failure to practice what he preached about governance and corruption undermines the Bank's credibility around the world, most damagingly among the Bank's clients in the hapless Developing World, and threatens to affect its operations. At issue, then, is a moral lapse of judgement, a flawed character; the institution itself is not at fault.

One may legitimately wonder who appointed the World Bank arbiter of global economic morality, the crusader-in-chief against corruption. Where was the Bank when all that corruption was occurring in all those countries it eagerly lent money for decades? And why is the culture of corruption often portrayed as a peculiar affliction of the poor, whether poor countries or poor people, when the very wealth of the rich is rooted and has historically been reproduced through the structural corruptions of slavery, colonialism, imperialism, unequal exchange, and enduring national and transnational class and racial hierarchies? It is the desire to protect privileged and unequal access to global resources that breeds in Euroamerica, the militarism of imperial wars abroad and assorted wars against the poor and racial minorities at home. The World Bank has been complicit in propping up corrupt governments and leaders around the world, from Carlos Menem's Argentina and Augusto Pinochet's Chile in Latin America, Hosni Mubarak's Egypt to

Mobutu Sese Seko's Zaire in Africa, Boris Yeltsin's Russia and post-Saddam Hussein's Iraq in Eurasia where billions of dollars routinely disappear in a quagmire of corruption. Not surprising, for some of the beneficiaries of this massive 'reconstruction of Iraq' corruption (that is a first: reconstruction in time of war) are giants of corporate America, including the well-connected Halliburton, formerly headed by Dick Cheney.

Perhaps the critics of Mr Wolfowitz in the financial and media establishments of Euroamerica were hoping for another Robert McNamara, US defence secretary from 1961-1968 and mastermind of another atrocious and unwinnable war, Vietnam, who served as president of the World Bank between 1968 and 1981. As World Bank president Mr McNamara sought to redeem himself by reinventing the Bank as a development agency committed to the 'basic needs' of the world's poor, and after he left the Bank he sought to rewrite and recast his wartime record in a more favourable light. This is one connection between Mr McNamara and Mr Wolfowitz. Both were fervent purveyors of destruction who ended up becoming fraudulent patrons of development. Haunted by American defeat in Vietnam, Wolfowitz's neo-con Iraq war sought to bury those ghosts and frighten the world into accepting the invincibility of the American war machine and the permanence of America's imperial supremacy. But like other ideologues in the twilight years of empire, they overreached and instead have hastened the end of the American empire.

The ease with which the two men moved from planning and waging real wars to pontificating about development from the gilded corridors of the World Bank shows the intricate and intimate connections between international financial institutions and the military industrial complex. The truth of the matter is that Mr Wolfowitz and the World Bank deserve each other; they are cut from the same cloth. He is not some strange and dangerous neo-con stain on an impeccably liberal institution devoted to eradicating world poverty as many seem to think in liberal circles in the United States or in anti-American circles in Europe.

Many of these critics are motivated more by their opposition to the Bush Administration than to the dreadful policies the World Bank has pursued over the decades in the global South. They relish the implosion of the neo-con movement, as one after another they are fired or leave the Administration totally discredited. Even *The Economist*[4] that once cheered them on now says they have become a 'laughing stock', lurching from one humiliation to another, discredited even in the conservative movement for their flawed thinking and execution, and for becoming the very incarnations of the arrogance of power that ostensibly inspired the founders of the movement

In the eyes of much of the world, which remains silent and invisible in the Euroamerican media, the reputation of the World Bank was damaged long before Mr Wolfowitz came on board, and neither the neo-cons nor neo-liberals represented much hope for world progress let alone peace and security. In the United States only social movements like '50 Years Is Enough'[5] seem to get the gravity of the situation, the connectedness of Mr Wolfowitz's personal and professional conduct with the depravity of World Bank policies.

For Africa the World Bank was fatally compromised by misguided neo-liberal structural adjustment policies (SAPs) which were imposed with religious zeal by the World Bank and its twin, the IMF, with the connivance of Euroamerican governments. To many African comment-ators and social activists the market fundamentalism of neo-liberalism bears some responsibility for Africa's 'lost' development decades of the 1980s and 1990s. These wasted years eroded the post-independence advances of the 1960s and early 1970s when Africa saw levels of socio-economic development it had not seen since the tragedy of European colonization. Instead of apologizing to the peoples of Africa for the socioeconomic wreckage of SAPs, the World Bank blithely continues to behave in its old discredited ways, posing as the institution possessing the secret of development. As far as I know no senior World Bank official has ever been fired for bad development advice in Africa or elsewhere that resulted in children dying, men and women losing their livelihoods, and countries groaning from deepening poverty; and now everyone is worked up about Mr Wolfowitz's girlfriend.

Predictably, as the scandal escalated Mr Wolfowitz turned to Africa to save himself. Once again Africa was cast as a foil for Euroamerica's morally impaired. He and his dwindling number of supporters stressed his focus on African poverty and development, claiming that World Bank 'aid' (loans) to Africa had increased under his tenure. The Bank, he declared, was halfway to the 2010 goal of doubling its 2004 'aid' levels to Africa . Shamelessly, African ministers of finance were either among the loudest supporters or quietest dissenters for a World Bank chief whom even his own staff called sleazy. African leaders of social movements reacted with outrage at the complicity of some of their ministers in attempts to save Wolfowitz by backing the lie that he had been 'good for Africa'. Liberia's finance minister even used the term 'visionary leadership'[6] to refer to Mr Wolfowitz and enthused: 'We can only say that we look forward to that continuing.' In contrast, representatives from Europe and Asia apparently pressed for a tough rebuke of Mr Wolfowitz.

The Congress of South African Trade Unions (COSATU)[7] demanded Mr Wolfowitz's resignation. 'This is not just because of his abuse of his office to promote, and give a huge pay rise to his girlfriend, but because of his consistently anti-working class and anti-poor policies. His corrupt promotion of his partner typifies the morality of the capitalist system of which he is such an enthusiastic supporter.' As COSATU wrote at the time of his appointment on 17 June 2005: 'We believe that Mr Wolfowitz embodies all the worst features of the international financial institutions – the World Bank and International Monetary Fund. Like them, he has been dedicated to entrenching the power of big business and multinational corporations, at the expense of the workers and the poor. He will do nothing to make the World Bank more accountable or responsive to the needs of the world's poor countries.' COSATU endorses the International Trade Union Confederation's call for 'proper transparency and democracy at the Bank and the International Monetary Fund'.

Protested Njoki Njoroge Njehu, executive director of Nairobi-based Daughters of Mumbi Global Resource Centre: 'Don't try to make Africa his saving grace. The impact of the World Bank's policy impositions of the last 20 years still devastates us every day. There are still kids out of school, hospitals without medicines, thousands of children dying before the age of five, and millions without safe water because of the Bank's policies. Paul Wolfowitz has done nothing to change that; he is no true friend of Africa. African politicians do African peoples no favours by making excuses for corruption and for the corrupt; Wolfowitz must resign'[8]

Added Nita Evele, an activist from the Democratic Republic of Congo based in Washington, DC:

> 'Corruption and the World Bank, corruption and Paul Wolfowitz: these are not new, and are not limited to his girlfriend. Congolese in the US protested outside the Bank on Saturday – a protest that called for Wolfowitz's resign-ation. But our initial and overriding purpose was to call attention to the way the World Bank, under Wolfowitz's direction, has facilitated the turning over of our country's vast mineral resources to multinational corporations for a song. If depriving the Congolese people, some of the most impoverished and abused by decades of violent history, of control over the resources isn't corruption, what is?'

It is often forgotten that the World Bank and the other IFIs were not created to promote development in the newly independent nations of Asia and Africa, let alone the countries of Latin America (which were collectively dubbed the Third World from the late 1950s, then re-labelled the South in the early 1980s, and the global South in the early 1990s). The IMF, originally established to provide temporary balance of payments support for the industrialized countries, only expanded its activities in Africa from the 1970s. The World Bank was originally intended to help in the reconstruction of devastated post-war Europe after which it cast its eyes to Asia and Latin America. It was also only in the 1970s that Africa became a major area of Bank activities. The Bank underwent notable shifts in its policies, moving from project lending for public sector development in the 1960s to 'basic needs' in the 1970s to macroeconomic structural adjustment from the 1980s.

The two institutions became increasingly indistinguishable in their policies and practices in this era of neo-liberal ascendancy and 'free' market governments in some key Euroamerican states – Ronald Reagan's America, Brian Mulroney's Canada, Helmut Kohl's Germany, and Margaret Thatcher's Britain all sought to roll back Keynesian policy making. Together the Fund and the Bank became part of the so-called 'Washington Consensus' and set out to construct a global free-market system. African countries facing rising balance of payment deficits because of their falling terms of trade and confronted by internal challenges became prime patients for the lethal medicine of economic stabilization and structural reform.

SAPs prescribed deregulation, liberalization, and privatization, which entailed retrenchment of the public sector, rolling back of the state, divestment from social sectors including health and education, and extension of the logic of the market to all aspects of social and economic life. The results were disastrous as recovery proved elusive and poverty grew. This led some, such as Joseph Stiglitz, once the Bank's chief economist, to critique the one-size-fits-all prescriptions of SAPs. Many of the new critics of orthodox structural adjustment policies merely repeated – without full acknowledgment of course – attacks previously made by so many African scholars and policy makers. Many of us in the 1980s and 1990s argued for the construction of democratic developmental states. We were amused when the Bank began talking of democracy, in predictably instrumentalist terms, as it added governance to its long list of conditionalities.

Africa doesn't need the World Bank for its economic growth and development. No country has ever become developed through the Bank: not yesterday's South Korea, today's China, or tomorrow's Malaysia; not the regional economic powers in the global South, whether South Africa in Africa, Brazil in South America, or India in South Asia. The reason is blindingly simple: the World Bank is not an institution geared for sustainable national development, but an instrument of global capitalist regulation. If it were for the alleviation of poverty, wouldn't the world's poor countries have more say in its operations and the Bank's leaders be chosen more competitively on merit, rather than confined to white men appointed by the US President?

It matters little, therefore, if the Bank is headed by white American men (all ten of its presidents have been white male American citizens) of impeccable moral rectitude or men of reprehensible moral turpitude, for the Bank is steeped in the structural imperatives of global capitalist production and reproduction which sustain the world's economic hierarchies.

April 28, 2007.

References

1   Steven R. Weisman, 'Turmoil Grows for Wolfowitz at World Bank', *The New York Times*, April 13, 2007, available at http://query.nytimes.com/gst/fullpage.html?res=9807E0DA 133FF930A25757C0A9619C8B63

2   See the following, Emad Mekay, 'World Bank Staff Seek Wolfowitz's Ouster,' IPS, April 12, 2007, available at http://www.ipsnews.net/news.asp?idnews=37328; James Westhead, 'Wolfowitz row 'Harms World Bank'', BBC News, available at http://news.bbc.co.uk/2/hi/business/6598251.stm; and the 'Wolfowitz Resign' website at http://wolfowitzmustresign.blogspot.com/

3   Here is a sample of the editorial and stories: 'Wolfowitz Must be told to resign now,' *The Financial Times*, April 12, 2007, available at http://www.ft.com/cms/s/2/18b3bad0-e914-11db-a162-000b5df10621.html; 'Paul Wolfowitz and the World Bank,' *The Economist*, April 19, 2007, available at http://www.economist.com/opinion/displaystory.cfm? story_id=E1_JDQDNTR; 'Principle and Practice: Wolfowitz's credibility as head of the World Bank is spent,' *The Times*, April 14, 2007, available at http://www.timesonline.co.uk/tol/comment/leading_article/article1652407.ece; 'Le départ de Wolfowitz,' *Le Monde*, April 15, 2007, available at http://www.lemonde.fr/cgi-bin/ACHATS/acheter.cgi?offre=ARCHIVES&type_item=ART_ARCH_30J&objet_id=98 4616&clef=ARC-TRK-NC_01; Naomi Klein, 'The World Bank has the perfect standard bearer,' *The Guardian*, April 30, 2007, available at http://www.guardian.co.uk/ commentisfree/2007/apr/27/comment.business; Editorial, 'Wolfowitz at the World Bank Door,' *Investors Business Daily*, April 13, 2007, available at http://www.ibdeditorials.com/IBDArticles.aspx?id=261357325252882; Editorial, 'Time for Mr. Wolfowitz to Go,' *The New York Times*, April 16, 2007, available at http://query.nytimes.com/gst/fullpage.html?res=9F01EFDE113FF935A25757C0A9619C 8B63; Editorial, 'Wolfowitz fall short,' *The Los Angeles Times*, April 16, 2007, available at http://articles.latimes.com/2007/apr/16/opinion/ed-wolfowitz16; Editorial, 'World Bank Power Play,' *Wall Street Journal*, April 13, 2007, available at http://online.wsj.com/article/0,,SB117643001072468665,00.html; and Editorial, 'Trouble at the World Bank: Beware a rush to judgment over the Wolfowitz pay flap,' *The Washington Post*, April 22, 2007, available at http://www.washingtonpost.com/wp-dyn/content/article/2007/04/21/AR2007042100961.html.

4   'The neocons' humiliation,' *The Economist*, April 19, 2007, available at http://www.economist.com/world/unitedstates/displaystory.cfm?story_id=9043308

5   50 Years is Enough, 'Wolfowitz Scandal Takes Bank Hypocrisy to New Heights,' April 20, 2007, available at http://www.50years.org/cms/updates/story/403

6   'Wolfowitz says he will stay World Bank head,' *USA Today*, April 15, 2007, available at http://www.usatoday.com/news/washington/2007-04-15-wolfowitz-world-bank_N.htm

7   COSATU Daily News, Week to 20 April, 2007, available at http://groups.google.com/ group/COSATU-Daily-News/browse_thread/thread/727d2ad3254cd2c6

8   50 Years is Enough, 'African Organizations Reject Minister's Praise for Wolfowitz,' April 16, 2007.

Chapter 15

The Class of 2007: The Rising Costs of Middle-Class Certification

Over the past month I attended four graduation ceremonies, more than I have ever attended in any one year. Indeed, this equals all the graduation ceremonies I have attended in my entire academic life. For someone not big on public ceremonies—I missed two of my own for the masters and the doctorate—one might wonder whether as I get older I have suddenly caught the graduation fever. More than anything else this is a tribute to fatherhood, that most endearing and enduring of emotions: pride in one's own. My two children graduated.

It started with my son whose commencement, as graduation ceremonies are called in the United States, took place about three weeks ago, and it ended with my daughter's commencement a week ago. In between were two graduation ceremonies I attended in my capacity as department head, one a special ceremony for African American students and the other the commencement ceremony for the College of Liberal Arts and Sciences, my university's largest college.

All four ceremonies were, in their different ways, moving and exciting. I found myself enjoying the cheerful band music, the festive rowdiness of the crowds, even the antics of the odd student jumping or waving wildly or screaming with joy on the stage, and the predictable commencement speeches laced with personal anecdotes, occasionally strained humour, and wise counsel about the challenges and opportunities of the real world out there. Each ceremony was a fascinating carnival celebrating multiple transitions for the students themselves and their families, infectious public performances of certification to the middle class or confirmation to the upper classes.

Clad in their sombre gowns, caps and hoods, sometimes adorned by more colourful accessories including the ever popular *Kente* among African American students, the students were a wonder to behold. Their excited families and friends would noisily shout, whistle, or stand up and clap when the students walked the stage and their names were called to receive their hard-earned diplomas. I did stand up and clap when it was my son's and daughter's turns and even did a little shouting. And of course we took rolls of pictures to relish later and send family and friends unable to partake in this wonderful celebration of the two young people's educational achievements, and as an indulgence of parental self-congratulation, a gesture in anticipation of the rewards of social class reproduction.

I beamed with joy and pride, immensely relieved that this day had come to pass, that my children had acquired the social capital of higher education increasingly indispensable in our contemporary world of knowledge economies characterized by ruthless national and transnational free-market capitalist competition. Amidst it all, there were the flashbacks, especially the memories of my daughter's sweet childhood and testing adolescence, some wistfulness about all those years of parenting and provisioning about to change, and long-awaited relief at the impending easing of strain on my pocket and fatherly anxieties. Finally, I thought, I might be able to go on a real holiday with my wife, not the extra day or two attached to some forgettable academic conference in some nondescript location that we often take.

Each graduation ceremony left me with a particular set of images that captured, as I reflected later, the changing terrain of American higher education in its transnational, racial, and gender dynamics. In the cavernous indoor sports arena where my son's graduation took place I was struck by the virtual absence of American students in the roll call of those graduating with engineering degrees. Many of the students were from India or of Indian descent, whose names the announcer tried hard not to mangle, although not always successfully. If many of the students were indeed from India rather than Indian American, it provided a small measure of the expanding technological frontiers of India, of the country's emergence as the world's fourth largest economy.

For the past few years India has had the largest number of foreign students in the United States, totalling 76,503 in 2005 (13.5 per cent of the total), followed by China with 62,582, South Korea 58,847, and Japan 38,712. Between them the four countries plus Taiwan (in sixth place after Canada) accounted for nearly half of all foreign students in the United States, still the leading destination of foreign students in the world notwithstanding the stringent immigration policies imposed after the terrorist attacks of 9/11. The majority of these students study in the scientific and technical fields. In contrast, the two leading African countries, Kenya and Nigeria, ranked in seventeenth and eighteenth place had only 6,559 and 6,192 students, respectively. At my son's graduation there was a smattering of students with Nigerian and Kenyan names, mostly in the social sciences and some in business. My son was one of only two students with a Malawian name. He majored in business administration.

At the commencement ceremonies on my campus, the enduring and often disturbing racial dimensions of American higher education were on full display. The fact that there was a special ceremony for Black students spoke volumes about the alienation many African American students feel on the large campuses of the historically white research universities, even among the public universities that profess a commitment to diversity. In its strategic plan, my campus proclaims a 'Great Cities Commitment', the ambition to become the country's leading public urban university. Yet, African American students make up less than 9 per cent of the total student population in a city where African Americans comprise the largest group (36.4 per cent, while Whites constitute 31.3 per cent, Hispanics 26 per cent, and Asian and Pacific Islanders 4.3 per cent). At the larger college convocation held a few days later, the African American students were noticeably scarce among the thousands of graduates. The boisterous good cheer of that earlier celebration was largely absent from their faces as they walked onto the stage in the massive indoor pavilion.

In 2004 the number of African Americans enrolled in American colleges reached 2.2 million (12.5 per cent of the total), up from 1.5 million in 1994 (10.3 per cent of the total). The percentage of the African American population with a college education has been rising steadily since 1950.[1]

Holders of Bachelor's Degrees Aged 25+ (Per cent)

Year	1950	1960	1970	1980	1990	2000	2005
African American	2.2	3.5	6.1	7.9	11.3	16.6	17.7
National Average	6.2	7.7	11.0	17.0	21.3	25.6	27.6

Large numbers of African Americans continue to be educated at the dozens of historically black colleges and universities (HBCUs),[2] forty of which are public four-year colleges and forty-nine private, and another fourteen two-year colleges, both public and private. Although comprising a mere 3 per cent of American's colleges and universities, the HBCUs enrol a quarter of African American students nationally and award a quarter of bachelor degrees and one-sixth of masters and professional degrees to African Americans.

My daughter went to an HBCU where she majored in Psychology. Having done her early schooling in Canada at a school with only two Black students, when we relocated to the United States she seemed eager for the Black experience, although the cultural meanings and class inflections of blackness for her seemed to shift over time. Therefore, I was not surprised when she chose to go to an HBCU. Thus, on her graduation what struck me was not the racial profile of the graduating class, or the specializations of the students, who were in all fields from the arts and humanities to the social sciences and natural sciences, to engineering and the professions, but their gender dynamics. There were far more women than men. The crowds were even larger than at the three graduation ceremonies I had attended earlier. The commencement was held in the sports stadium and by eight in the morning when it began, the stadium was filled to capacity, a testimony, if any were needed, of the high value many African American families place on higher education notwithstanding stereotypes to the contrary.

What I witnessed at my daughter's graduation is part of a national trend. Females now outnumber males at American college campuses. The gender gap has widened since the 1990s. In 1995, there were 7.9 million women students out of 14.3 million students (55.5 per cent), figures that rose to 9.9 million in 2004 out of 17.3 million students (57.2 per cent). The gap is particularly wide among African Americans: women made up

62.3 per cent of Black students in 1995 and 65 per cent in 2004. By 2005, the proportion of African American women with a bachelor's degree or higher was 18.9 per cent compared to 16.1 per cent for men. Looking at figures since 1950, however, the change appears less dramatic. African American men had surpassed African American women in levels of education only in 1970 and 1990. On many an occasion I have joked with my daughter about who she and her heterosexual friends will marry with the apparent shortage of college educated Black men. This is of course not a joke to many for whom the challenges of finding single Black men are widely publicized in the popular media, including respectable national papers such as *The Washington Post.*[3]

All these thoughts about the transnational, racial, and gender dynamics of American higher education were of course far from my mind as I watched and revelled in the graduation ceremonies, as we celebrated in the evening over dinner and drinks with family and friends. I was simply one immensely proud and happy father. My son and daughter were equally proud and happy. Like millions of graduating students across the United States and elsewhere in the world they were also relieved that a crucial period in their lives, for many a four- to six-year ordeal, had come to a successful end. The majority of students in the United States now earn their coveted degrees in six years rather than four.[4] The rate varies slightly for students in public and private colleges: in 1999–2000 it was 6.2 years and 5.3 years, respectively. My children mirror these trends. My son who went to public school finished in six years and my daughter who attended private school in five. It might be because I put a lot more pressure on my daughter to finish given the much higher cost of her college education.

One consequence of these trends is that while the United States ranks among the top five nations in the proportion of its younger adults, aged 18 to24, who enrol in college (with a participation rate of 35 per cent, behind Korea with 48 per cent, Greece 43 per cent, Finland 37 per cent, and Belgium 37 per cent), the completion rate is only 17 per cent, behind fifteen other industrialized countries.[5] Indeed, in comparative terms the proportion of younger adults with college education in the United States is now far below that of the older adults – those aged 35 to 64. Thirty-nine per cent of older adults in the country have a college degree—the same percentage as for the younger adults; the US ranks second in the first category and eighth in the second. Altogether, in 2005, 27.6 per cent of the US population aged 25 and above had a bachelors or higher degree.

Clearly, while the United States still boasts the world's largest and most diversified higher education system in the world, it is slipping behind other industrialized nations. The country has an astounding 4,355 degree granting institutions (and a further 2,252 non-degree granting institutions), 60.6 per cent of them 4-year colleges and the remainder 2-year colleges. The public colleges account for a quarter of the former and two-thirds of the latter. Altogether, in 2005 nearly 18 million students were enrolled in American colleges, 52 per cent in public colleges (42 per cent were undergraduate students). China, the new emerging economic superpower, is very close behind with 16 million students. The rate of higher education growth in China has been staggering: its college-age population enrolment rate doubled from less than 10 per cent in 1999 to nearly 20 per cent in 2006.

The relatively long completion period and high dropout rates in the United States can be attributed to many factors. The tendency to transfer colleges certainly plays a role: almost half of American students attend two or more institutions before they graduate. And many frequently change their majors. My son and daughter did both; they each attended two institutions and changed their majors, something quite inconceivable when I did my undergraduate studies in Malawi – where there was only one university. Also, many students are often ill-prepared for college and need remedial courses: in 2003–4, 15 per cent of first and second-year students at four-year public colleges and 12 per cent at private colleges took such courses.

Moreover, abetted by their 'helicopter' baby boom parents and the ubiquitous culture of mass consumption, instant gratification, and the dizzying obsolescence of tastes and fashions, American students tend to enjoy and seek much higher levels of material gratification – fancy cars, apartments, electronic gadgets – that would have been incomprehensible for my generation, and would surprise students in many other countries. So they often need to work or incur high levels of debt, which can sink their dreams for higher education. In 2002, only a quarter of students did not work; one-third worked full-time, two-fifths part-time. But students do not work simply to satisfy some proverbial material cravings; they increasingly have to do so to pay for their education. Rising cost is at the heart of the growing crisis of higher education in the United States. For students from working-class and even middle-class family backgrounds, higher education is increasingly unaffordable.

The cost of higher education has outstripped the rate of inflation and increases in student aid as colleges and universities have raised tuition fees either to cover declining public fiscal support or to raise their profile and brands in the ferocious competition for top quality faculty and students. In 2004–5, 75 per cent of the 2.6 million full-time and first-time degree/certificate seeking undergraduate students received student aid. There were of course variations based on the type of institutions and student background. But student aid from federal or state governments, the colleges themselves or private sources has become increasingly insufficient to cover the costs of higher education.

In 2006–7, for example, the average tuition fees per year for four-year colleges amounted to[6] $5,836 for public colleges and $22,218 for private colleges, up from $2,628 and $12,375 in 1986–7, respectively. When other costs are included such as books and supplies, room and board, and transportation the figures shoot to $16,337 for resident students in public colleges ($26,304 for out of state students) and to $33,301 in private colleges, compared to $7,528 and $18,312 twenty years earlier. In the meantime, Pell grants, the popular federal grant, which a generation earlier could finance public college tuition fees, was a paltry $4,050.

Not surprisingly, the net price of college education for students and their families has risen. For public colleges net tuition fees and other charges increased, in constant dollars, from $1,800 in 1996–7 to $3,100 in 2006–7, while for private colleges the rise was from $6,340 to $9,000. Consequently, four-year college education is increasingly out of reach for working-class students, many of whom are ending up at the two-year community colleges, thereby reproducing and entrenching America's unyielding class hierarchies that the tired rhetoric of the American Dream can no longer hide, if it ever could.

The largest cohort of dependent students in 2002 – 10.5 per cent – were from families earning more than $100,000; another 5.9 per cent came from families with incomes of $80,000-99,999, and 8.4 per cent with incomes of $60,000–79,999. Only 15.8 per cent of the students came from households with incomes of less than $40,000. The median household income in 2002 was $42,409.[7] Fewer students from the lower middle class have been receiving bachelor degrees. Their share dropped from 15 per cent in 1980 to 11 per cent in 2004,[8] while the share for the more affluent students rose from 72 per cent to 79 per cent during the same period.

Many needy students are increasingly resorting to private loans whose volume has grown correspondingly rapidly. In 2006 private loans reached $16 billion compared to $69 billion for federal loans.[9] Some predict that given the exponential growth rate – more than 1,000 per cent between the mid-1990s and 2006 and more than ten times the rate for federal loans – private loans will eclipse federal loans within a decade. Unlike the latter, the former are more risky and costly because of their variable interest rates, differentiation of borrowers according to their credit rating, and stringent repayment schedules. Previously, professional and graduate students were the most likely to resort to private loans, but in 2003–4 more than four-fifths of borrowers were undergraduate students. Adding salt to injury, some universities have been colluding with private loan companies by placing them on preferred lender lists and steering unwary students to them in exchange for bribes. The scandal broke early this month when the New York Attorney General began investigating several corrupt lenders and universities.

The result is that, as one aggrieved parent wrote, students are becoming a 'new indentured class',[10] owing large sums of money well into their middle age. He noted wryly that the average four-year student debt doubled from $9,200 in 1992 to $18,900 in 2002 (or $21,000 including credit card debt), and so did the debt incurred by parents for their children's education, from $18,572 in 1992-3 to $38,428 in 1999–2000. It is even worse for those in the professional schools. Law school graduates[11] reportedly owe $50,000–$80,000; medical school graduates[12] owe $120,000; and some doctoral students in education[13] owed more than $138,500. Such staggering costs not only increasingly exclude all but the wealthiest students from the professions, they also ensure that professionals avoid working for the relatively low-paying public sector, thereby impoverishing this sector and reinforcing the privatization of the economy and society.

The fact that my children completed their education without any student loans makes them part of a small, privileged group. Having incurred no loans for my own education, thanks to scholarships, I felt it was my obligation to provide them with a loan-free undergraduate education. It was of course not cheap. It was immensely gratifying when both of them told me, on their graduation, that they were deeply grateful for my assistance and encouragement, which more than made up for all those long years of belt tightening.

Education is one of the lasting gifts a parent can provide a child. And maybe my son and daughter will look after me when I am old. That is what I was taught as a child growing up in Africa, that children are their parents' future guardians, their ultimate existential and psychic insurance policy. But surely, society has a duty to ensure quality public higher education for all, not as a special privilege for the better heeled. It is a shame that a country as wealthy as the United States cannot provide such an education for the majority of its people, as it squanders trillions on misguided wars abroad and upholding racial and class polarizations at home. As we all await the dawn of public reason, I await news that my son and daughter have found good paying jobs, so that I can finally declare financial freedom from them.

May 28, 2007.

References

1. Institute of Education Sciences, National Center for Education Statistics, 'Percentage of persons age 25 and over and 25 to 29, by race/ethnicity, years of school completed, and sex: Selected years, 1910 through 2005' available at http://nces.ed.gov/programs/digest/d05/tables/dt05_008.asp
2. U.S. Department of Education, 'List of HBCUs—White House Initiative on Historically Black Colleges and Universities', available at http://www.ed.gov/about/inits/list/whhbcu/edlite-list.html
3. Krissah Williams, 'Singled Out: In Seeking a Mate, Men and Women Find a delicate Balance,' *The Washington Post*, October 8, 2006, available at http://www.washingtonpost.com/wp-dyn/content/article/2006/10/07/AR2006100701070.html
4. Institute of Education Sciences, National Center for Education Statistics, *Enrolment in Postsecondary Institutions Fall 2005; Graduation Rates 1999 and 2002 Cohorts; and Financial Statistics Fiscal Year 2005*, available at http://nces.ed.gov/pubs2007/2007154.pdf
5. The National Center for Public Policy and Higher Education, Measuring Up 2006: The National Report Card on Higher Education, available at http://measuringup.highereducation.org/_docs/2006/NationalReport_2006.pdf
6. College Board, *Trends in College Pricing*, Trends in College Series 2006, available at http://www.collegeboard.com/prod_downloads/press/cost06/trends_college_pricing_06.pdf

7.   Carmen DeNavas-Walt, et al. *Income in the United States 2002*, U.S. Census Bureau, 2003, available at http://www.census.gov/prod/2003pubs/p60-221.pdf

8.   Stephen Burd, 'Working Class Students Feel the Pinch', *The Chronicle of Higher Education*, June 9, 2006, available at http://chronicle.com/article/Working-Class-Students-Feel/25963

9.   Institute of Higher Education, *The Future of Private Loans: Who is Borrowing and Why*, December 2006, available at http://www.ihep.org/assets/files/publications/a-f/FuturePrivateLoans.pdf

10. Jeffrey J. Williams, 'A New Indentured Class,' *The Chronicle Review*, June 30, 2006, available at http://chronicle.com/weekly/v52/i43/43b00601.htm

11. Katherine S. Mangan, 'Bar Assn. Says Low Pay Keeps Law Graduates out of Public Service,' *The Chronicle of Higher Education*, September 5, 2003, available at http://chronicle.com/article/Bar-Assn-Says-Low-Pay-Keeps/25833/

12. Katherine Mangan, 'Medical Schools Told to Change Priorities,' *The Chronicle of Higher Education*, November 10, 2006, available at http://chronicle.com/article/Medical-Schools-Told-to-Cha/20901/

13. John Gravois, 'Trapped by Education,' *The Chronicle of Higher Education*, April 6, 2007 available at http://chronicle.com/article/Trapped-by-Education/2845

Chapter 16

Dancing with the Dragon: Africa's Courtship with China

Africa's courtship with China, a captivating dance of the elephant and the dragon, has intriguing implications for all concerned and the world at large. It is marked by, on the one hand, the grand political theatre of elaborate presidential tours and lavish summits, with their lofty declarations of equal partnership between the distant peoples of two ancient lands, by all those dramatic and diplomatic displays of statehood beloved of postcolonial or post-revolutionary societies enchanted by their sovereignty. On the other, it is driven by the explosive growth of economic exchanges, from thriving trade to increasing investment to mounting migrations, by the pursuit of the tantalizing promises of development embodied in the dreams of nationhood in the world's most populous country and its poorest continent. Choreographed by such powerful political and economic imperatives, it is a dance that arouses great interest in the media, among curious academics, cynical politicians, and concerned civil society activists. The commentaries swing unsteadily from the excited to the anxious, the celebratory to the condemnatory, and the sanguine to the suspicious.

The courtship has intensified since 2000. In that year the first ministerial conference of the Forum on China-Africa Cooperation[1] (or FOCAC) was held in Beijing in October, and attended by the Chinese president and premier, four African presidents and the OAU Secretary-General, as well as more than eighty ministers from China and forty-four African countries, representatives from seventeen regional and international organizations, and business people from Africa and China. The second ministerial conference was held in Addis Ababa in December 2003, and attended by the Chinese premier, six African presidents and three prime ministers, the heads of the African Union and the United Nations, and more than seventy ministers from China and African countries.

In November 2006 came the glittering Beijing Summit and Third Ministerial Conference of FOCAC,[2] which was attended by the leaders of forty-eight African countries, from Egypt to South Africa. China staged a dazzling performance, its biggest diplomatic party ever to celebrate the 'new strategic partnership' with Africa. The sights, sounds, and even culinary smells of Africa were everywhere; the spruced up streets of Beijing were emblazoned with the stereotypical Africa of elephants, zebras, and giraffes, a land that was finally open for engagement with the dragon flexing its global economic muscles, with the insatiable new factory of the world.

Besides these grand multilateral summits, bilateral visits between Chinese and African leaders have become commonplace; Chinese President Hu Jintao has visited Africa three times since taking office in 2003. Nor have the exchanges been confined to pageantry-loving politicians. Business people and economic agencies have joined in this carnival of economic cooperation. During the second FOCAC meeting the first China-Africa business conference brought more than 500 entrepreneurs and 21 cooperation agreements were signed worth $1 billion; while at the 2006 Summit business deals worth $1.9 billion were signed. In recognition of the growing economic importance of China, the African Development Bank– the continent's premier multilateral development agency – held its 42nd annual meeting in Shanghai in May 2007.[3] The meeting was attended by a record 2,500 representatives from Africa, Asia and other parts of the world. This was the second time the ADB held its annual board meeting outside the continent; the first was in 2001 in Spain.

The trade and investment figures tell an even more compelling story. Trade between Africa and China increased from $817 million in 1977 to $1.4 billion in 1991, jumping to $10 billion in 2000 and $39.7 billion in 2005. It reached $55.5 billion in 2006 and is projected to rise to $100 billion by 2010. By the end of 2006, about 800 Chinese companies were operating in Africa and they had invested $11.7 billion, up from about $6 billion in 2005, in sectors ranging from extractive industries, principally oil and minerals, to big infrastructural projects such as roads, railways, dams, and airports, and to services, especially telecommunications and retail trade. Chinese petty traders even began to appear on the streets of some African cities. The numbers of Chinese working or living in Africa for extended periods have reportedly swelled to 750,000.

What drives this explosive growth in economic ties between Africa and China? What is its current and likely future impact on Africa? Is China, to echo an article in the South African *Mail & Guardian,*[4] Africa's friend or foe, comrade or colonizer? There are of course no shortages of views, whether gleeful or gloomy; some reminiscent of the old rhetoric of Third World solidarity, of Afro-Asian dialogue or South-South cooperation, others full of trepidation, recalling Africa's tragic history of external pillage, and warning Africa to be wary of the strangers from the east bearing flashy but flimsy gifts of dependency and underdevelopment.

The commentaries from many Western opinion makers are predictably hysterical and hypocritical. Typical is the three part series in the *New York Times*[5] titled, 'New Power in Africa,' which explores 'China's deepening economic and political ties with Africa.' The language is one of possessive paternalism, simultaneously disdainful and dismissive of both Africa and China, while bemoaning and dreading the loss of historic Euroamerican hegemony over the continent. In this narrative, the Chinese are flourishing in Africa because being corrupt and authoritarian themselves, they are not averse to doing business with Africa's corrupt and authoritarian regimes; they pay no heed to the ostensibly enlightened trading and lending criteria of Western countries and their international financial institutions.

Moreover, Chinese business in Africa is profitable because the Chinese workers they bring are themselves used to poverty. 'While Western companies must provide relatively plush and private accommodations to attract expatriate workers, the Chinese employees … live in barrack-like conditions, several to a room.' As the Chinese move in, the authors lament, 'the Western presence, once dominant, has steadily dwindled, and essentially consists nowadays of relief experts working in international agencies or oil workers living behind high walls in heavily guarded enclaves.'

Thus corruption, authoritarianism, and poverty provide China with an unfair advantage in African markets. Since Western discourse on Africa is rooted in the moralistic language of the mercy-industrial complex, the narrative goes further. Chinese-African economic relations are judged in the calculus of human rights rather than commerce. And so Sudan and

Zimbabwe are trotted out as primary exhibits of the moral bankruptcy of the growing economic ties between China and Africa. For good economic measure, it is pointed out that China is using Africa as a training ground for its aspiring multinational corporations, and Chinese investment is leaving behind it 'a trail of heartbreak and recrimination', including the collapse of manufacturing industries, as well as cultural misunderstanding, and growing hostility. No polls or surveys are needed of course; China cannot be the beloved West, Africa's benevolent benefactor for centuries.

Never mind that democratic South Africa is one of China's two leading African trading partners (the other is Angola; China-South Africa trade was worth $8.5 billion in 2006), or that last year Africa accounted for a mere 3.2 per cent of China's total trade estimated at $1.76 trillion, or that China's main trading partners are the US itself, the EU, Japan, and South Korea – all countries considered democratic. US-China trade reached $203.9 billion in 2006 or 11.6 per cent of China's total trade (the US trade deficit was $148.7 billion). And while China has indeed overtaken Britain, its trade with Africa lags behind the US and France. Meanwhile, Africa-US trade[6] rose to $99.5 billion (the US had a trade deficit of $61.4 billion), marking an increase of 23 per cent over 2005. Even when it comes to oil, while China imported a third of its oil from Africa, this represented only 8.7 per cent of Africa's oil exports; Europe took 36 per cent and the US 33 per cent.

To many Africans, Euroamerica lacks any moral authority to criticize China's dealings with Africa because of its long and sordid history of slavery, colonialism, and neo-liberalism that accounts for much of Africa's underdevelopment. The reality of the Africa-China relationship is a lot more complex, and exhibits contradictory tendencies that are often ignored or oversimplified in the debate. To begin with, it is important to note how old Africa-China contacts are. It is not necessary in this context to trace the links to ancient Pharaonic times, which did exist, or even to Zheng's epic voyages between Asia and Africa in the early fifteenth century (1405–1433).

After the Second World War, several African countries and China enjoyed cordial relations in the polarized context of the Cold War that was soon overlaid by the Sino-Soviet split. During this era, the relations were as much ideological as they were economic, motivated by anti-imperialism as well as economic cooperation, by the multifaceted imperative of national liberation. The construction of Tazara railway was only the most graphic example of this multifaceted partnership, which also involved educational, cultural, and technical exchanges, and support for liberation movements fighting European settler colonialism in Southern Africa. This is to suggest that the tendency to distinguish between ideological and economic motivations, and sequester them in the past and present, respectively, is analytically unproductive.

But even then it was an unequal relationship, as Mwalimu Julius Nyerere readily recognized. Tanzania-China relations, he conceded, were between 'most unequal equals'. It is more unequal now because China is a lot stronger economically and otherwise than it was a generation ago. This leads some to view China's economic dealings with Africa in terms of imperialism. Clearly, China is driven by its voracious appetite for raw materials, and search for markets, and investment outlets, a familiar textbook definition of imperialism. In 2006 President Mbeki warned[7] 'against allowing Chinese forays into Africa to become a neo-colonialist adventure, with African raw materials exchanged for shoddy manu-factured imports, and little attention to developing an impoverished continent.' The South African commentator, William Gumede,[8] virtually accused China of becoming Africa's new colonizer. It is quite revealing that some of the loudest warnings against China's colonialist or neo-colonialist ambitions come from South Africa, Africa's largest economy with its own hegemonic ambitions across the continent.

Nineteenth and twentieth-century Western imperialism was made of much sterner stuff than is evident from or even possible with China's current engagement with Africa. Talk of China's 'Scramble for Africa' is quite disingenuous. Africa, for all its weaknesses, is simply not susceptible to classic colonialism, precisely because of its very encounter with Western imperialism and the protracted and horrendously costly struggles against it. This is not to argue that the relationship between China and Africa is not fraught with its own pitfalls. It is merely to call for more careful analysis, to avoid the hysteria of questionable historical analogies.

It is true that China's entry into Africa and world markets has ravaged textile manufacturing industries in many African countries. But it is well to remember the process of de-industrialization in these countries was facilitated by the disastrous neo-liberal policies of structural adjustment imposed with fundamentalist zeal by Western-controlled international financial institutions. Nor can the trading and tariff barriers against African manufactured exports in Western markets be discounted. At stake, for Africa, is not China's pursuit of self-interest, but the pursuit of Africa's own self-interest, for it stands to reason that every country seeks to maximize its self-interest.

Many Africans see China as an attractive alternative to Euroamerica. China is valued as a possible source of assistance and investment, as a development model, as a bulwark against Western hegemony – a kind of economic neo-Cold War leader, or as simply an invaluable major new trading partner. The first three assumptions cannot withstand the glare of geopolitical realities. At the Beijing Summit China announced an aid package of $3 billion, a $5 billion investment fund, and offered to cancel $1.3 billion of debt to 31 African countries, set up 30 hospitals, 30 malaria prevention centres, 10 agricultural pilot centres, 100 rural schools, and double the number of African students studying in China to 4,000. In mid-2006, China's foreign direct investment in Africa reached $1.2 billion.

For a continent of about 950 million this is an insignificant drop in the ocean, although the quality of Chinese 'aid' has historically tended to be higher than Western 'aid'. Expecting China to be a significant source of development assistance is gravely mistaken. Both friends and foes of China tend to argue that Chinese 'aid' comes with few strings attached, that it is free from the notorious conditions of Western 'aid'. Chinese development discourse assiduously promotes this perception and African leaders tired of being constantly lectured by the West are sometimes too eager to embrace it. But the proclamations of 'soft power' should not be allowed to conceal China's hardnosed superpower ambitions.

Chinese development 'aid' is as tied as any and it does not differ, in its composition, from Western aid, in so far as it is composed of loans, grants, and technical assistance. To date, China remains a small provider of 'soft loans' to the continent. This of course may change, perhaps soon if the $20 billion pledge for the next three years for infrastructure and trade financing announced at the ADB meeting in Shanghai is configured differently. What is clear is that China has its own conditions: economically its 'aid' recipients are expected to patronize Chinese firms and procure Chinese goods and services, and politically to adhere to the one China policy. And the jury is still out on whether the Chinese will resist, in their future aid packages, the pernicious Western habit of counting everything in their dealings with Africa as 'aid', from loans and debt relief, to technical assistance and educational scholarships.

Chinese investment is clearly growing, but there is little evidence so far that Chinese investors behave differently from other investors. They want high returns. They are not coming to Africa for philanthropic reasons but to make money. They are in the business of business. In fact, there are reports that because of their relative unfamiliarity with African workers, they sometimes act in an offensive, if not outrightly racist, manner. It was partly in response to this challenge that at the Beijing Summit the Chinese government issued a code of conduct for Chinese businesses in Africa, the so-called Nine Principles that called for respect for local laws, worker's labour rights, transparency, and environmental protection, among other things. More fundamentally, there is no 'Beijing Consensus' that is qualitatively different from the Washington Consensus as regards challenging the framework of the international economic system. In short, China's economic emergence does not contest let alone undermine, ideologically, the unipolar world of the post-Cold War era, even if it pluralizes the centres of economic power.

Notwithstanding the official rhetoric, it is important to note that the Chinese economic juggernaut is on an apparently inexorable capitalist path that offers no real alternative model for Africa. Indeed, for many progressive African critics of China's African policy, the Chinese model of development without democracy is anathema. The African social imaginary has always been guided by three fundamental quests: for self-determination, development, and democracy that brooks no trade off between them, especially following the democratic struggles and gains of the last two decades. India may provide a much better model in this regard.

This is not to downplay the enormous historical achievements of Chinese capitalism, the extraordinary capacity it has demonstrated, which is almost unprecedented in human history, to uplift hundreds of millions of people from abject poverty in such a short time. It is merely to caution against the tendency to view Africa as a developmental *tabula rasa* awaiting the inscription of models from abroad. Africa needs to

149

develop its own models, its distinctive paths to development, carved out of its specific and complex histories, rather than the histories of others, however inspiring.

Thus, it is simplistic, even mistaken, for Africa to see China as an economic bulwark against Euroamerica, let alone as the solution to its pervasive challenges of development. But China's emergence as an economic powerhouse does offer the continent new opportunities to diversify its economic partners. It is only in this sense that the 'China card' offers Africa some respite. Indeed, many commentators attribute Africa's relatively buoyant economic growth over the past few years—5.5 per cent in 2006 and a projected 5.9 per cent in 2007 and 5.8 per cent in 2008—directly to the continent's rising trading relations with China and Asia in general, and indirectly to the markets for raw materials in China and India, which have boosted global primary commodity prices.

The challenge for Africa is to turn the proceeds into investments for economic diversification and sustainable development, and avoid frittering them away in conspicuous consumption and capital exports to Western banks. Economic history, certainly the economic history of the continent, teaches us that the long-term trend is towards falling primary commodity prices and declining terms of trade for primary producers. In short, industrialization and diversification away from reliance on raw materials remain historical imperatives for Africa's future, which no amount of trade with China or Asia can offset.

More specifically, Africa needs to know more about China, in order to coordinate its policies on and define its interests and relations with China realistically. Knowing more about China falls into the realm of education and research: studying China seriously, its languages, history, and culture, as well as its economic and geopolitical interests and calculations. It also entails more vigorous educational and cultural exchanges, the establishment of centres of Chinese studies in African universities as the University of Stellenbosch in South Africa,[9] Nnamdi Azikiwe University in Nigeria, and the University of Zimbabwe have done, and the creation of independent think tanks on China that can advise African governments and businesses. Indeed, Africa ought to do this for all the major powers and regions of the world, including the West which we assume to know, sometimes superficially and often unstrategically, by virtue of our intimate histories of slavery, colonialism and neo-colonialism.

Coordinating Africa's China policy is a simple question of numbers. China is a country of 1.3 billion people and a $2.8 trillion economy. Africa's 54 countries combined have a total population of 945 million and an economy of $2.6 trillion (at purchasing power parity). There is simply no African country that, by itself, can negotiate effective terms of engagement with China, or any of the major powers and regional blocs, by itself. The imperative for African unity remains as pressing as ever, if not more so with the emergence of the new economic powers of Asia. The African Union and its organs such as NEPAD, as well as regional agencies like ECOWAS, SADC, the Maghreb Union, EAC, and COMESA ought to take the lead in this process.

But governments being what they are, it is unlikely that they can spearhead effective strategies for progressive engagement with China. They need the constant prodding of civil society organizations (CSOs) and activists. African civil society actors together with trade unions, working creatively and strategically with capital and the state, within and across national borders, can help to ensure that labour standards are respected, living wages are paid, and the human rights of African workers are upheld. Efforts need to be made to forge coalitions and network beyond Africa's borders, with groups and activists overseas, in this case in China and Asia more broadly.

The challenges of forging productive links between African and Chinese civil societies are immense. History serves as a double edged sword. It saves China from the pernicious legacy of slavery and colonialism that afflicts relations between Africa and Euroamerica, but it also deprives the Africa-China relationship of the intimacies of familiarity and the mediations of the enduring African Diasporic presence at the very heart of Euroamerica. In this context, the historic meeting between African and Chinese CSOs on the margins of the ADB meeting in Shanghai was heart-warming. It marked an important step that needs to become a regular feature of Chinese-African relations.

Together, CSOs as well as academics and other concerned groups must put the feet of governments and businesses in Africa and China to the fires of accountability and transparency. Certainly, the devastating environmental impact of Chinese companies working in Africa's extractive industries like oil, gas, mining, and logging, are no different from those of companies from elsewhere working in Africa, or Chinese companies operating in China itself. The convergence of interests of states and capital must be matched, and countered, by the solidarities of social movements.

It is the agency of the ordinary peoples of Africa that ultimately thwarted the colonial ambitions of Europe and the authoritarian propensities of Africa's own postcolonial ruling elites. This will also save Africa from any new or old colonial predators. Already Chinese firms and workers have become prey to rebel attacks in Niger and Ethiopia, as well as popular and political opposition in countries such as Zambia. China needs to learn more about Africa, as Africa needs to learn more about China, as their political and business leaders celebrate the incredible growth in economic relations between the peoples of these two remarkable lands.

September 4, 2007.

References

1. The First Ministerial Conference of the Forum on China-Africa Cooperation, available at http://www.fmprc.gov.cn/zflt/eng/bjzl/t404136.htm
2. Beijing Summit and Third Ministerial Conference of the Forum on China-Africa Cooperation, available at http://www.focacsummit.org/
3. The 2007 Annual Meeting of the African Development Bank, available at http://adb_english.people.com.cn/81415/5731101.html
4. Clare Nullis, Africa looks to China, India with Hope and Fear: Friend or Foe, Comrade or Coloniser?', Mail & Guardian, June 15, 2007, available at http://www.mg.co.za/article/2007-06-15-africa-looks-to-china-india-with-hope-and-fear
5. Howard French and Lydia Polgreen, 'New Power in Africa', Series, *The New York Times*, August 13, 18, 21, 2007, available at http://www.nytimes.com/ref/world/china_africa.html
6. U.S. Census Bureau, Foreign Trade Division, Data Dissemination Branch, 'Trade with Africa', available at http://www.census.gov/foreign-trade/balance/c0013.html#2007
7. Michelle Faul, Mixed Reaction to China's Africa Push,' *Mail & Guardian*, February 8, 2007, available at http://www.mg.co.za/article/2007-02-08-mixed-reaction-to-chinas-africa-push
8. Willian Gumede, 'Don't condemn Africa to Underdevelopment', *The Washington Post*, February 7, 2007, http://newsweek.washingtonpost.com/postglobal/william_gumede/2007/02/china_could_condemn_africa_to.html
9. University of Stellenbosch, Centre for Chinese Studies, available at http://www.ccs.org.za/scholarships.html

Chapter 17

The Contemporary Relevance of Pan-Africanism

Ghana holds a special place in our collective Pan-African imagination for its early independence under the illustrious leadership of President Kwame Nkrumah, whose dreams of African unity and regeneration remain as pressing as ever. In my youth Ghana acquired mythic status because it was an unwavering beacon of liberation for the rest of the continent yearning to be free from colonial barbarity; the first president of my homeland, Dr Hastings Kamuzu Banda, was a friend of Dr Nkrumah and spent many years in Kumasi, from where he returned to lead the nationalist movement in Malawi. And dare I mention that your football team, the Black Stars, beat us 12–0 in October 1962, two years before our independence! We of course attributed that to the fact that you were independent and we were still under colonial rule, which must have galvanized my parents' generation in their fight for independence!

I feel especially humbled and honoured that I have been asked to speak on 'The Contemporary Relevance of Pan-Africanism' on this august occasion to launch the Kwame Nkrumah Chair in African Studies at the Institute for African Studies, University of Ghana. First, let me thank the Director of the Institute, Professor Takyiwaa Manuh, who I have known for many years for inviting me. Let me also commend her and her colleagues and the university at large for securing the resources to create this important Chair in memory of one of Africa's most remarkable leaders. President Nkrumah was not only a great Pan-Africanist, but also a distinguished intellectual in his own right, a true philosopher-king. It is important for our universities to create endowed chairs as a mechanism of recognizing, nurturing and celebrating intellectual excellence. And it is crucial for our societies to develop new cultures of philanthropy in which individuals and corporations support and endow public and private institutions including universities. Partnership between the state, capital, civil society and academe is indispensable for the realization of the quintuple dreams of African nationalism—decolonization, nation-building, development, democracy, and regional integration—four of which remain to be fully realised.

As this is my first visit to this wonderful country and given the importance of the occasion, I trust you will understand if my prepared remarks go over the time I have been allotted. I also seek your indulgence if I start my presentation with a brief historical account of Pan-African-ism given the fact that I am a historian. More importantly, I believe we cannot fully appreciate the contemporary relevance of Pan-Africanism without understanding its past. The past, the present, and the future are always interconnected, they are intersected historical processes.

Pan-Africanism encompassed various political, cultural, and intellect-ual movements based on a series of shared presumptions and objectives. It was inspired by the desire to instil racial pride among African peoples on the continent and in the Diaspora, to achieve their self-determination from European domination, to promote solidarity among them, and to foster their social and economic regeneration. Thus, Pan-Africanism had two main objectives: first, to liberate Africans and the African Diaspora from racial degradation, political oppression, and economic exploitation; second, to encourage unity or integration among African peoples in political, cultural, and economic matters. Pan-Africanist ideas were derived from the experiences of and struggles against slavery, colonialism and racism, as well as internationalist ideas of democracy, Marxism and socialism, and nationalist ideas from other parts of the colonized world, such as Ghanaian philosophy. So Pan-Africanism was a complex move-ment, which had diverse origins, contexts, objectives, ideologies, and forms of organisaization. It was also gendered in terms of the relative participation of men and women, and in the construction of its ideo-logies, as an imaginary that was primarily nationalist; nationalist imagin-aries have, historically, tended to be masculinist.

At least six versions or imaginaries of Pan-Africanism can be identified: Transatlantic, Black Atlantic, continental, Sub-Saharan, Pan-Arab, and global. Proponents of the first imagined a Pan-African world linking continental Africa and its Diaspora in the Americas. The second version confined itself to the African Diasporic communities in the Americas and Europe, excluding continental Africa, as articulated in Paul Gilroy's book *The Black Atlantic,* in which the cultural creativity and connections of the African Diaspora in the United States and Britain are celebrated, while continental Africa is largely ignored. The third focused primarily on the unification of continental Africa. The fourth and fifth restricted themselves to the peoples of the continent north and south of the Sahara, and in the case of Pan-Arabism, extended itself to western Asia or the so-called Middle East. While Gamal Abdel Nasser proudly saw Egypt at the centre of three concentric circles linking the African, Arab, and Islamic worlds, Sheikh Anta Diop argued for the fundamental cultural unity of Africa rooted in the civilizations of the Nile valley including Pharaonic Egypt. The sixth sought to reclaim the connections of African peoples dispersed to all corners of the globe.

Each version, as a discourse or a movement, developed at different times and in different ways. For example, while transatlantic Pan-Africanism developed as a movement of ideas, with little formal organization apart from periodic conferences, and predated – indeed spawned – continental Pan-Africanism, it was the latter which first found institutional fulfilment with the formation of the Organization of African Unity (OAU) in 1963. The connections and reverberations between these Pan-Africanisms were, and continue to be, intricate, complex, and contradictory, spawning both narrow territorial nationalisms and broad transnational movements, including dozens of regional integration schemes. Pan-African movements were often complimented and constrained by other transnational movements, those organized around religion, for example, or colonial linguistic affiliations.

The nationalists who led the movements for independence almost invariably subscribed to some form of Pan-Africanism, to the notion of a shared, collective African identity that was in opposition to European identity. There were several reasons for this. First, it reflected the over-determination of race in the colonial world, the fact that globally colonialism imposed the subordination of the 'darker' to the 'lighter' races, and Africans everywhere seemed to be under some form of European oppression and exploitation. Second, the nationalists were linked through intricate institutional and ideological networks, for example, through education in regional and metropolitan universities, participation in regional and international political organizations and social movements, and the cultural traffic between Africa and the Diaspora. Third, the project of nation-building was seen both as one confined to, and transcending, the colonial borders, of forging coherent postcolonial nation-states around the territorial space drawn up by the colonialists, states which would eventually be integrated together. But the internal demands of nation-building proved more pressing and enduring than those of Pan-African integration. As nationalism intensified in each colony, indeed, as independence was achieved, the struggles and visions of the future were increasingly anchored to the interests of the nation, at the expense of Pan-Africanism.

Transatlantic Pan-Africanism had its roots in the dispersal and dehumanization of African peoples to the Americas and Europe through the Atlantic Slave Trade. The centres of this triangular trade, which connected Western Europe, Western Africa, and the Americas, became centres for the development of Pan-Africanism. As an ideology and a movement it first emerged among the enslaved Africans in the Diaspora because they were the earliest to bear the full brunt of European racism, oppression, and exploitation. Regardless of where they came from in Africa or what social position they had held in African society or now held in the Americas, they were all lumped together as racially 'inferior'. So they were more inclined to see Africa and Africans as a unit than the Africans on the continent itself who remained isolated or attached to their ethnic groups or nations. The lead taken by the African Diaspora in the Caribbean and the United States in organizing Pan-Africanism can be attributed to the fact that racial ideologies there were more severe than in Latin America. Also, Britain was a colonial superpower and later the United States became a global superpower.

Africans in the Diaspora were constantly being reminded of Africa by their European masters who tried to impress upon them that Africa was primitive. Repudiating this thinly veiled justification of slavery required Diaspora intellectuals to focus on Africa and demonstrate that it made major contributions to world civilization. Consciousness of Africa was also sustained by the continuous flow of people, ideas, values, visions, practices, and expressive culture from Africa to the Americas and vice-versa. After slavery was abolished there were waves of African students. From the Americas came the 'Back to Africa' movements. Beginning at the turn of the nineteenth century, groups of free Africans from the Caribbean, Canada, the United States, and Britain moved to Sierra Leone and Liberia. There were also migrations from Brazil to West Africa. The new immigrant Diaspora communities played a crucial role in the construction of African modernities and in the development of Pan-Africanism. Among the most renowned Pan-African intellectuals was Edward Blyden, who migrated from St. Thomas at a young age and settled in Liberia. He saw Africa as the product of a triple heritage: the indigenous, Islamic, and Christian traditions; a concept that was further developed by Kwame Nkrumah in his treatise on consciencism, and Ali Mazrui, the Kenyan intellectual, in the film series, *The Africans: A Triple Heritage.*

Analysis of transatlantic Pan-Africanism tends to focus on the development of nationalist movements and ideologies. Pride of place has gone to the Pan-African congresses associated with the great African American scholar-activist, W. E. B. Dubois, who famously declared that the 'problem of the twentieth century is the problem of the colour line'. Between 1900 and 1945, five Pan-African congresses were held in Europe attended by delegates from the continent and the Diaspora, mostly from the English-speaking countries. The early congresses called for increasingly substantial colonial reforms, while the 1945 Manchester congress, the last to be held outside the continent, categorically demanded independence for African and Caribbean colonies. Delegates such as Nkrumah and Jomo Kenyatta of Kenya returned to their respective countries to lead nationalist movements to independence, which was largely achieved in the following three decades.

There were of course other movements besides the Pan-African congresses. The Caribbean, a region that experienced both slavery and colonial rule and was thus uniquely placed to connect the experiences of slavery in the Americas and of colonialism in Africa, produced many of the leading Pan-African thinkers and organizers, such as Marcus Garvey from Jamaica, and George Padmore and C. L. R. James, the illustrious revolutionary thinkers from Trinidad. Garvey was the founder of the Universal Negro Improvement Association in 1914 in Kingston, which was relocated to the United States in 1915 and quickly became the largest African American mass movement the country had ever seen. The UNIA established its own journal, the *Negro World*, and a shipping line, and the flamboyant Garvey preached fervently for 'Back to Africa' and the creation of a United States of Africa, one largely founded on capitalist principles. The annual UNIA conventions were attended by delegates from more than twenty-five countries. The movement eventually collapsed, thanks to state machinations, aided by opposition Garvey garnered from other civil rights activists, including Dubois, who had more scholarly and socialist inclinations.

During the 1930s both Dubois' congresses and Garvey's conventions were moribund. In their place emerged a series of Pan-African organizations, such as the League of Coloured Peoples and the International African Service Bureau, both formed in England, which vociferously protested the Italian invasion of Ethiopia in 1935, an invasion that shook Africans everywhere. In the United States, Paul Robeson, the famous singer and activist, founded the Council on African Affairs, and African students formed the African Students Association, both of which organized meetings and called for African development and independence. In Africa itself Pan-African sentiments were expressed through the lively African press and emerging political associations. In West Africa there was the National Congress of British West Africa, formed in 1920, and the West African Students Union, formed in 1925, while in South Africa the African National Congress was created in 1911. All three organizations highlighted the abuses of colonialism and called for African solidarity and struggle for emancipation. In the Francophone world the Universal League for the Defence of the Black Race was founded in 1924 and called for the formation of a unitary Black state embracing Sub-Saharan Africa and the West Indies.

From the 1950s, as African and Caribbean colonies gained their independence, Transatlantic Pan-Africanism waned as the nationalists concentrated on national development and regional integration. The Pan-African conferences hosted in Accra in 1958 – the Conference of Independent African States and the All African Peoples Conference – for example, were largely confined to continental Africans and state actors or leaders of nationalist movements. The attention of African and Caribbean leaders increasingly turned inwards to the OAU and the Caribbean Common Market, respectively. No wonder the sixth Pan-African Congress of 1974 held in Tanzania attracted relatively little interest. In the meantime, in the United States, struggles for civil rights were gathering momentum and scoring some legislative victories. In Latin America, where the politics of racial identity had historically undermined Pan-Africanism, there was rising African Diaspora or racial consciousness, as manifested in the four Congresses of Black Culture in the Americas held between 1977 and 1984. There were connections between these processes: the nationalist achievements in Africa and the Caribbean inspired civil rights struggles in the United States, while civil rights activists in the US provided crucial support to liberation movements fighting against settler regimes in Southern Africa by applying pressure on the American government and companies.

The traffic and flows between Africa and the Americas which facilitated and sustained transatlantic Pan-Africanism also involved periodic and cumulative cultural exchanges. For example, in the nineteenth and early twentieth-centuries African American missionaries played a critical role in the spread of Christianity in several parts of the continent, especially in West and Southern Africa. The influence of the cultural practices of the African Diaspora on African expressive culture has also been remarkable. Many forms of popular music in twentieth century Africa, from rhumba and jazz, to reggae and rap, were imported from the African Diaspora. Congo's celebrated rhumba was heavily influenced by Cuban music; South African jazz bore strong American influences; Senegalese reggae borrowed from Jamaican reggae, and so on. In the realm of literature, there were close connections between the literary movements of Africa and the Diaspora, most significantly the Harlem Renaissance and the Negritude movement in the 1920s and 1930s. In the arts, more broadly, there were Pan-African festivals, such as the Colloquium of the World Festival of Black Arts and Culture (FESTAC) held in Nigeria in 1977. And in the United States the African elite often received their academic and political education in the HBCUs before colonial universities were belatedly established in the twilight years of decolonization or the historically white universities opened their segregated doors in the aftermath of the civil rights movement.

Clearly, Pan-Africanism played a major role in the struggles for emancipation and self-fashioning in Africa and the Diaspora in the twentieth century in all spheres from the political to the economic, the cultural to the intellectual. Since independence there have been divergent conceptions of Pan-Africanism that are sometimes encapsulated, rather simplistically, in antagonist dualisms: continentalism versus globalism; continentalists versus regionalists; and radical unionists versus functionalist gradualists. Additional contestations have centred on which comes first, economic or political integration; or who the primary architects of Pan-Africanism should be: states or civil society, presidents or the people; or what the basis of a Pan-African identity should be: national or racial, consciousness or citizenship.

Our Pan-Africanist commitments must transcend these unproductive dichotomies. In my view, Pan-Africanism remains a powerful force in the twenty-first century both because its objectives are far from achieved and because the new challenges facing Africa and the Diaspora require Pan-African responses. In other words, the past that created Pan-Africanism is not over, and for Africa and the Diaspora the present will remain impoverished and the future incomplete without it. Thus, the imperatives for Pan-Africanism are simultaneously historical and contemporary, ideological and instrumental. The historical imperatives include the continued marginalization of Africa and the Diaspora and the unfinished business of emancipation for Africans at home and abroad. The contemporary imperatives encompass the current processes and projects of globalization, the growth of African international migrations and expansion of new Diasporas, the resurgence or reconfiguration of Pan-Africanism among the historic Diasporas, and the revitalization of African regional integration efforts. Progressive Pan-Africanism provides a countervailing ideology to the triumphant neo-liberalism of the post-Cold War world, and offers alternative possibilities to mobilize all manner of capital – financial, social, cultural, and intellectual – for socioeconomic development in Africa and the Diaspora.

Despite the enormous historical achievements of decolonization and civil rights, African and Caribbean states remain marginalized in the world and African Diasporas in their host countries. The pace, breadth and depth of the strides we have made since independence and civil rights over the last fifty years vary enormously between countries and regions, among social classes and genders, across periods and sectors. Nevertheless, our states and societies are still largely pawns rather than players on the world stage. This will not fundamentally change unless we pool all our resources – demographic, political, economic, cultural, and imaginative – to fight for our collective emancipation and empowerment.

Pan-Africanism remains a powerful force through which Africa and the Diaspora can reinforce each other's struggles, help reposition each other, become each other's keepers: African states have a responsibility to raise the costs of marginalizing the Diaspora, while the Diaspora have a responsibility to lower the costs of engagement between Africa and the global North.

The present has its own contexts and challenges that demand, and facilitate, Pan-Africanist redress. Several stand out including the new forms of globalization, democratization, migration and Diasporization. Contemporary globalization entails, on the one hand, a process of intensifying global interconnectedness among countries and communities, characterized by increased velocity of flows, from capital to commodities, ideas to images, visions to viruses, religions to reflexivities; and on the other, a project of global capitalist restructuring underpinned by neo-liberal ideologies and policy interventions known across Africa by the infamous name of structural adjustment programmes (SAPs). The catastrophic regime of neo-liberal capitalism has led to the decomposition of the developmental state in the global South and the welfare state in the global North, which has undermined the socioeconomic standing of both Africa and the Diaspora. While globalization currently represents a triumph of capital over other social classes, it has provoked the rise of new civil society organizations and transnational social movements, whose growth is facilitated by the very intrusive tentacles and information technologies associated with globalization. Communications between Africa and its Diasporas, both old and new, have never been better which creates new possibilities for forging Pan-African solidarities.

One of the dynamics that characterizes contemporary African politics is democratization. Needless to say, democratization is a complex and contradictory phenomenon, but it has recast the contexts and conceptions of Pan-Africanism. There is ample evidence that since the turn of the 1990s the number of states following and abiding by features of democratic governance – principally elections and multi-party politics – has increased. This despite many reversals, and the manipulations of Africa's dictators, and the fact that in many countries the new democracies amount to little more than recycled fractions of the same bankrupt political class. And despite the fact that elections are often marred by harassment and intimidation, violence, vote rigging and human rights abuses, not to mention campaigns to allow incumbent presidents to stay beyond constitutional limits, as happened in my own country when the venal President Muluzi who succeeded the Banda dictatorship following the country's democratization in 1994 desperately, but unsuccessfully, sought a third term.

But even if the roots of the old leviathan remain deeply embedded in Africa's rocky political soil, its branches have been shaken by the strong winds of social struggles for popular participation. This means Pan-Africanism can no longer be an elite project, let alone a state-led project. Civil societies, both in Africa and the Diaspora, have a profound role to play in constructing the architecture of a Pan-Africanism befitting the conditions, demands, perils, and possibilities of the twenty-first century.

The rising rates of African international migration also create new conditions and prospects for Pan-Africanism. It is becoming increasingly clear, or it ought to, to African policy makers and intellectuals that the Diaspora and Pan-Africanism may constitute the most reliable vehicles for enhancing Africa's presence in the world system. The Pan-Africanism of the twenty-first century must take the Diaspora option seriously, which requires devising creative strategies for knowledge and skill circulation, the formation of national, regional, and continental knowledge networks that facilitate brain mobility, from academic exchanges to consultancies and temporary return migrations, to the transmission of information and vigorously defending Africa which is routinely defamed in Euroamerica with little social cost. In short, the Diaspora, both the historic and contemporary, constitutes Africa's eyes and ears in the world, the interpreter of the world to Africa and Africa to the world. It is indispensable to the globalization of Africa and the Africanization of globalization. The provision of dual citizenship by several countries including Ghana is a move in the right direction. The formation of the African Union ushered in a new phase in Africa's long search for continental integration and unity with the Diaspora. Notwithstanding its structural weaknesses and idealistic ambitions, the African Union (AU) is a much more robust organization than its predecessor, more committed to the pursuit of development, democracy, and human rights than the Organization of African Unity (OAU) which was preoccupied with the politics of decolonization, national sovereignty, and presidential camaraderie. In part, this reflects the conjunctures, the different moments, during which the two organizations were created. The first independence of the 1950s and 1960s that ushered in the OAU paid homage to state sovereignty, the seductions of state power; the second independence of the 1990s and 2000s, acknowledged the contribution of civil society, the sanctions of popular disaffection. The OAU was largely a presidents' club, the AU is potentially more people friendly. The difference between the two is democratization, the dreams of the first Uhuru for the symbols, and of the second for the substance, of nationhood and statehood. Unlike the OAU, which represented the triumph of continental Pan-Africanism over trans-Atlantic Pan-Africanism, the AU gestures tentatively towards a global Pan-Africanism for the twenty-first century that could create a new compact between Africa and its Diaspora. The conceptual and concrete challenges of pursuing this project are immense. People of African descent are spread in various regions of the world, experience different degrees of sovereignty and marginalization, and encompass historic, contemporary, and overlapping Diasporas. The AU has designated the Diaspora as Africa's sixth region and allocated it representation in the Economic Social and Cultural Council:[1] 20 civil society organizations (CSOs) out of a total of 150. It is not yet clear how the Diaspora will enter the mainstream of the AU. Indeed, some argue that of greater importance than the integration of the Diaspora in African regional structures is the need to strengthen connections and communication between ordinary Africans and the Diasporas. I don't think the two are mutually exclusive. The incorporation of the Diaspora in the AU's Pan-African project represents a return to the future in so far as the very notions of African unity and integration are derived from the Diaspora imaginary, arising out their homogenization and racialization in the lands of their dispersal.

In 2004 and 2006 the AU organized two important meetings: the Conferences of Intellectuals from Africa and the Diaspora (CIAD I and CIAD II). CIAD I was held in Dakar, Senegal and CIAD II in Salvador, Brazil. They brought together hundreds of intellectuals and a handful of presidents, although there was little real dialogue between the politicians and the intellectuals. Then in September 2007, the AU held the Regional Consultative Conference for the African Diaspora in Europe in Paris. In the meantime, the AU 'has mandated South Africa to present in the first half of 2008 the African Union-African Diaspora Summit[2] at the level of

Heads of State and Government. The theme of the Summit is 'Towards the realization of a united and integrated Africa and its Diaspora: A shared vision for sustainable development to address common challenges.' The essential objective of the Summit is to produce a practical programme of action for co-operation between the continent and its Diaspora.

There can be little doubt that the imperatives for contemporary Pan-Africanism are both old and new, so are the contexts, objectives, and key players. For one thing, it is no longer driven by demands for political independence in Africa and the Caribbean and political enfranchisement in the rest of the Diaspora which inspired and preoccupied earlier generations of Pan-Africanists. Now the key players include states controlled by Africans on the continent and the Diaspora in the Caribbean, and Diaspora state actors are now at the highest levels of government, as in Canada, the United States, and Brazil. Also, while the elites still dominate Pan-Africanist networks within Africa and the Diaspora and between them, flows of various kinds and levels of intensity are more common than ever. Thanks to these, both Africa and the Diaspora are more conscious of their being 'African' and 'Diasporic' than ever before, and of the complex ties that connect and separate them. These flows include people, cultural practices, productive resources, organizations and movements, ideologies and ideas, images and representations. But as before, they share national and social marginalities in the global racialized hierarchies of power and privilege. And as President Nkrumah, one of Africa's most foresighted and brilliant minds taught us, that will not change until we unite, until Pan-Africanism becomes our guiding praxis.

Speech given at the Launch of Kwame Nkrumah Chair in African Studies, Institute of African Studies, University of Ghana, Legon, September 21, 2007.

References

1.   African Union, Statutes of the Economic, Social, and Cultural Council of the African Union, available at http://www.africa-union.org/ECOSOC/STATUTES-En.pdf
2.   African News Switzerland, The African Union-African Diaspora in Europe, September 11-12, 2007, available at http://www.african-news.ch/?p=209

Chapter 18

The 2007 Kenyan Elections:
Holding a Nation Hostage to a Bankrupt Political Class

Kenya's last election has left it in deep political crisis. The opposition refused to accept the results which have been questioned by local and international observers. Three days of violent protests left more than 120 people dead. While there was relief and even celebration among some supporters of the 'victorious' President Mwai Kibaki, the frustration and fear that gripped the country was almost unprecedented in forty-four years of independence. A proud country that likes to see itself as an oasis of stability in a volatile region is being held hostage by a bankrupt political class. Many Kenyans are filled with a sense of shame and anguish, as well as fortitude to salvage their country's fortunes and future.

Lost in the electoral shenanigans and post-election turmoil has been a historic opportunity to consolidate the country's newly minted democracy, to confirm its democratic credentials in the region and on the continent. Instead Kenya now faces a prolonged period of political uncertainty that will play itself out in unpredictable ways from the streets to parliament, severely testing the fragile fabric of public order, social cohesion, and inter-group relations, especially those structured around the complex inscriptions of ethnicity, class, gender, and generation. Some worry that Kenya might turn into East Africa's Côte d'Ivoire, a once stable and relatively prosperous postcolony in West Africa that descended into chaos and civil war because of its failure to manage the combustible politics of democratic transition.

The opinion polls pointed to a close election. They were proved right. But only one out of fifty polls conducted in the lead up to the elections showed President Kibaki in the lead; the rest pointed to a possible narrow win by the opposition candidate, Mr Raila Odinga. The latter maintained his lead during the early counts of the presidential vote, but when the final results were announced by the Electoral Commission of Kenya, he trailed by 231,728 votes. President Kibaki was declared duly elected with 4,584,721 votes against Mr Odinga's 4,352,993 votes. Election observers expressed surprise, the opposition cried foul, riots erupted, and the country teetered on the brink of crisis.

What a difference five years makes. In 2002 President Kibaki was inaugurated in broad daylight before an ecstatic crowd of a million people in Uhuru Park in Nairobi; this time he was hurriedly inaugurated in the evening less than an hour after being declared winner before a small and dour crowd of officials. The intoxicating euphoria of 2002 had given way to widespread anger and anxiety. In 2002 the masses, brutalized by decades of one-party rule, rediscovered their voices and will; the nation was united in its hopes for the future, believed fervently in the possibilities of productive change. This time, many felt betrayed and disempowered, robbed of their votes and voices.

Whatever the future holds for Kenya and its tortured journey from dictatorship to democracy, the present crisis has a complicated history rooted in the political economies of colonialism, neo-colonialism, and neo-liberalism that have characterized Kenya over the last century. This is to suggest that the present moment, the current political crisis, is rooted in complex historical forces that go beyond the ubiquitous 'tribalism' beloved by the Western media in discussing and explaining African politics, or the excessive obsession with personalities often found in the African media itself. This is of course not to dismiss the role of ethnicity or particular leaders, it is merely to point out the need to put both in the context of broader historical forces that have propelled Kenya to this moment, and might impel it out of it.

The Kenyan elections promised to achieve something extraordinary: unseating an incumbent president through the ballot box after only five years in power. This would have been unprecedented in Kenyan history, and is rare in Africa where incumbents typically serve the constitutional two terms and some even try to rig their way into illicit third terms. This is a tribute to the power of incumbency to win or rig elections, the inordinate advantages enjoyed by ruling parties to use the sanctions and seductions of state power.

The manipulation of electoral processes and results by ruling parties is of course not confined to Africa: remember the US elections of 2000, and President Putin's recent attempts to prolong his rule? It is not uncommon for ruling parties in many so-called mature democracies to call elections opportunistically, redraw electoral districts in their favour, or 'bribe' the electorate with contrived economic goodies. However, it can be argued that the national costs of electoral malpractices are much higher for African and other countries in the global South that are struggling against the challenges of internal underdevelopment and political and cultural subordination than for the more globally hegemonic Western countries.

Save for the disputed victory of the president himself, the government suffered a political tsunami as a score of Cabinet ministers and the vice-president lost their parliamentary seats. Altogether, the Party of National Unity (PNU), cobbled together only a year before the election, under whose banner President Kibaki ran, won only 37 seats. The victorious opposition party, Orange Democratic Movement (ODM), led by Mr Raila Odinga took 100 seats, and the rest (parliament has 210 directly elected members) went to the Orange Democratic Movement-Kenya (ODM-K), the party of the third major presidential candidate, Mr Kalonzo Musyoka, and other smaller parties.

Swept away also were power brokers of the former dictator, President Daniel arap Moi, including the once feared Mr Nicholas Biwott and the tycoon Mr Kamlesh Pattini an infamous architect of one of Kenya's largest corruption scandals, as well as Mr Moi's own ambitious three sons. In a sense, the election signified a rejection of leading politicians associated with Presidents Moi and Kibaki. While the two represent different presidential administrations, one dictatorial and the other democratic, they are associated in the popular imagination, and were painted by the opposition, as old men leading corrupt regimes. Remarkably, Mr Moi campaigned indefatigably for his successor, to the obvious glee of the opposition.

Thus the contest between the octogenarian Mr Kibaki and the flamboyant Mr Odinga became a generational struggle for power. It is one of the ironies of contemporary Africa that countries that have enjoyed political stability since independence, such as Kenya, Malawi, and

Senegal, are still ruled by the nationalist generation that brought independence, while the countries with more turbulent histories have long made the generational transition. In this sense, the Kenyan election was a contest between the older and the younger generations, between the Kibaki generation, in power since independence, and the Odinga generation that came of age after independence.

The first Kibaki government was elected in 2002 on a strong anti-corruption platform. Impoverished and exhausted from twenty-four years of authoritarian and corrupt rule by the Moi administration, the country was hungry for a clean government that would bring to justice corrupt former officials and lead a transparent and accountable administration capable of reviving the economy and pursuing develop-ment. But the drive against Moi-era corruption scandals stalled, and new corruption scandals sprang up. The new administration's anti-corruption credentials were irreparably damaged when the government's own anti-corruption czar, Mr John Githongo, fled to exile in the United Kingdom in 2005.

But the Kibaki administration delivered on the economy. The country's economic growth rate jumped from 0.6 per cent in 2002 to 6.1 per cent in 2006. Buoyed by this robust growth, the government unveiled its ambi-tious Kenya Vision 2030[1], a development blueprint to turn Kenya into a newly industrializing 'middle income country providing high quality of life for all its citizens by the year 2030'. President Kibaki and his PNU ran on this economic record, while the opposition claimed it could achieve even faster growth unadulterated by corruption. One sought continuity, the other promised change. In reality, there was little difference in the programmes of the PNU and ODM and their contending presidential candidates.

As is often the case in such contexts, the absence of policy differences was more than made up for by personality. Here Mr Odinga bested the president. Mr Odinga was a millionaire businessman, who had once been a political prisoner, and most importantly, he was the son of the nationalist icon and former vice-president, Mr Oginga Odinga. Odinga campaigned vigorously to achieve what had eluded his father. He appealed to the youth and people from disaffected regions, while assiduously assuring domestic and foreign business interests who preferred the wealthy, elderly and gentlemanly President Kibaki that he had long shed the socialist inclinations and firebrand reputation of his younger days.

The electoral contest between continuity and change partly reflected the glaring mismatch between growth and development, both socially and spatially, and tapped into deep yearnings for a new socioeconomic dispensation, a restless hunger for broad-based development which had been frustrated by neo-liberal growth. Kenya's economic recovery and growth from 2002 largely benefited the middle classes rather than the workers and peasants, who make up the bulk of the population. Even among the middle classes, the benefits flowed unequally between those in the rapidly expanding private service sectors and those in the decapitalized public sector, which has been under assault since the days of structural adjustment in the 1980s.

For many Kenyans, therefore, the economy may be doing well, but they are not. As dependency theory used to postulate in the radical 1960s and 1970s, growth is not synonymous with development. Neo-liberal growth is even less likely to lead to broad-based development because people are secondary to profits; public to private good. In Kenya, as in much of Africa and indeed the wider world since the triumph of neo-liberalism, the gap between the rich and the poor has widened, so that the sense of economic insecurity has increased among large numbers of people even as their countries' economies grow. This partly helps explain the tightness of the vote and the prospect of a government losing elections at a time of rapid economic growth.

If the economic growth of recent years in Kenya stoked expectations of development, the unequal distribution of wealth thwarted those expectations and engendered popular frustration, while democracy gave a new vent to express the frustrations. In the authoritarian past there was no political alternative to the one-party state. Now the discontented electorate could transfer its hopes for development to the opposition, even if their investment in the opposition was unlikely to yield different dividends.

But class is not a reliable predictor of political loyalty and voting behaviour even in the so-called developed countries. Often far more powerful are the constructed identities of ethnicity or race. In Kenya, as elsewhere in Africa, ethnic identities have greater political salience than racial identities. This is not simply because politicians mobilize ethnicity for electoral purposes, which they do – Kenyan politicians are notoriously adept at playing the ethnic card. Rather, elections for members of parliament are local or regional political events, latched onto the *national* presidential election; they are spatialized performances in which both the candidates and voters are located in particular constituencies and tend to share some common identity, ethnic or otherwise.

It is clear that many members of parliament lost elections in their constituencies to competitors from their *own* ethnic groups. In such cases, party allegiance, the record of the incumbent, and personalities all played a role. The ethnic card is played most effectively in the large cities with their ethnically diverse populations where ethnic consciousness can be mobilized. In such contexts party allegiance loomed exceptionally large as a proxy for ethnicity. Only the president is subject to both *local* and *national* constituencies, and hence the enhanced ethnicization of the presidential election.

The complex interplay of local, regional, and national elections is of course not confined to Kenya or Africa for that matter. Look at voting patterns across Europe and North America and the different regional strategies political parties tend to employ to appeal to voters in various regions, not to mention the use of race. Nor is the ethnicization of electoral politics a peculiar African predilection. With the notable exception of the US, no major Western country has ever elected a black person president or prime minister. And even in the United States, few Blacks win state wide offices. Yet nobody labels electoral contests and results in Western Europe and North America as 'racial', let alone 'tribal'; they are given more dignified names.

Media reports on the Kenyan elections and especially reports of the protests following the inauguration of President Kibaki almost invariably include references to 'tribes' and 'tribalism' as primordial identities untouched by history, as ancient hatreds immune to modernity, as pathological conditions peculiar to Africa. Forgotten is the simple fact that both Mr Kibaki and Mr Odinga could not win the elections based on voting from their so-called 'tribes': two ethnic groups out of the country's many ethnicities. While the presidential candidates received overwhelming electoral support in their home provinces, to win the presidency ethnic coalition building is essential, for the president has to win at least twenty-five of the votes in at least five of Kenya's eight provinces.

The ethnicization of politics in Kenya is not a reflection of some atavistic reflex, or simply the result of elite political manipulations or primordial cultural affectations among the masses, even if the elites do indeed use ethnicity and the masses are mobilized by it. It is salutary to remember that some of Kenya's ethnic groups only emerged or developed their current identities under British colonial rule. Few can trace themselves to the remote past notwithstanding the work of some historians to distinguish their ethnic communities with long and pristine pedigrees. Imagined ethnic and national histories are of course not about the past, but the present; they are part of the discursive and political arsenal for claim-making in the present and for the future.

As we have learned from African studies, we need to distinguish between 'moral ethnicity', that is, ethnicity as a complex web of social obligations and belonging, and 'political ethnicity', that is, the competitive confrontation of 'ethnic contenders' for state power and national resources. Both are socially constructed, but one as an identity, the other as an ideology. Ethnicity may serve as a cultural public for the masses estranged from the civic public of the elites; a sanctuary that extends its comforts and protective tentacles to the victims of political disenfranchisement, economic impoverishment, state terror and group rivalry. In other words, it is not the existence of ethnic groups (or racial groups) that is a problem in itself, a predictor of social conviviality or conflict, but their political mobilization.

Ethnicity in Kenya is tied in complex and contradictory ways to the enduring legacies of uneven regional development. During colonial rule Central Kenya, the homeland of the Kikuyu, became the heart of the settler economy, while Nyanza, the Luo homeland, languished as a labour reserve that furnished both unskilled and educated labour to the centres of colonial capitalism. Not surprisingly, the Kikuyu bore the brunt of colonial capitalist dispossession and socialization, and were in the vanguard of the nationalist struggles that led to decolonization. For this reason they came to dominate the postcolonial state and economy. Capitalist development and centralization of power reinforced domination of the Kenyan economy by the Central Province and the Kikuyu, a process that withstood the twenty-four-year reign of President Moi, a Kalenjin from the Rift Valley, and was reinvigorated under President Kibaki's first administration.

Central Province and Kikuyu dominance of Kenya's political economy bred resentment among other regions and ethnic groups. It fed into constitutional debates about presidential and political centralization of power, and the regional redistribution of resources that dominated Kenyan politics until 2005, when the draft constitution supported by the president and Parliament was rejected in a referendum. The ODM was born in the highly politicized maelstrom of the run up to this referendum.

This narrative tends to ignore an important qualifying fact, that not all Kikuyus are dominant and not all Luos are disempowered. Colonial, neo-colonial and neo-liberal capitalisms have bred class differentiations within communities as much as they have led to uneven development in the different regions. In other words, Kikuyu and Luo elites have much more in common with each other than they do with their co-ethnics among the peasants and workers – who also have more in common with each other across ethnic boundaries than with their respective elites. This is a reality that both the elites and the masses *strategically ignore* during competitive national elections, because the former need to mobilize and manipulate their ethnic constituencies in intra-elite struggles for power, and the latter because elections offer one of the few moments to shake the elites for the crumbs of development for themselves and their areas.

Kenyan politics exhibit familiar African trends. The country started its independence with a hurriedly negotiated multiparty system between the nationalists and the departing imperial power that could not withstand the homogenizing imperatives of nationalism and the intoxicating and intolerant demands of Uhuru: nation-building, development, and democratization. Before long, Kenya joined the African race towards the one-party state, as the pre-independence opposition party KADU (Kenya African Democratic Union) folded voluntarily into the ruling KANU (Kenya African National Union) in 1964, while the post-independence radical Kenya People's Union formed in 1966 by former vice-president Oginga Odinga, the father of the ODM leader, was violently suppressed.

Kenya became a de jure one-party state under President Moi, who took power in 1978 following the death of the founding President Jomo Kenyatta. Moi was confronted by on the one hand the political tensions engendered by the attempted coup of 1982, and on the other a slowing economy that stagnated under the onerous weight of structural

172

adjustment programmes imposed by the international financial institutions – the World Bank and International Monetary Fund – and Western governments. By the end of the 1980s, it was clear that while the country remained relatively stable in a tumultuous region its early promise had been squandered under a reign of authoritarianism, corruption, and structural maladjustment.

As in much of Africa, from the late 1980s and throughout the 1990s, the unproductive power of one-party rule faced growing popular opposition. The struggles for the 'second independence' by the restive masses and organized civil society scored limited victories in the 1992 and 1997 elections, and finally seized the prize in the elections of December 2002 when the ruling party, KANU, lost to the opposition National Rainbow Coalition (NARC). It was a new day: democracy expanded as political and civil freedoms spread, so did the economy as the stagnation of the Moi years receded, but the social and structural deformities of the postcolony remained as entrenched as ever. It is in this context that Kenya's current crisis can best be understood.

The last five years have seen the growth of both democracy and the economy, but the marriage between democracy and development remains unfilled. The economic growth rates under President Kibaki resemble those in the early post-independence years under President Kenyatta. The difference is not only that neo-colonial capitalism of the Kenyatta era, which had a nationalist face, has given way to contemporary neo-liberal capitalism, which has a neo-colonial soul. Democracy has reconfigured old challenges and brought new ones that the society and state have yet to manage satisfactorily as the results of the last elections amply demonstrate.

As the suffocating lid of state tyranny is lifted during moments of democratic transition the suppressed voices and expectations of civil society surge, but the stresses and strains arising from the competitive grind of democracy often find articulation in the entrenched identities, idioms, and institutions of ethnic solidarity. The challenge in Kenya, as in other divided multicultural societies, is the need to balance group and national interests through further democratization, devolution of power, and power sharing. In so far as ethnic interests and cleavages are only one among many other possible bases of political contestation – class, religion, region, and gender – there is need to think about group interests beyond ethnicity.

The current trials and tribulations facing Kenya will not be resolved without the emergence of a leadership that is truly up to the challenge; a leadership that pursues a *national* project of profound social transformation, that eschews narrow and short-sighted exclusionary politics and neo-liberal economic growth. Kenya, and Africa as a whole, has no historic alternative to building truly democratic developmental states if they are to chart the twenty-first century more prepared and empowered than they did the disastrous twentieth century marked by the depredations of colonialism and neo-colonialism.

The current leadership, both the 'victors' and 'losers', seem keen to retain or gain power at all costs. The power struggle is as sinister as the differences among the leaders are small. But often it is the very narcissism of minor differences that breeds gratuitous violence and viciousness, as histories of genocide demonstrate. The leading politicians engaged in combat whose followers are tearing their lovely country apart are members of the same recycled political class, both committed to neo-liberal growth and offering no real solutions to Kenya's enduring challenges of growth and development, choiceless democracy and transformative democracy.

Most of the major figures in the three leading parties, PNU, ODM, ODM-K, served in the Moi and Kibaki administrations at one time or another. Their politics do not differ in any significant ways. Indeed, it is a mark of the promiscuity of the political class that the three parties were formed quite recently, and politicians shop for parties with the consummate ease of well-heeled customers. In a sense, then, the interests of the politicians and national interests of the population are not coterminous, although overlaps do exist and are invoked at certain moments. The political animus between the Kibaki and Odinga camps is rooted in the now infamous secretive Memorandum of Understanding (MOU) on the distribution of Cabinet positions and power drawn up by the opposition parties that hurriedly formed NARC to fight the ruling party in the 2002 elections. NARC was a marriage of convenience for a splintered opposition determined to win, but it failed to survive squabbles over the spoils of victory. Before long, Mr Odinga and his followers began complaining that Mr Kibaki had reneged on the MOU and thus began the slide to political impasse and crisis.

President Kibaki's contested 'victory' has deprived the country of the opportunity to see that the opposition offers little more than a recycling of policies and politicians, as has been witnessed in other African countries that are now into their third or fourth cycle of competitive multiparty elections. As this has become evident the attraction of elections as engines of fundamental socioeconomic transformation has dimmed in many countries and the search for new forms of politics is underway. In Kenya the disputed results of this election may have done the same. Only time will tell, perhaps long after the violence has subsided. What can be predicted is that the Kibaki government will be paralyzed in the new parliament, where it controls less than a fifth of the seats, and might even be brought down by a vote of no confidence, although the power of the government to secure or 'buy' support from self-serving parliamentarians cannot be ruled out, as has happened in Malawi and other countries where the president's party is in the minority. And a popular uprising, can never be ruled out.

Kenya's current political tragedy is part of a much larger story. The absence of articulated and organized institutional and ideological alternatives under neoliberalism is at the heart of the political crisis facing contemporary Africa and much of the world. It has led to the ossification of politics, and in some countries, the premature abortion or aging of elections as instruments of transformative change. The spectre of choiceless democracies is not confined to countries in the global South, for in many parts of the global North including the United States the ideological divide between the major parties is often indecipherable, the result of which is political apathy as nearly half the population has exited the electoral process. For more fragile societies, the danger is not apathy, but anarchy. As a keen observer of Kenya, a country where I spent many fruitful years studying and teaching in the late 1970s and 1980s, I hope the country can avoid such a fate. Perhaps the ferocity of the reaction to the botched elections will serve as a wakeup call to the political class and the troubled citizenry to chart a more productive future for their beloved country. A good beginning would be for the contending parties to agree to a binding independent and internationally monitored investigation of the election results.

December 31, 2007.

175

Reference

1. Ministry of State for Planning, *Kenya Vision 2030*, Government of Kenya, available at http://www.planning.go.ke/

Chapter 19

The Africa Cup of Nations:
For the Love of Football and Leisure:

If there is one passion people across Africa share - it is football. From Cape to Cairo, Senegal to Somalia, football is the sport of sports within neighbourhoods and nations. It is a contagious communal ritual of celebration and competition, revelry and rivalry; a spectacle where mass cravings for pleasure are harnessed for profit by the entertainment industry, where the career and celebrity dreams of needy male youths, and increasingly female ones, are made and unmade, and masculinities and nationalisms are performed with all their convivialities and chauvinisms.

When I visited Ghana in October 2007, football fever was already in the air as the country prepared to host the Africa Cup of Nations early in 2008. The airport was emblazoned with announcements of the tournament, which pits the giants of African football against each other, including Ghana itself, which has won the cup four times, the same as Cameroon, while Egypt, the record holder, has five victories, The teams are fondly known by their nicknames, the Black Stars of Ghana, the Indomitable Lions of Cameroon, the Pharaohs of Egypt, the Super Eagles of Nigeria, the Lions of Atlas of Morocco, etc. Altogether, sixteen teams, divided into four groups, advance through the knock-out rounds in the tournament. In regional terms, West Africa clearly dominates: this time it has eight teams competing, followed by Southern and North Africa each with four; no teams are represented from East and Central Africa.

One could dissect this uneven regional representation and attribute it to the differentiated histories of the sport, the varied fan and funding bases, the patterns of insertion into the global football fraternity characterized by the recruitment of African players for overseas professional leagues (which has accelerated since 1990), the improved performance of African teams during World Cups, and the selection of South Africa as World Cup host in 2010. To be sure, the growth of African international football labour migration, especially to Europe,[1] replicates the history of exploitative African-European exchanges. Many national squads will be featuring players who have made their fame and fortune in overseas teams and tournaments. When it comes to football, African countries seem to embrace and celebrate their transnational players in a way they have yet to do with their other professionals – doctors, lawyers, scientists, engineers, and professors who are scattered across the global North in even larger numbers than the football maestros.

This only serves to underscore the mass appeal of football, the seductive power of entertainment, the collective lure of leisure. Footballers, together with musicians, and increasingly the stars of Nollywood and its continental imitations, are the supreme icons of Africa's creeping celebrity culture. Across the continent, certainly among male youths, the names of Africa's football stars are legendary. Ghana's Michael Essien, Nigeria's Austin 'Jay-Jay' Okocha and Obafemi Martins, Cameroon's Samuel Eto'o Fils, Côte d'Ivoire's Didier Drogba, and for the older fans Cameroon's Roger Milla, Ghana's Abedi Pele, and Liberia's George Weah, each of whom was variously voted as Africa's or Europe's or the world's player of the year at the peak of their careers, are revered for their acrobatic skills on the pitch, and venerated for the wild possibilities of their cosmopolitan lives.

Until recently the topic of sports or the theme of popular culture in general was not taken too seriously in African studies, preoccupied as the field was with the weighty subjects of self-determination, development and democratization; with the structural conditions and transformations of African economic, political, and cultural life. Scholastic indifference to sports and popular culture also emanated from pervasive suspicions of the city, as well as the romanticization of the rural which was bred as much by anthropological and nationalist discourses as by quests for African difference and authenticity by Euroamerican tourists and African traditionalists. Both thought the African city was unreal, a leftover colonial space, a social and imaginary dessert, empty of the nurturing and sustaining reservoirs of indigenous custom and tradition.

Thus, pitted against rural Africa, urban Africa tended to be dismissed or devalued as a context for vibrant African life and creativity, for popular culture, for leisure. Forgotten was the simple fact that the city in Africa – think of Cairo, Fez, Ibadan, or Mombasa – is as old as the city anywhere, and that more and more Africans call cities home; soon more than half of the continent's inhabitants will be city dwellers, a landmark the world reached for the first time in history last year. Leisure is about the ordinariness and extraordinariness of daily life. It is both the poetry and prose of life's pleasures and pressures; of the promises and possibilities of effective and affective living. Studying leisure constitutes serious intellectual work; as a field of knowledge it is as contemplative and consequential as any field of scholarly inquiry, indeed, it offers us a unique entry into the heartbeat of social life, enabling us to feel and fathom the textures of daily life.

As someone who was born and bred in a city, and as a novelist and student of social history, I am always struck by the stiff and suffocating unreality of much academic writing on Africa, especially that fuelled in recent years by the unrelenting gloom of Afro-pessimism, in which African social life is depicted as one long and unrelieved tale of deprivation, disease, despotism, and destruction. For too long academia has overlooked the Africa I see when I visit family and friends, of their small joys of living: the sights and sounds of children playing; people walking the streets; entertaining indoors and visiting each other; the gaiety in restaurants; the rowdiness in bars and nightclubs; the intoxicating ecstasy at football and boxing matches; the uninvited and unpaid storytellers in buses and taxis; the carnivalesque crowds at political rallies or gathered on street corners watching and listening to some aspiring or accomplished comedian, preacher, and acrobat, laughing, clapping or booing; the sartorial displays of fashion and delight in 'dressing well'; of people relishing the wonders of nature at beaches and in the countryside; of men and women breaking the monotonous rhythm of their labours with song and cheerful conversation; of families assembled at home telling stories, watching television, or listening to the radio; of friends gossiping and playing; of lovers indulging in the whispers and gratifications of intimacy.

The power of football transcends the momentary ecstasies of victory or the agonies of defeat. The Africa Cup of Nations animates continental conversations and connections. It represents popular Pan-Africanism at play, the flipside of the presidential Pan-Africanism of summits. It is an exhilarating performance that can even help uplift nations wounded by the traumas of war and conflict, as happened to Rwanda, a country haunted by memories of the 1994 genocide, which was electrified with collective joy when it qualified for the tournament for the first time in 2004. Similar outpourings of national enchantment and hope for qualifying teams have been noted in Liberia in 1996 and Côte d'Ivoire in the 2006 World Cup. And even in the harrowing life of refugee camps or for the amputated victims of war in Sierra Leone football has been known to provide remedial pleasure, the social rehabilitation of recreation.

It is gratifying to see that many African scholars now take football and leisure in general as seriously as the so-called popular masses. There are a range of recent studies,[2] such as *Football in Africa, Africa, Football, and Fifa, The African Game, Leisure in African History* , and my own *Leisure in Urban Africa,* which examines the conceptions, content, and contexts of leisure: the ways in which leisure activities from football to films, music to tourism have been produced and consumed in African cities from the nineteenth century to the present. The history of football in Africa, introduced a little over a hundred years ago, throws into sharp relief the complex connections between indigenous and imported traditions of sports; colonialism and nationalism; the constructions of African modernities; the transnational flows and counter-flows of leisure activities between Africa and the rest of the world including the Diaspora; and the formation of gender, ethnic, class, and national identities and their intersections.

Success at the Africa Cup of Nations offers ordinary people inestimable pleasure and pride and their states a prestige that might even buy temporary legitimacy and national unity for beleaguered regimes. To the wider world, to people who have never been to Africa but think they know the continent from the stereotypical images reproduced by the racist Western media and the mercy industrial complex, the tournament presents an unfamiliar image: of Africans having ordinary fun with the extraordinary fanfare of sporting events the world over.

Let the games begin!

January 19, 2008.

References

1 Gerard Akindes, 'Football Academies and the Migration of African Football Labor to Europe,' *Journal of Sports and Social Issues* 31, 2 (2007): 143-161, available at http://jss.sagepub.com/cgi/content/abstract/31/2/143.

2 See Gary Amstrong and Richard Giulianotti, eds., *Football in Africa: Conflict, Conciliation and Community* (New York: Palgrave Macmillan, 2004); Paul Darby, *Africa, Football and FIFA: Politics, Colonialism and Resistance* (London and New York: Routledge, 2002); Andrew Dosunmu and Knox Robinson, *The African Game* (New York: PowerHouse Books, 2006); Emmanuel Akyeampong and Charles Ambler, eds., *Leisure in African History*, Special Issue, *The International Journal of African Historical Studies*, 35 (1) 2002; and Paul Tiyambe Zeleza and Cassandra R Veney, eds., *Leisure in Urban Africa* (Trenton, NJ: Africa World Press, 2003).

Chapter 20

Remembering Martin Luther King: Beyond the Sanitization of a Dreamer

I am writing this on Martin Luther King Day. This is one of only four holidays named after an individual in the United States, an indication of the hallowed status the Rev. Dr Martin Luther King, Jr. occupies in the pantheon of American heroes. It was not of course always so. Few remember, or want to know, how widely unpopular Dr King was in the media and among many whites, including liberals, as well as more militant blacks, at the time of his death forty years ago. Now, Dr King is universally celebrated, acclaimed as one of the greatest orators in American history; his 'I have a dream speech' seared in the national memory, a familiar ditty even to school children and in commercial jingles.

Dr King is embraced by conservatives and liberals alike, whites and blacks, each espousing their preferred version of his message, finding inspiration and justification in selective words from the bounty of eloquent speeches. Dr King has become a historical icon, a symbol for all seasons, a sanitized dreamer. Forgotten in popular representations is the fact that in the years and months leading to his tragic assassination on the balcony of the Lorraine Motel in Memphis he was reviled even by the liberal establishment for his principled opposition to the Vietnam War.

When historical figures turn into symbols, they often fall prey to popular simplification and political sanitization. The greater their historical role, the greater the pressures for universal reclamation and acclamation, and the greater the temptation to turn them into empty vessels ripe for commodification and celebrity worship. We have witnessed this happen to Nelson Mandela – it is hard today to find anyone anywhere including South Africa itself who would own up to once despising him, denouncing him as a 'terrorist', a 'communist', or baying for his blood. He is now a secular saint. Forgotten are the protracted struggles, the incalculable sacrifices, and the ostracization. Even fair-weather friends forget: none other than former president Bill Clinton[1] recently claimed that his wife, Hillary Clinton, is tougher than the lifelong freedom fighter.

If the heroism and courage of foreign icons like Mandela can so easily be forgotten, there is even greater temptation to disrobe Dr King's life and struggles of their profound meanings. America's popular culture prefers uncomplicated idols, and its political discourse loves the moralistic binaries of good and evil, right and wrong, heroes and villains. And there is no greater spectre that has haunted America since its founding four centuries ago than race and racism spawned by the country's two original sins: the genocide and dispossession of its native peoples and the enslavement and exploitation of Africans.

Dr King represents America's enduring and unfulfilled quest to transcend these sins, to raise its low moral worth to match its enormous material wealth, both of which arose out of the two original sins and their reproduction over the generations. That is why Dr King's message is often reduced to symbolic racial reconciliation, and his civil rights struggles are bled of the substantive demands for racial equality, namely, the need to address the distribution of economic resources and power. Lest we forget, it was economics that engendered slavery, rather than racism as such, although following the fateful embrace of slavery and racism, economics and race worked inseparably to reproduce each other.

This is to suggest that Dr King, both the man and the message, have been wilfully oversimplified. He was a complex man who led a complex movement that left a complex legacy. Dr King and the civil rights struggles were focused on three principal goals: civil enfranchisement of African Americans and other racial minorities; anti-militarism, which he force-fully articulated in his opposition to the Vietnam war; and economic equality embodied in his Poor People's Campaign. To read or listen to his *Beyond Vietnam: A Time to Break the Silence*[2] is to appreciate the true measure of the man, his unflinching courage in challenging the powerful forces of the military-media-industrial complex whose ideologues proceeded to attack him viciously. And let us remember he had gone to Memphis to participate in a strike by black sanitation workers when he was assassinated. He had launched the Poor People's Campaign, and hoped to assemble a 'multiracial army of the poor' to march on Washington and force Congress to enact a poor people's bill of rights. For this he faced opposition from many of his fellow civil rights leaders and lieutenants, and the intense hostility of the capitalist media and establishment.

Dr King clearly understood that civil rights, anti-militarism, and the struggle against poverty were inseparable; that racism, imperialism and inequality were each other's keepers; that civil freedoms at home were unsustainable with persistent poverty and wars of aggression abroad. He understood that the Vietnam War drained resources that could be used to improve living standards for the poor; that civil and political rights (e.g. the right to vote), economic, social, and cultural rights (e.g. right to education, housing, and economic well being), and solidarity rights (e.g. the right to peace), were interrelated, interdependent, and indivisible. In today's human rights discourse, he would be regarded as a champion of the holistic conception of human rights, an advocate of social democracy, and a supporter of progressive internationalism.

This is not the complex man of Martin Luther King Day celebrations. Happily, the scholarship on both Dr King and the civil rights movement has grown in its quality and quantity. Increasingly scholars are paying close attention to his economic and social philosophy,[3] as they have done to his moral and political philosophy in the past. The work of the King Papers Project,[4] which has published six out of a projected fourteen volumes of primary source documents, has been indispensable in this regard. Sadly, however, translating such scholarship into popular knowledge remains as daunting as ever in a politically disaffected society hungry for uplifting leadership. Dr King fills that void as an object of reverence. And so in the popular media and political speeches we are sold the King of innocuous dreams, not revolutionary action; the King of beautiful sermons against racism, not the courageous agitator against racial and economic inequalities; the prophet of racial unity at home, not international peace as well. Yesterday, in his speech at Dr King's former church in Atlanta, Senator Obama[5] focused largely on unity and personal responsibility, while Senator Clinton,[6] at a black church in Harlem, boasted of the transforming experience that hearing Dr King speak had on her as a young suburban white girl.

Ironically, the inauguration of the Martin Luther King holiday in 1983, opposed by President Reagan and many conservatives, accelerated the transformation of Dr King from a complex historical figure and a normal and flawed human being into a lofty saint, the immaculate and incontrovertible embodiment of the American Dream itself. Thus sanctified, he could be appropriated by all and sundry. To the triumphalist white right and their black ventriloquists, the Shelby Steeles,[7] he was the prophet of a postracial society, which they imagined America had already become, where people were judged by the content of their character, not by the colour of their skins, notwithstanding the shrill protests of the disorganized left and aging civil rights activists. Alternatively, some would try to deflate his sainthood by pointing to his personal failings: his alleged womanizing, chauvinism, plagiarism, messiah complex – sometimes gleefully recycling notorious FBI smears.

Predictably, politicians have been the most shameless in their appropriation of Dr King as a safe, uncontroversial, and universal icon. They commemorate him on highways, boulevards, statues, monuments, and stamps, but ignore the fierce urgency and complexity of his messages. In the fight for Democratic Party leadership before the last election he was resurrected, but reduced to a verbal bat between the Clinton and Obama campaigns. The former claimed he was a dreamer, but President Johnson was the one who legislated and implemented civil rights, to the chagrin of the latter who are affronted by this irreverence, this apparent insensitive racial slight. The real racial slight is less about the history of civil rights legislation forty years ago – the respective roles of Dr King and President Johnson – than the assumption by the Clinton team that forty years after the belated enfranchisement of African Americans only a white president is still entitled to legislating black aspirations. Underlying this is the insinuation that black leaders have no right to aspire to the presidency itself; the conceit that the rather disagreeable Senator Clinton was the reincarnation of President Johnson, the doer, while the oratorically gifted Senator Obama resembled Dr King, the dreamer.

Dr King was of course not simply a dreamer; he was part of a massive movement that forced politicians including the president and Congress to enact civil rights laws that had been resisted for generations. This brought to an end legalized segregation, but left unchanged many of the structures that had sustained the unequal life chances of African Americans and

European Americans. President Johnson did not want civil rights legislation any more than President Reagan wanted Martin Luther King Day. The rhetorical spat between the Clinton and Obama campaigns shows the enduring power of Dr King to influence contemporary American politics. But it also betrays how his bold, radical vision for America has been cheapened and devalued by the rhetoric of colour-blind racism and the superficial politics of personalities and aspiring dynasties. His legacy will remain unfulfilled if he continues to be remembered only for his eloquent speeches as a dreamer. This incredible man, who died at the tender age of thirty-nine, deserves a lot better than that.

January 21, 2008.

References

1. ABC News, 'Bill: Hillary Tougher than Mandela and Rabin', January 7, 2008, available at http://blogs.abcnews.com/politicalpunch/2008/01/bill-hillarys-t.html
2. Martin Luther King Jr., 'Beyond Vietnam—A Time To Break Silence', April 4, 1967, American Rhetoric, Online Speech bank, available at http://www.americanrhetoric.com/speeches/mlkatimetobreaksilence.htm
3. Christopher Phelps, 'The Prophet Reconsidered', *The Chronicle Review*, January 18, 2008, available at http://chronicle.com/article/The-Prophet-Reconsidered/27391
4. The Martin Luther King, Jr. Research and Education Institute, The King Papers Projects, available at http://mlk-kpp01.stanford.edu/
5. Barack Obama, 'Speech at Ebenezer Baptist Church', *Time Magazine*, available at http://thepage.time.com/obamas-speech-at-ebenezer-baptist-church/
6. Raymond Hernandez, 'At King Event, Clinton Denounces GOP Leadership,' *The New York Times*, available at http://www.nytimes.com/2006/01/17/nyregion/17speech.html
7. Shelby Steele, *The Content of Our Character: A New Vision of Race In America* (New York: Harper Perennial, 1991).

Chapter 21

The Political Wonder That Is Obama

It was a dazzling performance, historic in its possibilities: a black man electrifying America's imagination, pulverizing the ferocious Clinton machine, collecting electoral victories with deceptive and decisive ease, seemingly unstoppable on his amazing journey to the US presidency. That is the political wonder that is Barack Obama. It is an incredible story that has confounded pundits and scholars within the country and appears incomprehensible to many outside the United States. I watched this intriguing political drama with growing incredulity ever since Senator Obama declared his candidacy in Springfield, Illinois, the home of the revered Abraham Lincoln, in January 2007. I watched it through the long season of silly preoccupations with his blackness and serious concerns about his electability; during his first astounding victory in Iowa on January 3 and his bitter defeat in New Hampshire five days later; to his stunning successes on Super Tuesday; and his subsequent momentum that sealed him an unbroken chain of victories in ten states from Virginia to Maine, Wisconsin to Hawaii.

Even more extraordinary are the margins of victory for the young black male senator: he won by more than 55 per cent in 20 states compared to 4 states for the older white female senator, by 65 per cent and higher in 10 states as opposed to only one for Senator Clinton, and by over 75 per cent in 3 states – a feat the latter has not achieved anywhere. For Senator Clinton to have caught up with Senator Obama, let alone to win the nomination, she would have had to beat her rival in the remaining contests by double digit margins.

What accounts for Obama's meteoric rise from an obscure community organizer in Chicago to the celebrated frontrunner in the Democratic Party's nomination? How was he able to overwhelm the fabled Clinton electoral machine, forcing her once assumed inevitable candidacy to gasp for its political breath, a prospect that was unimaginable only a few weeks before when upstart Obama was expected to perish in a Clintonian tsunami on Super Tuesday. His momentous appeal can be attributed to four sets of votes: against Bush and Billary; and for him and the future.

Seven years of the disastrous Bush presidency – perhaps the worst in US history – have left most Americans deeply despondent at home and widely distrusted, if not despised, abroad. They despair over the unending and horrendously costly wars in Afghanistan and Iraq, which are draining an economy reeling from a housing crisis and staring at recession. They deplore bitter partisanship, opportunism, and callousness that have permeated and poisoned the political culture. The chickens of neo-liberalism and neo-conservatism, consummated during the Bush presidency, have come home to roost and the ugly results have been rather disquieting to many Americans, leaving them yearning for new beginnings, for change. The huge and in some cases unprecedented turnouts at Democratic Party primaries and caucuses, easily eclipsing those of the Republican Party, were eloquent testimonies to America's desire to transcend the Bush years.

It was a vote against the republicanization of America, that began with the contested civil rights settlement of the late 1960s and early 1970s, and which has finally run its course. Conservative principles and posturing increasingly sound like an old broken record out of step with the tempestuous rhythms of the times. This is what the Obama phenomenon has tapped into, a deep emotional need for change, for hope, for escape from the mean, fearful post-9/11 era. Watching him at his exhilarating multiracial rallies was to witness a more hopeful America gesturing to the future, a different America from that of Senator McCain who was often surrounded by dour old white men, an embarrassing public portrait that history is desperately seeking to leave behind.

If many Americans saw redemption in the Democratic Party, within the party itself many were increasingly recoiling from a Clinton coronation, from a dynastic restoration of a Billary presidency. As former president Clinton aggressively and angrily campaigned for his wife, Senator Clinton claimed experience from her husband's presidency, thereby both unwittingly suggesting that Hillary's presidency would be as much Bill's as the latter's was hers. It was perhaps in South Carolina that the electorate, beginning with African Americans, fully woke up to the insufferable conceit of the Clintons, their blatant sense of entitlement when they sought to demean Senator Obama's candidacy and diminish the Rev. Martin Luther King's legacy. As Mr Clinton was stripped of his honorary status as America's first black president, bestowed upon him with poetic playfulness by Toni Morrison, who proceeded to endorse Mr Obama, Mrs Clinton began to lose the black vote by embarrassingly overwhelming margins.

While the race card divorced the Clintons from Black America, negative campaigning reminded the rest of the electorate of the unprincipled politics of the Clinton administration, the emptiness of triangulation, the moral decrepitude of the impeached president, which paved way for the moralizing terror of the Bush administration. While some trumpeted the good old days of the 1990s, others remembered that it was under Bill Clinton's watch that the Democratic Party lost both houses of congress, many governorships and state legislatures, and the rightwing agenda of dismantling the welfare state was pursued with vigour. As Cassandra R Veney stated on *The Zeleza Post*, Clinton was not a friend of black people whether in America or Africa, contrary to the popular mythology.[1] The fresh senator from Illinois benefited from the rising discontent with the Clintons, which overshadowed the historic importance, in gender terms, of Senator Clinton's own candidacy.

But Obama did not simply ratchet up negative victories. He won because of the redemptive potential of his candidacy: the promise to redeem white America from the enduring guilt of slavery and segregation and Black America from the gutter of second class citizenship and limited expectations; to renew the seductive narrative of the American Dream, restore hope to an eternally optimistic people, and rebrand the country's tattered image in the world. Not surprisingly, his mesmerized audiences received his soaring oratory with the ecstasy of converts at a religious revival or revelers at a rock or rap concert. Obama possesses that most elusive and valuable of political attributes – charisma – that is often embodied in, and projected onto, a leader in times of national crisis when the population is yearning for civic salvation. And America desperately longs for racial reconcialiation at home and popular paternalism abroad.

However, Obama's astonishing electoral successes go beyond charisma, or the appeal of his blackness to a postracial America exemplified in his biography as the son of a Kenyan-Kansan couple who was raised in Hawaii and Indonesia and went to Ivy League colleges; They are also a tribute to the brilliance of his organizational skills. Senator Obama skillfully built a remarkable electoral machine, a modern mass movement that combined old style community organization, hardball party politics, and digital mobilization. Through this he was able to recruit volunteers, energize supporters, raise staggering amounts of money – $36 million in one month alone – and establish a formidable campaign presence throughout the country.

Whereas the Clinton campaign concentrated on the large states, reminiscent of the farcical candidacy of former New York mayor Rudy Giuliani in the Republican primaries, and assumed the contest would be over on Super Tuesday, the Obama camp prepared for a protracted campaign in every state, big and small, ignoring no community, rich and poor, men and women, democrats, independents and republicans, and all racial and ethnic groups, in a methodical drive to win votes and delegates and, more grandly, to build a new democratic majority. No wonder he has extended his support across all demographic groups including those claimed to be bedrock Clintonites, giving the lie to the claim that Obama is only attractive to blacks, the young, men, and those earning more than $50,000, while Clinton had a lock on white women, the elderly, Hispanics, and blue-collar workers.

I suspect his organizational prowess will be studied more closely than the boisterous rhetoric of his speeches. Obama out-financed, out-organized, and out-maneuvered Senator Clinton at every turn except when it came to launching negative attacks, which did not seem to work, not least because he refused to be swift-boated. On this basis alone, he proved the superior candidate.

The votes for Senator Obama of course also represented a vote for the future as seen most poignantly in the way his candidacy fired up the imaginations of the youth. In a way this was a generational contest, between the post baby-boom and post-civil rights generations and the depression and baby boom generations. Senator McCain, seventy-one, the presumptive Republican nominee and Senator Clinton, sixty, the fading Democratic aspirant represented the latter, whereas Senator Obama, forty-seven, was born a year after John F. Kennedy, another inter-generational icon. For older and establishment politicians including African Americans, some of whom recanted their earlier support for Senator Clinton, the Obama juggernaut has been quite bewildering.

It shows that there might be a new postcivil rights generation – in terms of both age and sensibility – that does not find the idea of a black president such an improbable proposition. This hip hop and multi-culturalist generation has grown up seeing blacks occupying high political offices in unprecedented numbers – from mayors to governors to senators to judges to cabinet secretaries – and as professionals, not simply as idols of popular culture in sports and entertainment. This is to suggest there may be a cultural shift taking place in American society, a new social imaginary of citizenship might be emerging, underpinned by the very limited dispensations of the civil rights settlement the Republicans have worked so hard to overturn, as well as by new product-ions and consumptions of popular culture, and transformations in domestic and global racial geographies as articulated in demographic shifts and the circuits of globalization.

What are the implications of the Obama candidacy for the Pan-African world? He will be a fascinating footnote if he fails to win the nomination. But if he does he will generate enormous pride among people of African descent everywhere, and should he proceed to capture the presidency he will write a new chapter in the history of the African Diaspora in the Americas. He will not of course be the first Diasporan African to assume a position of national leadership. Rulers of African descent are known in the histories of India and Andalusian Spain, for example. Even in the racially checkered history of the Americas several leaders of African descent emerged as presidents. Examples include from Mexico, Jose Maria Morelos (1765–1815), the revolutionary leader of the Mexican War of Independence and Vicente Guerrero (1732–1831), the second president of Mexico; and from Venezuela there is Jose Antonio Paez (1790–1873) who served as president three times. Thus, the United States is more than a century behind Latin America on this score.

However, as inspiring as his ascent would be, the import of his achievement would be more symbolic than substantive. In other words, a President Obama would not fundamentally alter the structural and social impediments that have long faced African Americans, nor would it significantly temper the imperialist impulses of the United States in Africa and other regions in the global South. This is because as important as the presidency is, it is only one centre of power in the American hegemon dominated by the military, prison, corporate, and media industrial complexes. And Senator Obama is not, in any meaningful way, a radical, let alone a revolutionary figure; if he was he would not have gone this far in the deeply conservative American political system and culture. He is as ensconced in the American mainstream as are all the white men and the white woman who have sought the presidency during this election cycle. That does not mean I will not welcome, or even celebrate his victory. After all, I have made a small contribution to his campaign, my first in an American election, and his victory would be a welcome return on that investment. More importantly of course, it will offer us all some respite from the unrelenting terror and mediocrity of the Bush years.

February 20, 2008.

Reference

1   Cassandra Veney, 'The Myth of Bill Clinton,' *The Zeleza Post*, January 16, 2008, available at http://zeleza.com/blogging/u-s-affairs/myth-bill-clinton-cassandra-r-veney.

Chapter 22

The Whiteness of Airports

As a frequent traveller, I am struck by how much international travel has changed over the last three decades, much of it for the worse. Especially distressing is the manic security at airports which began with the hijackings of the 1970s and escalated following the 9/11 terrorist attacks in the United States, and which has been ratcheted up with every new threat, real and imagined. It now takes ingenuity to even travel with toiletries. On my recent trip from Chicago to Johannesburg via Paris my hair shaving cream was confiscated at Charles De Gaulle airport because, so explained the security attendant, a young black woman, the container was more than 100 ml. My pleas that I was in transit and the offending package had passed US airport security and my grooming for the next two weeks depended on it fell on deaf ears, notwithstanding her sympathetic smile.

The deregulation of the airline industry, imposed with fundamentalist market zeal by the intolerant overseers of neo-liberalism in Western capitals from the 1980s, seems to have engendered less efficiency and a decline in services, including the quality of airline food except for business or first-class travellers which is not the lot of most academics or the flying public. Flight delays seem worse than I remember them. All this could of course simply reflect the nostalgic impulses of ageing. I cannot dispute that flying has become more pleasant since the banning on smoking. And airports are larger, better stocked with restaurants, bookstores, and upscale stores; they have been turned into malls for the weary traveller anxious for the addictive fix of shopping. They are certainly more crowded with the democratization of travel and explosion of mass tourism. But they remain largely white.

The whiteness of airports was quite evident on my recent trip. Chicago has a large community of 'people of colour' – as non-whites are strangely called. 42.5 per cent of the city's population of 2.9 million is African American (as compared to 31.3 per cent white non-Hispanic). But you wouldn't know that travelling out of O'Hare International Airport, the world's second busiest airport. To be sure, you see many Blacks among the airline and security attendants, serving in restaurants and shops, but their numbers decline perceptibly among the passengers boarding flights. If these are relatively small on domestic flights, notwithstanding variations according to destination, they are even more so on international flights. On my flight to Paris, which was full, I could count the number of Black people on one hand.

The flight from Paris to Johannesburg showed that the racialization of travel was not confined to the Eurozone of the North Atlantic, but had a more global reach encompassing Africa. There were only a handful of Black people on my flight to the southernmost tip of this massive continent, another confirmation that whites, who constitute a minority of the world's population, consume a disproportionate share of the world's resources and services including space and travel.

I have been intrigued by the whiteness of airports ever since my first trips to and from Europe in the late 1970s. Later when I moved to North America I was astounded by the fact that excluding African-born migrants there were so few African Americans or African Canadians on flights to Africa, far fewer in fact than on flights to Europe. Africa, I soon learned, was not an object of tourist desire for those of the African Diaspora with the means to travel, despite the seductions of heritage tourism engendered by the acclaimed television series, *Roots*. For generations the African Diaspora has been taught to be ashamed of Africa, to be afraid of the contaminating backwardness of Africa, to regard the continent as a land of persistent pathology rather than potential pleasure. To this day, I meet many African American professionals who have been to the citadels of Europe or the beaches of the Caribbean, but not to Africa. Many more of their white compatriots have fewer qualms in going, although the Africa they seek to consume is the stereotypical Africa of animals (or orphanages for the socially enlightened among them), the Africa of the mercy industrial complex, not the Africa of modern infrastructure, industries, and institutions. In contrast, on the flights I have taken to Japan, China, and South Korea I was impressed by the noticeable Asian presence, both of returning Asian visitors and of the Asian Diaspora.

The perils of the whiteness of airports came home to me on a trip to Venezuela in June 2006. There were very few Black people on the flight from Miami to Caracas. My first surprise when we landed was the number of Blacks I saw among the airport workers and taxi drivers. Venezuela's blackness expanded the further I travelled out of the smart districts of central Caracas into the dense *favellas* that carpet the hillsides of this sprawling city and the deeper I went into small towns several hours drive from Caracas, some of which were up to seventy or eighty per cent black. My hosts, two Afro-Venezuelan professors, told me Blacks comprised at least half of Venezuela's population of twenty-six million. Even Hugo Chavez, the country's irrepressible president who delights in poking at the eyes of US imperialism, has some African ancestry; the country's disaffected white elite contemptuously calls him 'El Negro'. ·

The superficial whiteness of Latin America is evident when travelling to Brazil, which I visited following my trip to Venezuela. By all measures the African presence in Brazil is massive. Estimates of Africa's demographic weight vary because of the very contentious and complicated history of racial construction in Brazil, but most scholars agree that the Afro-Brazilian population constitutes nearly half of Brazil's 188 million people. This makes Brazil, as President Lula boasted at the opening of the Second Conference of Intellectuals from Africa and the Diaspora (CIAD II) co-sponsored by his government and the African Union, the second most populous African country after Nigeria. While Brazil readily accepts and indeed embraces Afro-Brazilian culture as the foundational matrix of Brazilian culture, Afro-Brazilians themselves remain politically and economically marginalized.

This was disturbingly clear at CIAD II itself, which was held in Salvador, the capital of Bahia, one of the centres of Afro-Brazilian culture and politics. Yet few of the conference organizers and attendants at the opulent convention centre located in the white part of this overwhelmingly black city were Afro-Brazilian – to the astonishment of many African delegates. Surprise turned to shock when a group of Afro-Brazilian activists, comprising mainly workers, community organizers and students, stormed the conference on the last day demanding racial quotas, as affirmative action is called. When they started singing 'Inkosi Sikelele Africa', the anthem of the African liberation struggle, it finally brought home to the African delegates the emptiness of Brazil's carefully cultivated myth of 'racial democracy'. Many of us sang in solidarity, choking with great emotion, and I even saw a few shed tears of mutual recognition. The Africans finally saw the Brazil shielded from them on their flights and in their hotels and in the polite rhetoric of South-South solidarity.

There are of course exceptions to the whiteness of airports in the Atlantic world, none more glaring than Haiti, as I witnessed on my trip there in July 2007. There was a sea of black faces as I approached the gate for the flight to Port-au-Prince at Miami International Airport. The few whites wore their intrusion visibly. It was the first exception I had encountered to the whiteness of airports in Euroamerica. But it was also quite revealing, a testimony to Haiti's isolation and marginalization in the Americas, its contrived status as a pariah nation, shunned by white America, feared since the revolution of 1791–1804 that freed the enslaved Africans and presaged the collapse of slavery in the Americas and the onset of national liberation in Latin America. This was Haiti, proudly, uneasily black, proclaiming its blackness loudly in a world where its sister Caribbean islands have largely become playgrounds, extended beaches, tourist havens for Euroamerica. If this had been a gate for flights to these other islands the whiteness of the airport would have reasserted itself as a stubborn law of nature in a world of globalized Apartheid.

Flights to post-Apartheid South Africa throw into sharp relief the racial politics of global travel and tourism, which is underpinned by the enduring imperatives of racial capitalism. South Africa of course did not invent racial capitalism. This has characterized the Atlantic world since its emergence in the fifteenth and sixteenth centuries on the back of African slavery and Amerindian genocide. It merely purified it. Similarly, post-Apartheid South Africa has not dismantled racial capitalism, it seeks to pluralize it. Modern travel and tourism are driven by the unyielding demands of global capitalism, which remains profoundly racialized.

Travel and tourism facilitate the social construction of space as a commodity that can be consumed and controlled. Thus, the consumptive and representational values that characterize international tourism are derived from, and help reproduce, Euroamerican material and discursive hegemonies. And so it is Hollywood not Bollywood let alone Nollywood movies that are shown on international flights, and bland McDonaldized fare rather than more palatable Asian or African cuisine that is served, and the planes that ply the world's skies are themselves largely manufactured by Euroamerican corporations.

It is therefore not surprising that the global tourism industry continues to be dominated by Euroamerican travellers and destinations. In 2007 the number of world tourist arrivals reached a staggering 900 million, 6 per cent higher than in 2006. Africa accounted for 44 million arrivals compared to Europe's 480 million, Asia's 185 million. In percentage terms this translates into 4.9 per cent, 53.3 per cent, and 20.6 per cent for Africa, Europe, and Asia, respectively.[1]

What is surprising is that even where this is not the case, in the popular imagination the quintessential tourist remains white. Many a black tourist in the Caribbean and in parts of Africa has been anguished and even angered at the preferential treatment accorded to white tourists, a troubling testimony to the deeply internalized valorization of whiteness and devaluation of blackness in postcolonial societies. The South African foreign minister was once forced to remind her compatriots that two-thirds of the tourists visiting the country in 2005 came from other African countries.

The mismatch between black travel and white tourism was captured most poignantly this morning on South African television news. Two reports caught my attention. One was a tourism awards ceremony attended by beautiful people desperately mimicking white Hollywood stars, in which South Africa bagged several prizes – Cape Town for the best African tourist destination and the Durban International Conference Centre for the best African convention centre. The other was a report on grotesque xenophobic violence against immigrants from Zimbabwe and other African countries in the Johannesburg township of Alexandria, in which dozens were brutally beaten and raped. The violence made the headline of *The Star* newspaper: 'Fear and loathing in Alex,' the paper screamed.[2]

As I read the paper on my flight from Johannesburg's Oliver Tambo International Airport to Port Elizabeth, the following paragraph jumped at me:

> 'No detailed studies had been done on xenophobia and effective ways to address it successfully, SAHRC (South African Human Rights Commission) CEO advocate Tseliso Thipanyane said. "But it is clear that this problem is getting worse. We need to call an urgent meeting to look at the

problem and find meaningful ways to sort it out. It's a peculiar problem in our country where the attacks happen in poor communities and informal settlements *directed at African people, particularly those darker than ourselves* (my emphasis)."'

For a society with a long, ugly history of racialized violence, I find the xenophobic colourization of African travellers, tourists, and immigrants troubling, but not totally surprising. The wounds of Apartheid, which preached the irredeemable inferiority of South Africa's own blacks as well as the country's splendid exceptionalism in the African continent, remain deep indeed. As I read the paper, I looked around me. There were less than ten people of colour on the flight, or to use Apartheid nomenclature, that is, Africans, Coloureds, and Indians, out of more than a hundred passengers. There were about a dozen Japanese tourists as far as I could make out.

The rest of the passengers were white. Whatever their concerns, I imagined, marginality and its violent vulnerabilities was not one of them. They surely could take comfort from the whiteness of the flight, indeed from the whiteness of the global order embodied on my trip from Chicago to Paris, Paris to Johannesburg, and now Johannesburg to Port Elizabeth. Political Apartheid in South Africa may be dead, but global economic Apartheid is alive and well. That is what the whiteness of airports is all about: the racialized class privileges of travel and tourism that have enabled a minority of the world's population from a small corner of Eurasia to traverse the globe over the last half millennia and discover, conquer, shape, consume, despoil, and name places, oblivious to the interests and gaze of the natives.

May 14, 2008.

References

1   *UNWTO World Tourism Barometer*, http://pub.world-tourism.org: 81/WebRoot/Store/Shops/Infoshop/Products/1324/080206_unwto_barometer_01-08_eng_excerpt.pdf.

2   Solly Maphumulo, et al. 'Fear and Loathing in Alex,' *The Star*, Johannesburg, May 13, 2008.

Chapter 23

The Racialized Complexes of Xenophobia

The Pan-African world has been watching with mounting horror the xenophobic violence that has gripped several South African townships over the past two weeks which has resulted in the wanton destruction of many lives and property. Fifty-six people have been murdered, thousands seek sanctuary in police stations, churches, community halls and 'safe havens' or camps, and many more are fleeing back to their countries of origin as several governments desperately try to repatriate their nationals.

Our horror reflects our immense investment in the success of the rainbow nation born out of our collective abhorrence of Apartheid South Africa as the supreme embodiment of the barbaric crimes committed against peoples of African descent over the last half millennium: slavery, colonialism, and racism. It also reflects deep disappointment that migrants from the neighbouring countries and the rest of the continent are being treated with such vicious contempt notwithstanding their countries' unwavering support and sacrifices for the liberation of South Africa from the historic nightmares of Apartheid.

To date, 35,000 people are internally displaced and more than 26,000 have fled to Mozambique alone, and 25,000 Zimbabweans are fleeing through Zambia. The scale of the violence has shocked South African civil society and humanitarian organizations, pummelled the rand and business confidence, and dented South Africa's image across the continent, shaking the South African state and its embattled lame-duck president out of their stupor of political indifference, policy incoherence, and operational incompetence on migration and the poor.

The current cycle of xenophobic violence – there have been several others – is a depressing testimony to the failures of post-Apartheid South Africa to resolve the interconnected challenges inherited from the political and racial economies of Apartheid: *domestically* the deracialization and reduction of social inequalities and *externally* the reinsertion of South Africa into independent Africa from its Apartheid laager of isolation. While South Africa has made remarkable progress since 1994, not least in terms of economic growth, national integration, democratization at home, and reincorporation into African and world affairs, social inequalities persist and are in fact deepening, and the dangerous and occasionally deadly myth of South African exceptionalism endures.

The South African poor are still awaiting the fruits of uhuru as the black middle classes expand and the white rich maintain their monopolies of wealth and privilege even if they are now joined by politically well-connected 'native' beneficiaries of black economic empowerment. In the meantime South Africa, historically constructed as a sub-imperial metropole ever since the mineral revolution of the late nineteenth century, continues to attract labour migrants from the subregion and further afield. These post-Apartheid migrants are no longer channelled predominantly into the declining mining industry, but find themselves competing for economic survival with South Africa's poor in the townships.

The demise of Apartheid ended internal 'influx' controls into the previously designated 'white' cities and opened South Africa to new waves of African immigrants. Circumscribed by its conformities to neo-liberal economic policies on the one hand and its commitments to a Pan-African agenda on the other, the ANC government has thus far failed to stem domestic racial and social inequalities and develop a sound and sustainable immigration policy. This is the combustible brew that has blown up: the struggle for resources among the disaffected South African poor and the disenfranchised immigrants, whose very social and spatial intimacies engender the violent narcissisms of minor difference.

Whatever their debilitations and marginalizations from the post-Apartheid dispensation, the township poor have citizenship on their side, which they periodically wield violently to dispossess the immigrants, for petty primitive accumulation (342 foreign-owned businesses have been looted or destroyed), for national attention, to make claims for redress from the neo-liberal state. As is typical in such struggles, the former blame the latter for taking their jobs, opportunities, and women (the gendered inflexion of xenophobic bigotry), and the escalation of crime –

never mind that levels of crime in South Africa are much higher than in the countries where most of the immigrants come from, itself another tragic legacy of Apartheid.

But there is more to this depressing carnage of xenophobic violence than material conditions. Nor is South Africa unique in its eruptions of xenophobia in the Pan-African world, let alone the world at large. Remember the state-sponsored expulsions of between 155 and 213 thousand West Africans, including 50 thousand Nigerians from Ghana in 1969; 1.3 million Ghanaians from Nigeria between 1983 and 1985; the killings and mass expulsions in Libya in the 1980s and 1990s; the tit-for-tat expulsions of nearly 150 thousand people between Eritrea and Ethiopia in the late 1990s; and of tens of thousands from Côte d'Ivoire during its boom years. The list of xenophobic violence across Africa is a long and depressing one indeed.

One could of course blame the incongruity of Africa's porous national boundaries on the legacies of colonialism, the universal propensity of governments and the media to blame foreigners for domestic crises, and the rise of chauvinistic and explosive nationalisms in response to the stresses of neo-liberal globalization. In the case of Africa's former settler societies from Algeria to South Africa, via Kenya and Zimbabwe, there is an added dimension: the cruel bequest of deeply racialized and internalized superiority and inferiority complexes. The current xenophobic violence in South Africa is being meted out to what some in the country call 'those Africans', or more popularly, the *makwerekwere*. None of the fifty people who have been killed is white. The anger is *intra-racial*, directed at other black Africans.

Pius Adesanmi discussed the social pathologization and discursive ridicule of the *makwerekwere* in an earlier blog on *The Zeleza Post*.[1] African commentators and visitors to South Africa are often confounded by the pervasive sense of South African difference, of exceptionalism, the lingering racist Apartheid myth that South Africa is an outpost of civilization, of modernity, on the 'dark continent'. Ignorance of other African countries is of course not peculiar to South Africa, nor is the sense of misguided national superiority. I have encountered it in many other countries: from Zimbabwe to Jamaica to Kenya, not to mention Britain, Canada, and the United States. It is the deadly mantra of xenophobic nationalism: 'We are better than you, you are less than us.'

Across the Pan-African world, measures of the 'better than, less than' national discourses mutate and are articulated in peculiar local idioms, but they revolve around two axes: the relative levels of material development and the magnitude of the white presence. Thus, Western-ness and whiteness remain imprimaturs in the scale of human worthiness – the reason why Diasporan Africans feel superior to continental Africans, why within the Diaspora the light-skinned have historically enjoyed better opportunities than their darker skinned compatriots, why shades of blackness have become a shameful basis for distinguishing African immigrants among black South Africans, why the latter's xeno-phobic rage is not directed at white immigrants but at 'those Africans', the despised *makwerekwere.*

Racialized superiority and inferiority complexes have stalked the Pan-African world for decades, stoking the mistrust that sometimes degenerates into interpersonal and intra racial animosity and even violence. This violence is the flipside of the collective Pan-Africanist struggles and ideals for the unity of African peoples and their collective liberation and empowerment. South Africans and all of us could benefit from a more systematic and sustained education about our shared pasts, present, and futures in a world that has devalued and continues to devalue our lives and humanity.

May 26, 2008.

References

1   Pius Adesanmi, 'Makwerekwere: Black South Africa's Instant-Mix Kaffirs', *The Zeleza Post*, available at http://www.zeleza.com/blogging/african-affairs/makwerekwere-black-south-africa-s-instant-mix-kaffirs.

Chapter 24

Africa's Global Summits: The Rise of the Continent or Back to the Scramble?

Hardly a few months now go by without a major summit between Africa and the world's leading economic powers. In November 2006, there was the glittering Beijing Summit that brought leaders from forty-eight African countries to China and signalled China's entry into the world's second largest continent. Then in December 2007 came the second African Union-European Union Summit[1] held in Lisbon, Portugal, followed in early April 2008 by the first India-Africa Forum Summit.[2] Then came the fourth Japan-Africa Summit, otherwise known as the Tokyo International Conference on African Development,[3] which was attended by forty African heads of state.

Despite differences in their agendas and atmospherics, the summits are remarkably similar in their soaring rhetoric and Spartan results. Premised on tense (with Europe) or tepid (with Asia) histories, they promise a new era of strategic partnership based more on trade and investment rather than aid, although summit declarations dutifully announce increased levels of development assistance from the summit hosts to their African visitors. Each summit seeks to signal the changing face and fate of Africa, its march from the margins of the global system to the centre, Africa's final discarding of its assumed dependencies on the mercy industrial complex and the clutches of charity.

What accounts for all this sudden attention, Africa's new moment in the sun? Undoubtedly, it has a lot to do with the rise of China and the latter's relentless drive to secure new sources of raw materials, markets and investment outlets, which has shaken Europe from its neo-colonial complacencies and complicities, and awakened the other two Asian powers, Japan and India, to the economic possibilities of African partnership. It can also be attributed to the restructuring of African political economies themselves: the emergence of new contexts of politics and conditions of production; the expansion of capitalism and release of entrepreneurial classes from the shackles of state capitalism or socialism. Changes in the international and domestic divisions of labour of course manifest themselves unevenly across Africa, but there is no question that Africa is enjoying its fastest economic growth in a generation.

Analyses and commentaries of Africa's growing relations with the world's old and new economic powers tend to be presented in terms of imperial, solidarity, and globalization imperatives. According to the first perspective, Africa is too weak to have agency, so what is happening is nothing but a new scramble for the continent. In this narrative Africa's poverty dooms it to powerlessness, to eternal victimhood, to either exploitation or charity. Ironically, it is a discourse most loudly propagated by Western commentators and policy makers, whose own countries' engagements with Africa supposedly embody compassion while those of their competitors, specifically China, entail the opposite; it is even sometimes grudgingly conceded that China's behaviour is reminiscent of old-style European colonialism, something postcolonial Europe has of course transcended.

If some see Asia as the continent's new colonizer, many others believe the machinations of the old economic powers of Euroamerica harbour imperialist attitudes and practices. The critics include those who prefer to see the role of the new economic powers in Asia as a manifestation of the solidarity imperative of post-war Third-worldism. To many leaders and analysts in Africa and its new partners in China and India, the new partnerships are part of what was once called Afro-Asian dialogue, which spawned the Non-Aligned Movement during the Cold War, and which has now mutated into South-South cooperation. Not only do these countries share histories of colonization and pillage by Europe, in so far as they are developing countries, they may also serve as development models for each other.

To those for whom the language of solidarity strains credulity in this era of fierce global competition for resources, markets, and capital, globalization provides a better analytical frame. China and India and their businesses scouring Africa and the globe for resources represent important new players, no better and no worse than other historical

206

actors. We have entered a post-Western world characterized not so much by the decline of the West as such, but by the rise of the Rest as Fareed Zakaria puts it.[4] What we are witnessing are the amoral dynamics of globalization, the growing connectedness between communities, countries and continents as flows of capital and commodities, ideas and images, peoples and practices, values and viruses accelerate. This is a perspective that eschews the politicized language of imperialism and the moral vocabulary of solidarity.

In reality, globalization is as much a description of a historical process as it is the prescription of an ideological project. In other words, globalization is not new: the world has been globalizing for a long time. What gives contemporary globalization its apparent novelty, besides the compression of time and space facilitated by new information and communication technologies, is the supremacy of neo-liberalism, the drive for global capitalist restructuring. In other words, we live not simply in an age of globalization, but neo-liberal globalization. The distinctions between the old imperialism and the new globalization should therefore not be overdrawn.

What has changed is history: precisely because of the long sordid histories of old imperialism, which created generations of resistance including struggles for independence that created many of the world's nation-states, contemporary globalization cannot operate through the arsenals of colonial conquest and the apparatuses of the colonial state. This is of course of little solace to the countless victims of neo-liberal globalization, whose livelihoods and prospects have diminished as they lose out in the relentlessly widening divides between rich and poor.

It is not too long ago that Africa was written off as irrelevant to the global economy, a continent irretrievably doomed to eternal marginality and poverty. I have always been suspicious of discourses about Africa's marginality. I fail to see how Africa could ever have been marginal to its peoples, now rushing towards a billion, and the tens of millions more in the Diaspora. And as a historian I am only too aware that over the past half millennium Africa has been central to the construction of the modern world system in all its dimensions – if the pivotal role of the Atlantic Slave Trade and colonialism are factored into the emergence of industrial capitalism in the Atlantic world and the rise of global Euroamerican hegemony. Clearly, Africa has always been deeply integrated into the world economy, just as the African Diasporas were firmly incorporated into the economies of the Americas, but this has not been historically beneficial to the continent and its peoples. The problem, then, is not Africa's marginalization from the world, but its modes of engagement with the world.

Thus the global summits represent neither the rise of Africa nor the continent's descent into a new scramble, but rather a particular moment in Africa's long involvement in global affairs which will either bring or save us from further historical grief. The challenge for Africa in its global relationships is not, in my view, the intentions of its old or new partners, let alone its incorporation into the global system. It is about the form of these relationships and Africa's own agency. It stands to reason that China and India, no more than the classic colonial powers of Europe and the neo-colonial powers of the United States and Japan, seek to promote their own interests with or without Africa's connivance. It is up to African leaders and civil societies to ensure that these relationships benefit their countries. We owe it to ourselves to be the guardians of our own interests. It is a responsibility that simply cannot be transferred to others for whatever reason, including vulnerabilities to imperialism, the seductive affectations of solidarity, or the inexorable drive of globalization.

June 9, 2008.

References

1   'Africa-EU Summit 2007', available at http://www.africa-union.org/root/AU/
     Conferences/2007/December/eu-au/AU_EU.htm
2   'Africa-India Forum Summit,' available at http://www.africa-union.org/root/au/
     Conferences/2008/april/India-Africa/India-Africa.html
3   'The Fourth Tokyo International Conference on African Development,' available at
     http://www.ticad.net/ticadiv-index.shtml
4   Fareed Zakaria, *The Post-American World and the Rise of the Rest* (New York: Norton,
     2008).

Chapter 25

The Curse of Oil Returns and the
Search for New Energy Futures

Fourteen years ago I had the strange experience of being named by the then Malawi opposition party, the United Democratic Front (UDF), as Shadow Minister for Industry and Energy. Strange because I knew nothing about either field. The UDF went on to win the elections, thereby ending the thirty-year old dictatorship of President Kamuzu Banda, but I was spared the capricious life of a cabinet minister, preferring to continue the far less glamorous one of an academic.

There are of course moments when I wonder how I would have fared as a politician; how a minister of energy in the struggling economy of a non-oil producing African country could respond to the recent spike in oil prices that wrought havoc around the world. Of course one need not be an energy expert to feel the effects of an oil crisis, which affects all aspects of life involving material production and physical transportation, from the costs of driving and flying to those of power and food.

Oil prices skyrocketed from $10 in 1998 to about $140 a barrel in June 2008; more than doubling over the course of one year alone. Some predict the price is headed towards a staggering $200 a barrel. In the late 1990s, *The Economist*[1] and other financial papers that pronounce authoritatively on economic trends declared the dawn of the era of cheap oil, claiming that OPEC and the curse of oil had finally been broken. Detroit resumed its profligate ways and banked its future on gas guzzling SUVs, and searches for alternative fuels lost steam.

But the curse of oil returned with a vengeance, an indictment against all those hasty predictions, a repudiation of the self-appointed overseers and soothsayers of the world economy. Governments are reeling from its dangerous provocations of the masses, especially as the soaring oil prices coincide with, indeed contribute to, rising food prices. This lethal combination of escalating fuel and food prices has sparked demonstrations, road blocks, and riots in more than thirty countries from France to Senegal, Britain and Haiti, where the government was brought down. The car manufacturing and transport sectors have been hit particularly hard, including the air industry, with some major airlines teetering on the verge of bankruptcy.

The incendiary politics of oil leave no country untouched, including the world's largest economy and its biggest oil consumer. In the United States the cost of gas surpassed the psychological watershed of $4 a gallon, which is still relatively low compared to many parts of the world (the lowest is in Venezuela at 12 cents a litre and the highest in Eritrea at more than $9 a litre). Worried about a backlash from both developed and developing countries, and the long-term implications of high oil prices, Saudi Arabia called an emergency meeting of forty ministers from the world's leading oil producing and consuming countries, as well as twenty chief executives from big oil companies.

There was no shortage of culprits for the crisis. Blame was placed on either supply or demand. Some also faulted the role of financial markets and speculators. The supply factors included disruptions of production, both actual and anticipated, in some of the leading oil exporting countries: Iraq ravaged by an unending war; Nigeria facing a low-intensity insurgency in the Niger Delta; Iran threatened with severe sanctions and even military attack by the US or Israel over its nuclear programme; and Venezuela embroiled in a war of nerves with the US. Also, there are those who argue that low oil prices reduced investment in oil production or refining capacity; the last oil refinery in the US, for example, was built in 1976. The alarmists go further and warn that oil production has peaked as available physical supplies have entered a period of inexorable decline; the oil age is drawing to a close.

Even if correct, and the evidence is conflicting and not equally compelling for each of these explanations, the supply problems do not adequately account for the oil crisis. Some attribute it to increasing demand in the emerging industrial powers, especially China and India. These new economic juggernauts have an insatiable appetite not only for oil but for many other primary commodities whose prices they have helped push to record highs. The crisis is beginning to impact them as well: China, currently the world's second largest oil consumer after the US, was forced to cut subsidies and raise consumer fuel prices And in India swelling oil prices have pushed the inflation rate to more than eleven per cent, the highest level in thirteen years.

Again, the evidence is a lot more complex and contradictory: oil demand has indeed increased, but not all oil on the market is being sold – unsold inventories of Iranian heavy crude are growing. This has led other commentators to reproach the financial markets and speculators. One contention is that the rise in oil prices reflects the relative decline of the US dollar – in which oil futures are traded – against the world's other major currencies, especially the Euro. The other blames the oil companies for unconscionable price gouging, or sees this as a speculative bubble created by investors seeking new streams of profits unavailable in stagnant sectors or imploding financial instruments such as the subprime mortgage market. Speculators may affect oil price volatility, but there is little evidence of hoarding.

Experts will of course continue to debate the merits of these arguments. As with any crisis, its impact was quite uneven among and within countries and between social classes. As usual, it was the poorer countries and lower social classes that bore the disproportionate costs and burdens of rising oil prices. And within regions oil exporting and oil importing countries fared quite differently. In the case of Africa, while Nigeria, Angola, Algeria, and Libya were raking in billions of dollars, Egypt, Senegal, and Cameroon were rocked by riots and many others were groaning from the record prices that threatened to derail any economic growth achieved in recent years.

Crises not only have differentiated impacts, they also tend to generate varied responses and opportunities. Many countries saw the oil crisis as a threat to national security, but the twin fuel and food crises were increasingly also being seen as strategic threats to major parts of the world, especially to the fragile new democracies, where some governments could be toppled by hungry and fuel-deprived mobs. One response has been to intensify oil exploration and production. Even in the US, President Bush and the presumptive Republican Party presidential nominee, Senator John McCain, called for the lifting of the twenty-seven year federal moratorium on offshore oil drilling. In Africa, the race is on for the discovery of black gold: Ghana, Tanzania and

211

Uganda are among the latest to announce their membership of the exclusive oil and gas club.

But looking for more oil is not enough in so far as the problem is not simply one of lowering energy costs but also consuming environmentally safer forms of energy. In short, in so far as global warming is real and needs to be reversed for the sake of the earth and our survival as a species, we need to develop and depend on renewable forms of energy; energy that is both cheap and clean. Thus more innovative energy sources and comprehensive policies are required.

If I had accepted and lasted as minister of energy I would be paying a lot of attention to several alternative forms of energy with which Africa is abundantly blessed. There is of course hydro power, which has already been extensively developed in various parts of Africa, although its full power has yet to be fully exploited. It is often said that tapping the power of the mighty Congo River alone could provide electricity to the whole continent. Far less developed are wind power and solar energy; technologies for both have advanced immensely in recent years, although unevenly. Then there is geothermal energy, tapping the heat buried deep in the earth.

Biofuels have been attracting a lot of attention lately. Much of the focus has been on ethanol derived from crops such as maize, wheat, beet, and vegetables, which unfortunately threatens food supplies and has according to some exacerbated the growing food crisis. Less threatening and more promising are efforts to extract fuel from grasses, trees, and algae that are not ordinarily consumed and that can be produced in lands unsuitable for food production. Finally, there is nuclear power, of whose raw material, uranium, Africa is a major producer. The development of nuclear technology is often conflated with nuclear weapons, which are seen as the monopoly of certain countries, as some kind of privilege for adult nations and unsuitable for the rest. And for environmentalists, nuclear power represents the ultimate energy of mass destruction.

Developing these alternative and sustainable sources of energy requires vast research and business investments. Some governments on the continent have been making such investments. For example, using its oil windfall, Algeria has built an experimental solar-thermal power station which is expected to be opened in 2009, and in South Africa there are efforts, among the most advanced in the world, to develop a new type of safe and simple nuclear reactor.

However, most African countries are not making the necessary investments in exploring and developing new forms of energy. This is terribly unfortunate, for alternative energy is likely to be one of the biggest enterprises of the twenty-first century, and Africa has the necessary natural resources to be a major innovator and beneficiary. What is needed is the full mobilization of its human capital.

June 22, 2008.

References

1   *The Economist*, 'Cheap Oil: The Next Shock,' March 4, 1999, available at
     http://www.economist.com/displaystory.cfm?story_id=188181

Chapter 26

The Dawn of the Obama Era:
In Memory of the Ancestors

The Obama era has begun. Like millions of people in the United States and around the world today I sat glued to the television watching the historic inauguration, relishing the man and the moment, its substance and symbolism. Tomorrow, of course, the hard work starts and the harsh realities facing the new president will break today's magical spell. America's daunting challenges will puncture the bubble of messianic expectations invested in the young president. The extraordinary euphoria that has gripped this nation and parts of the world is obviously unsustainable, and it will inevitably evaporate in the predictable whirlwind of stumbles, setbacks, even scandals, not to mention the structural obstacles of this mighty but beleaguered capitalist and imperial power that will constrain bold changes, truly progressive transformation.

The challenges are immense indeed: ending two foreign wars in Iraq and Afghanistan that have depleted the nation of treasure and trust and abandoning its misguided commitment to the 'war on terror' (which even Britain, one of America's staunchest allies, thinks is a mistake); managing the economic crisis and administering an effective stimulus package that will halt the economic recession and restore growth; expanding access to health care and improving the quality of education and overcoming the inequities of the prison industrial complex that has devastated African American and other minority communities; pursuing sound and sustainable domestic and global environmental policies; and promoting smart foreign policies and allegiance to multilateralism. The biggest challenge facing President Obama is how to manage the relative decline of American global supremacy in a world of new and emerging powers and growing intolerance against authoritarianism, whether within or between nations; in short, a more global and nationalistic world impatient with the old injustices and hungry for development, democracy, and self-determination.

The indefatigable anti-Apartheid and human rights campaigner, Archbishop Desmond Tutu[1] put it best yesterday at a congregation of black leaders from around the world convened to celebrate the life of Dr Martin Luther King and the inauguration of President Barack Obama. He urged the new president 'not to squander the promise of this moment, and to return America to the moral high ground once again. The world is waiting for America to be a leader once again, but not an America of bully-boy tactics,' he urged. 'A leader that says, "Climate change is here, let's not pussyfoot around" ... An America that won't tolerate abominations like Guantanamo Bay. No! Torture is torture, the world is waiting for an America that says, "No to torture!". An America,' he continued, 'that ratifies the International Criminal Court, sending a message to despots in places like Zimbabwe, Sudan, Burma and Tibet that "there is no impunity, there is nowhere for you to hide".' If the impending inauguration of Obama is possible, Tutu argued, then so is all of this. 'God has been waiting,' Tutu said, 'to hear us say: "Yes We Can!"'

From his inaugural address,[2] which invoked some key moments and motifs of American history, and crossed generational and racial divides, it is clear President Obama understands many of these challenges and is eager to confront them as effectively as possible. The speech was more sombre than soaring. Eschewing the false optimism beloved by American presidents and politicians, he called for a new era of responsibility. He painted a grim picture of the problems facing the country:

> 'That we are in the midst of crisis is now well understood. Our nation is at war against a far-reaching network of violence and hatred. Our economy is badly weakened, a consequence of greed and irresponsibility on the part of some but also our collective failure to make hard choices and prepare the nation for a new age. Homes have been lost, jobs shed, businesses shuttered. Our health care is too costly, our schools fail too many, and each day brings further evidence that the ways we use energy strengthen our adversaries and threaten our planet.

216

These are the indicators of crisis, subject to data and statistics. Less measurable, but no less profound, is a sapping of confidence across our land; a nagging fear that America's decline is inevitable, that the next generation must lower its sights.

Today I say to you that the challenges we face are real, they are serious and they are many. They will not be met easily or in a short span of time. But know this America: They will be met.

On this day, we gather because we have chosen hope over fear, unity of purpose over conflict and discord.'

He called for bold and swift action and strongly repudiated the policies of the Bush administration and the ideological bickering of the past few decades:

'The question we ask today is not whether our government is too big or too small, but whether it works, whether it helps families find jobs at a decent wage, care they can afford, a retirement that is dignified. Where the answer is yes, we intend to move forward. Where the answer is no, programs will end. And those of us who manage the public's dollars will be held to account, to spend wisely, reform bad habits, and do our business in the light of day, because only then can we restore the vital trust between a people and their government. Nor is the question before us whether the market is a force for good or ill. Its power to generate wealth and expand freedom is unmatched, but this crisis has reminded us that without a watchful eye, the market can spin out of control. The nation cannot prosper long when it favours only the prosperous. The success of our economy has always depended not just on the size of our Gross Domestic Product, but on the reach of our prosperity; on our ability to extend opportunity to every willing heart —not out of charity, but because it is the surest route to our common good.'

Finally, he promised a new compact with the world:

'And so, to all other peoples and governments who are watching today, from the grandest capitals to the small village where my father was born: know that America is a friend of each nation and every man, woman, and child who seeks a future of peace and dignity, and that we are ready to lead once more ...

To the Muslim world, we seek a new way forward, based on mutual interest and mutual respect. To those leaders around the globe who seek to sow conflict, or blame their society's ills on the West, know that your people will judge you on what you can build, not what you destroy. To those who cling to power through corruption and deceit and the silencing of dissent, know that you are on the wrong side of history, but that we will extend a hand if you are willing to unclench your fist.

To the people of poor nations, we pledge to work alongside you to make your farms flourish and let clean waters flow; to nourish starved bodies and feed hungry minds. And to those nations like ours that enjoy relative plenty, we say we can no longer afford indifference to the suffering outside our borders, nor can we consume the world's resources without regard to effect. For the world has changed, and we must change with it.'

Only the next few weeks and months and years will tell whether these promises will be kept, whether the faith placed in the Obama Administration by millions of people in the United States and around the world for transformative change is misplaced or not. The scholar in me does not expect profound changes in the conduct of America's domestic and foreign policies. But I celebrate the new president nonetheless. I have noticed many of my scholarly and activist colleagues and friends share the same ambivalence, a kind of cautious excitement. Excitement that the long history of struggle has brought this country a black president, and caution because many of the country's structural features and deformities will remain unchanged for the foreseeable future. Given the ugly weight of race in American history, the election of President Obama diminishes the symbolic and substantive stranglehold of race on American society and political economy. That is to be welcomed.

But this is a day for rejoicing, not predicting the future. In the words of Donna Brazile,[3] a Democratic strategist and chairwoman of the Democratic National Committee's Voting Rights Institute:

> 'This is the day for which so many prayed, so many marched and so many more sacrificed. This is a day of jubilation and celebration. This is the day to rejoice and recommit ourselves to restoring the American dream for us all ... Yes, of course, racism still exists in America. But if a black man can become president of the United States of America, then aren't all Americans now free to believe they can achieve any goal they set for themselves?'

It is for these struggles and promises that this is indeed a historic day. In one of the most memorable lines in his address, President Obama reminded his audience of the historic gravity and possibilities of the moment: 'And why a man whose father less than sixty years ago might not have been served at a local restaurant can now stand before you to take a most sacred oath.'

Rupert Cornwell[4] wrote with understated astonishment in the British paper *The Independent*:

> 'The most powerful man in the world is black ... Let us savour history today. Tomorrow for Barack Obama the hard part begins – the small matters of largely reinventing his country, trying to bring a semblance of order to an ever more turbulent world, and staving off economic Armageddon ... Today in one sense is a destination, the end of a journey lasting 233 years, from the very foundation of a country with its own original sin of slavery. There have been many milestones along the road: among them emancipation, Jackie Robinson and the integration from 1947 of baseball which truly was then the national pastime. Then came the 1954 Supreme Court ruling, Brown vs Board of Education, that desegregated America's schools, followed by the great civil rights acts of the 1960s. The dream set out 45 years ago by Martin Luther King on the steps of the Lincoln Memorial –

at the opposite end of the Washington Mall from where Mr Obama will speak today – may not have been entirely realized. The colour of a person's skin still does matter in America – but how far America has come.'

This is a deeply emotional moment for African Americans, unimaginable for centuries, inconceivable to their ancestors who endured the indescribable savagery of slavery and segregation, astounding even to the post-civil rights offspring often hindered by the abiding bigotries and excuses of low expectations. This day is a tribute to their struggles, their unshakeable faith in their humanity, their hopes that they could shift the trajectory of their nation's cruel history. Their slave ancestors built the Capitol where the new president was inaugurated and the White House where he will be living for the next four years and perhaps eight. It was in these buildings that the drama of African American subjugation and emancipation was played out, where new chapters of the American story were written in blood and tears, where European dreams and African nightmares confronted each other generation after generation.

Connecting the two sites is Pennsylvania Avenue, which has been, as *The Los Angeles Times*[5] noted yesterday, 'the scene of hate, oppression, possibility and progress.' The paper observed that the new president's triumphant motorcade:

> '…will retrace the path of Ku Klux Klan marches and roll past the ghosts of hotels and movie theaters that used to turn away people like him. This historic stretch, book-ended by the Capitol on one end and the White House on the other, has witnessed many of the milestones that made an Obama presidency possible. The Emancipation Proclamation and the Civil Rights Act of 1964 were signed here. But it's doubtful that even a Harvard-educated wonder can get his arms around the scope of the civil-rights drama that has played out on this 1.2-mile slice of real estate. There are places more infamous for their scars – Selma, Birmingham – but none captures the sweep of the story the way Pennsylvania Avenue does, where laws were passed to enslave people and laws were passed to free them, and at least a

dozen of Obama's predecessors would sooner have considered him a piece of property than a peer.'

It is a poignant coincidence that President Obama's inauguration came a day after Martin Luther King Day. The Obama presidency was made possible by the civil rights movement symbolized by Dr King's leadership. Writing in *The Washington Post*, Dr King's son, Martin Luther King III, stated,[6] 'Forty-five years ago, my father, Dr Martin Luther King Jr., proclaimed his dream for America "that one day this nation will rise up and live out the true meaning of its creed." His words, spoken in Lincoln's shadow on Aug. 28, 1963, will echo profoundly on Jan. 20, 2009. The ideals that Abraham Lincoln and my father championed will advance when Barack Obama takes the presidential oath of office.' But the civil rights leader concluded with a sombre thought: 'As bright a day as Nov. 4 was in our nation's history, it is important to remember that Barack Obama's election is not a panacea for race relations in this country. The 13th Amendment abolished slavery, yet segregation ran rampant for a hundred years. Blacks were given the right to vote in 1965, but it took 43 years for an African American to rise to the nation's highest office. Though it carries us further down the path toward equality, Barack Obama's election does not render my father's dream realized.'

This caution was echoed by one of Dr King's lieutenants and trail blazer for President Obama, the Rev. Jesse Jackson, in an op-ed piece in *The New York Times*,[7] in which he asked: 'What would Dr King, who spent much of his life changing conditions so that African Americans could vote without fear of death or intimidation, think of the rise of the nation's 44th president? I can say without reservation that he would be beaming. I am equally confident that he would not let the euphoria of the moment blind us to the unfinished business that lies ahead. And he would spell out those challenges in biblical terms: feed the hungry, clothe the naked and study war no more. Dr King spent his 39th birthday working ... That's the model we should follow this week – and beyond. We should celebrate the election of our new president. And then we should get back to work to complete the unfinished business of making America a more perfect union."

Clearly, President Obama owes much to Dr King, but he is not the latter's predictable heir. The two not only belong to different generations, what President Obama himself calls the Moses and Joshua generations,[8] they represent different political projects. President Obama lacks Dr King's burning moral and political fervour to overhaul American society and politics; his drive is to run the country more efficiently. For Dr King, racism, poverty, and war were intertwined, American imperialism abroad and racism at home reproduced each other. But President Obama seems wedded to maintaining American power, albeit with softer gloves than the bare knuckled arrogance of the Bush-Cheney Administration. Warns Michael Honey:[9] 'Like Lyndon Johnson, Obama risks his domestic agenda by getting bogged down in a quagmire in Afghanistan.' Already his lukewarm reaction to the Israeli invasion of Gaza is cooling enthusiasm for him in some parts of the world. Reports William J. Kole:[10] 'Muslims want to know why Obama hasn't joined the chorus of international criticism of Israel's Gaza offensive. Last week posters of him were set on fire in Tehran to shouts of "Death to Obama!"'

President Obama confronts progressives with challenges they didn't face with the manifestly banal and uncompromising President Bush. They must go beyond making predictable critiques if they wish to influence the new administration, to keep its feet to the fire in carrying out some of its own more enlightened campaign promises. They need to constantly engage both his administration and America. To quote John Nichols:[11]

> 'Obama knows not just the rough outlines of the left-labor-liberal-progressive agenda, but the specifics. He does not need to be presented with progressive ideas for responding appropriately to an economic downturn, to environmental and energy challenges, to global crises and democratic dysfunctions. He has, over the better part of a quarter century, spoken of, written about, and campaigned for them.'

He continues:

> 'The way to influence Obama and his Administration is to speak not so much to him as to America. Get out ahead of the new president, and of his spin-drive communications team. Highlight the right appointees and the right responses to deal with the challenges that matter most. Don't just

critique, but rather propose. Advance big ideas and organize on their behalf; identify allies in federal agencies, especially in Congress, and work with them to dial up the pressure for progress. Don't expect Obama or his aides to do the left thing. Indeed, take a lesson from rightwing pressure groups in their dealings with Republican administrations and recognize that it is always better to build the bandwagon than to jump on board one that is crafted with the tools of compromise. Smart groups and individuals are already at it.'

He concludes with a pertinent historical analogy:

'Franklin Roosevelt's example is useful here. After his election in 1932, FDR met with Sidney Hillman and other labor leaders, many of them active Socialists with whom he had worked over the past decade or more. Hillman and his allies arrived with plans they wanted the new president to implement. Roosevelt told them: "I agree with you, I want to do it, now make me do it." It is reasonable for progressives to assume that Barack Obama agrees with them on many fundamental issues. He has said as much. It is equally reasonable for progressives to assume that Barack Obama wants to do the right thing. But it is necessary for progressives to understand that, as with Roosevelt, they will have to make Obama do it.'

As I watched dignitaries from the three branches of government coming to be seated for the inauguration, the audacity of the moment was unmistakable: the new black president will be accompanied by only one black justice, the widely despised Clarence Thomas, and one black senator, Roland Burris, Senator Obama's briefly contentious replacement, nominated by the impeached Illinois Governor. The contrast between the white faces of power and the colourful sea of people, estimated at nearly two million, stretched for two miles over the Washington Mall and all across the capital, was palpable.

The two images underscore the symbolic significance of this moment; that American history had turned, if not a new chapter, at least a new page. The festive crowds had turned out to witness history and celebrate their rendezvous with history. Their ecstasy on the Mall and across the nation was as infectious as it was intense, almost unprecedented and not seen in the inaugurations of any of President Obama's immediate predecessors. That did not stop the pundits from trying to find parallels in past inaugurations, many settling on the mystique of John F. Kennedy, another youthful president with a beautiful family, and much promise. Indeed, for Matt Bai,[12] the inauguration of President Obama marks the end of 'America's 50-year quest to find a truly transformational leader' à la Kennedy.

It is easy to be cynical about such theatrical political events as the inauguration, the ritualized performance of the American transfer of power. The claims trotted by pundits and the new president express the typical bombast of American exceptionalism. Writing yesterday, the astute British journalist, Gary Younge,[13] puts it this way:

'Not for the first time, ridiculous claims will be made for this particular historical moment. Some will say this could not happen anywhere else, without acknowledging that putting one in three black men born at the turn of this century in jail could not happen anywhere else either. A black man in the White House seems so unlikely precisely because a black man in prison, dead or impoverished is so much more likely. Some will claim that Obama's advance shows that anyone in America can make it, regardless of race or class, without acknowledging that, in fact, class fluidity and racial uplift are in fact in retreat, and have been for several years. And yet others will insist that a black face will help promote US interests abroad, without acknowledging that the face of American foreign policy for the last eight years has been Colin Powell and Condoleezza Rice. Those who hold that America is a land of boundless opportunity and relentless progress are no fans of fact or history.'

But rituals and celebrations are the poetry in the prosaic lives of individuals, families, communities, and nations, the spice that seasons human existence. The explosive fervour for President Obama is not to be derided. To quote Younge again:

> 'For those on the left who have sneered at this joy, tomorrow is their last chance to join the rest of the people whose liberation they claim to champion. Anxious to get their disappointment in early and avoid the rush, they have been keen to point out the various ways in which Obama will fail and betray. Their predictions may well prove correct. The best is not the same as adequate. He has been elected to represent the interests of the most powerful country in the world. Those will not be the same interests as those of the powerless. And yet, in the words of Friedrich Engels: "What childish innocence it is to present one's own impatience as a theoretically convincing argument." Obama was the most progressive, viable candidate possible in these circumstances. A black American, propelled to office by a mass popular campaign pledging income redistribution and an end to torture and the war in Iraq, has defeated the Republicans and is about to replace the most reactionary president in at least a generation.'

The millions of Americans and others around the world who are rejoicing at Obama's accession to the presidency are not simply overjoyed by Obama's personal success, although many are, nor are they delusional optimists, although some may be, but they are also, in the most elemental sense, projecting their own hopes and dreams for different lives, for better futures. Younge again puts the point most eloquently:

> 'The global outpouring of support for Obama suggests a constituency for a world free of racism and war, and desperate to shift the direction of global events that is in dire need of leadership and an agenda. Dancing in the streets tomorrow afternoon doesn't mean you can't take to those same streets in protest from Wednesday. As one African American activist said shortly after election day: "As much hell as we've caught over the past few hundred years, we should enjoy this one."'

President Obama starts office with incredible support, with approval ratings of eighty-three per cent. The poll ratings are simply dizzying, higher than for any incoming president in recent memory. Writes Jonathan Freedland:[14] '79 per cent [of Americans are] optimistic about the next four years, according to the *New York Times*, a degree of goodwill that trumps the numbers that greeted the previous five presidents.' As befits America, his image has become a hot commodity, stamped on all manner of merchandise. As political leaders and cultural icons tend to, especially in moments of national crisis and angst, the new president serves as the *tabula rasa* upon which millions of people yearning for change seek to rewrite their collective lives. The fact that they are likely to be disappointed is not an argument against the dreams themselves, nor does it invalidate the struggles that made this moment possible.

The presence of President Obama also recasts struggles and representations of the African Diasporas in various parts of the world. We are all familiar with the electrifying impact of President Obama's election in countries in the Americas and Europe, places with large and often marginalized African Diaspora populations. The excitement extends to Asia including Iraq, the burial ground of American imperial hubris, where the country's estimated two million Blacks have apparently made Barack Obama a model to follow.[15] Even in India, according to Lakshmi Chaudhry,[16] where Indians of African descent tend to be racially despised, the country has 'been overwhelmed by the undisguised pleasure of seeing a brown-skinned underdog triumph against all odds over a white establishment ... Many Indians believe Obama's victory makes all things possible for people of colour everywhere – including the many American grandchildren, nieces, nephews and cousins who, thanks to globalization, are part of the Indian extended family.'

In another insightful article, 'What Obama Means to the World,' Gary Younge[17] reminds us of the special role African Americans have occupied in the global political and cultural imaginary, facilitated by the standing of the United States, as victims of oppression and beacons of redemption against American imperialism and racism, as powerful producers and custodians of American popular culture. The progressive image of African Americans was severely damaged by Colin Powell and Condoleezza Rice, who became the black faces of 'the most reactionary US foreign policy in at least a generation. When Secretary of State Powell addressed the Earth Summit in Johannesburg in September 2002, he was jeered ...' President Barack Obama reprises the more heroic image and role of African Americans.

But he does more: his rise challenges Europe and other multiracial societies to look hard at their own histories and societies.

'Political conversation in France, Britain and Germany, in particular, went almost effortlessly from how to keep immigrants out to how descendants of (mostly) immigrants could ascend to the highest office in the land – or why they could not ... In almost every instance the simple, honest answer to the question "Could it happen here?" was no. The Obama story was indeed about race. But at its root it was essentially about white people. Would they vote for him? Would they kill him? It's not clear whether white Europeans would be any more comfortable with electing a black leader in their own countries than some Republicans were here. Having basked in a smug state of superiority over America's social, economic and racial disparities, Europeans were forced by Obama's victory and the passions it stoked to face the hard realities about their own institutional discrimination, which was not better or worse – just different ...

'To this day "immigrant" and "nonwhite" are often used synonymously in France. Indeed, given the conflation of immigration and race in Europe, the fact that Obama's father was an immigrant was in some ways as significant as the fact that he was black. In that sense every country potentially has its Obama, depending on its social fault lines. For the broader symbolism of his win has less to do with race than with exclusion ... [Obama's] central appeal was not so much that he looked like other Americans as that he sounded so different – and not just in comparison to Bush. For if Obama represents a serious improvement over his predecessor, he also stands tall among other world leaders. At a time of poor leadership, he has given people a reason to feel passionate about politics. Brits, Italians, South Africans, French and Russians look at Obama and then at Gordon Brown, Silvio

Berlusconi, Thabo Mbeki, Nicolas Sarkozy and Vladimir Putin and realize they could and should be doing a whole lot better.'

In conclusion, Younge observes:

'Much of this is, of course, delusional. People's obsession with Obama always said more about them than him. Most wanted a paradigm shift in global politics, and, unable to elect governments that could fight for it, they simply assigned that role to Obama. His silence during the shelling of Gaza, however, was sobering for many. As a mainstream Democrat he stands at the head of a party that in any other Western nation would be on the right on foreign policy, the centre on economic policy and the centre-left on social policy. Come inauguration day, that final symbolic set piece, the transition will be complete. The rest of the world must become comfortable with a black American, not as a symbol of protest but of power. And not of any power but a superpower, albeit a broken and declining one. A black man with more power than they. How that will translate into the different political cultures around the globe, whom it will inspire, how it will inspire them and what difference that inspiration will make will vary. From inauguration day people's perceptions of Obama will no longer hinge on what he is but on what he does.'

Whatever indeed happens under the Obama Administration, its inauguration today has already changed the face of American politics. The African ancestors brought to these lands in chains are watching, but for once, probably with a smile. The long struggle for citizenship among their descendants has entered a new age, the Obama era.

January 20, 2009.

References

1   Ari Berman, 'Desmond Tutu, Black Leaders Celebrate King & Obama,' *The Nation*, January 19, 2009, available at http://www.thenation.com/blogs/state_of_change/399270/desmond_tutu_black_leaders_celebrate_king_obama?rel=hp_currently
2   Full transcript can be found at ABC news, http://abcnews.go.com/Politics/Inauguration/story?id=6689022&page=1
3   Donna Brazile's commentary can be found at http://edition.cnn.com/2009/POLITICS/01/20/brazile.milestone/index.html?eref=rss_topstories
4   Rupert Cornwell, 'Obama's inauguration: A day for hope', The Independent, January 20, 2009, available at http://www.independent.co.uk/news/world/americas/obamas-inauguration-a-day-for-hope-1451398.html
5   Faye Fiore, 'Obama Rides Through History on Pennsylvania Avenue,' *The Los Angeles Times*, available at http://articles.latimes.com/2009/jan/20/nation/na-pennsylvania-avenue20
6   Martin Luther King, Jr., 'The Dream This Jan. 20', *The Washington Post*, available at http://www.washingtonpost.com/wp-dyn/content/article/2009/01/18/AR2009011801437.html?referrer=emailarticle
7   Rev. Jesse Jackson, 'Dr. King's Last Birthday,' *The New York Times*, available at http://www.nytimes.com/2009/01/19/opinion/19jackson.html?_r=2&emc=eta1
8   David Remnick, 'The Joshua Generation: Race and the Obama Campaign,' *The New Yorker*, November 17, 2008, available at http://www.newyorker.com/reporting/2008/11/17/081117fa_fact_remnick
9   Michael Honey, 'Barack Obama needs to carry out King's vision,' *The Progressive*, January 13, 2009, available at http://www.progressive.org/mag/mphoney011309.html
10 William J. Kole, 'As Challenges mount, ardour for Obama cools abroad', available at http://www.newsvine.com/_news/2009/01/18/2326420-as-challenges-mount-ardor-for-obama-cools-abroad
11 John Nicholls, 'How to Push Obama,' *The Progressive*, January 2009, available at http://www.progressive.org/mag/nichols0109.html
12 Matt Bai, 'The Long Search for Kennedy's Successor,' *The Independent*, January 20, 2009, available at http://www.independent.co.uk/news/race-for-whitehouse/the-long-search-for-kennedys-successor-1451327.html
13 Gary Younge, 'Celebrate the moment. From then, it's not who Obama is, but what he does,' *The Guardian*, January 19, 2009, available at http://www.guardian.co.uk/commentisfree/2009/jan/19/obama-inauguration
14 Jonathan Fredland, 'Magical spell that will open a new American era,' *The Guardian*, January 20, 2009, available at http://www.guardian.co.uk/world/2009/jan/20/barack-obama-inauguration
15 Jill Dougherty, 'Black Iraqis make Obama a model to follow,' January 19, 2009, available at http://edition.cnn.com/2009/WORLD/meast/01/19/obama.black.iraqis/index.html?iref=newssearch
16 Lakshmi Chaudhry, 'Slumdog President,' *The Nation*, January 15, 2009, available at http://www.thenation.com/doc/20090202/chaudhry?rel=hp_currently
17 Gary Younge, 'What Obama Means to the World,' *The Nation*, January 15, 2009, available at http://www.thenation.com/doc/20090202/younge?rel=hp_currently

Chapter 27

Waiting for the Obama Dividend: The Future of Africa-US Relations

Africa has been delirious with excitement and great expectations following the recent election of President Barack Obama. But the celebrations are now giving way to the hard realities of political normalcy. Many observers across the continent and the United States wonder what President Obama will bring to Africa beyond hope and pride. Will there be any significant shifts in American foreign policies towards the continent beyond the traditional paradigm that sees Africa in humanitarian, not geostrategic, terms? The US has seen Africa as a global pawn rather than as a global player, notwithstanding the polite rhetoric about Africa's great potential, or the growing anxieties about China's economic 'invasion', and new security preoccupations in which Africa is seen as a soft underbelly in the 'war on terror'.

For some commentators it will be enough if the Obama Administration continues the so-called humanitarian policies of President Bush exemplified by PEPFAR (the President's Plan for Aids Relief shorn of its repressive restrictions,[1] augmented by the expansion and reauthorization when it expires in 2012 of the African Growth and Opportunity Act (AGOA).[2] Others believe that US African policies should be remade to focus single-mindedly on peacemaking to end the continent's remaining big wars in Sudan, eastern Congo, and Somalia.[3]

During the presidential campaign, the Obama team identified three objectives in its Africa policy: first, to accelerate Africa's integration into the global economy; second, to enhance the peace and security of African states; and third, to strengthen relationships with those governments, institutions and civil society organizations committed to deepening democracy, accountability and reducing poverty in Africa.[4]

As laudable as these goals might be, the devil is in the detail and, in the implementation. The rhetoric is compromised by both the weight of history and the inherent contradictions of unequal power, the persistent incongruence of American and African interests. The Obama Administration would go a long way in transforming US-African relations if it adopted the following five-pronged agenda.

First, it needs to abandon the growing militarization of United States Africa policy spawned by the misguided 'war on terror' and concretized by the formation of African Command (AFRICOM), which is widely opposed by African states and civil society groups. Militarism has been the bane of African development and policies predicated on more militarization, whatever the justification, are counterproductive.

Second, the United States should promote and effectively coordinate with regional African peacemaking initiatives. Failure to do so produced the strategic blunder in Somalia when local interests were subjugated to America's blind ideological opposition to the largely moderate Islamist forces that had taken power and were consolidating their rule over this beleaguered country. America's complicity with the ill-fated Ethiopian invasion cost it goodwill in Somalia itself and across the continent.

Third, backing rather than bucking progressive democratic regimes, experiments, and struggles will bring both Africa and the United States long-term political dividends. The United States has a sordid record of coddling autocracies and ignoring electoral malpractices when it suits its short-term interests; the former remains evident with the twenty-eight year old Mubarak dictatorship in Egypt and the latter was demonstrated during Kenya's rigged elections of December 2007. If it seeks to win friends and influence Africa's peoples, hungry for democracy, the US must embark on sustained engagement with the continent's democratic states and civil societies.

Fourth, the United States should support Africa's efforts for sustainable development which have been undermined by the ideological regime of neo-liberalism that undid much of Africa's post-independence development momentum. The Wall Street financial meltdown which triggered the global economic crisis has confirmed the utter bankruptcy of neo-liberalism. The Obama Administration secured a huge bailout for the American economy; at the very least it should support long-standing efforts to cancel Africa's ill-gotten debts.

In this regard, it is also critical for the United States, together with other states and agencies in the global North and Africa itself, to bolster more transparent investment practices and forestall the kind of massive corruption perpetrated by Western corporations such as Halliburton[5] – recently charged $559 million to settle a bribery case involving Nigeria. This merely underscores the fact that corruption in Africa, a bane on development, is often facilitated by Western corporations and oiled by Western banks.

Finally, the United States would assist Africa immeasurably if it backed the restructuring of institutions of global political and economic governance from the UN Security Council to that detested trinity, the World Bank, IMF, and the World Trade Organization (WTO). The US also needs to take leadership in environmental matters befitting its role as the world's biggest polluter and consumer of global resources. The US can do this by, among other things, supporting international protocols and funding existing agreements for climate adaptation and mitigation among the developing countries, and by negotiating new and more robust arrangements to combat global warming and other environmental threats.

It hardly needs pointing out that 'Fair Trade' would boost African economies far more than so-called 'Foreign Aid' can ever hope to. The Doha Development Round was in part frustrated by the refusal of the developed countries led by the United States and the European Union to liberalize world agricultural markets and terminate their agricultural subsidies without removing their own agricultural subsidies. As *The New York Times*[6] once reminded its readers, in an article entitled 'Harvesting Poverty: The Long Reach of King Cotton', focusing on the high price West African farmers pay for US farm subsidies: 'If the United States terminated its cotton subsidies, commodity prices would rebound to more realistic levels, allowing third-world cotton farmers to compete and earn a profit on their crops. And by terminating trade-distorting farming subsidies, Washington would defuse a potent source of feverish anti-Americanism.'

It is doubtful the Obama Administration will embark on a fundamentally transformative path that includes all these elements. African states and policy makers should shed any illusions that the Obama Administration will give Africa any special treatment because of the president's personal connections to Kenya or the Democratic Party's tepid multilateral internationalism. Lest we forget, the Rwanda genocide occurred under President Bill Clinton.

But the tone can be expected to change, certainly if President Obama keeps his word. In his first interview with *Al Arabiya* he said that in his dealings with the Muslim world his Administration would 'start by listening' because 'all too often the United States starts by dictating' when 'we don't always know all the factors that are involved'.[7] The problem is that African leaders do not always know or clearly express their countries' best interests; so they ought to be clear about what they want to say to his administration. Some believe the appointment of Dr Susan Rice, the former Assistant Secretary of State for African Affairs in the Clinton Administration, as Ambassador to the United Nations, a Cabinet position, signals the high position Africa is likely to feature in the foreign policy of the Obama administration.

The challenge for Africa, as with any American administration and other major powers for that matter, is for its leaders and thinkers to clearly articulate and fight for Africa's fundamental interests cohered around the triple dreams of development, democracy, and self-determination. This entails a three-pronged strategy in Africa's dealings with the United States: strengthening coordination within Africa itself so that the continent speaks with a more unified voice on critical global issues; promoting collaboration between Africa and the global South for more leverage in negotiations with the global North over international challenges from trade to security to the environment; and bolstering connections with the African Diaspora as Africa's eyes and ears in the streets and corridors of power in Euroamerica.

The African Diasporas in the United States and elsewhere in the global North have made critical contributions to Africa: from the development of Pan-Africanism by the historic Diasporas, out of which the nationalist struggles for independence were incubated; to remittances by the new Diasporas that currently constitute the largest inflows of 'foreign aid' for many countries. The tentacles of the Diasporas today are extensive, encompassing cultural and social institutions as well as political and civil society organizations, and they extend from classrooms to Congress, the pulpit to the presidency. Africa and the Diaspora need to mobilize each other for their mutual benefit under President Obama, the first African

Diasporan leader of this powerful country, and make his administration do the right thing for Africa.

The Obama presidency in itself might free the relations between the continent and the United States from their predictable historical shackles. Unburdened by the white guilt of his predecessors, President Obama can speak more truthfully to his African counterparts, and unencumbered by reflex suspicions of white Euroamerican leaders African leaders might be prepared to listen more openly. President Obama is already an example to many Africans of the possibilities of electoral democracy, and any criticisms he might express of dictatorial and corrupt African states will not be so easily deflected. Indeed, they are likely to be welcomed by many ordinary Africans. But by the same token, they will not hesitate to turn against his Administration, if he continues America's historic bullying of their weaker and smaller countries. Their racial pride will quickly evaporate: after all they are used to being ruled and misruled by black leaders in their own countries.

January 31, 2009.

References

1   Dana Hughes, 'Will Obama Give Africa More Than Just Pride,' *ABC News*, January 23, 2009, available at http://abcnews.go.com/ International/President44/story?id=6711854&page=1

2   Micheal Madill, 'Obama is good and bad news for Africa,' *The Independent*, January 22, 2009, available at http://www.independent.co.ug/index.php/obama-makes-history/92-obama-makes-history/526-obama-is-good-and-bad-news-for-africa

3   John Pendergast and John Norris, 'Obama, Africa and Peace,' Enough Strategy Paper, January 13, 2009, available at http://www.enoughproject.org/files/publications/Jan1309ObamaAfricaPeace.pdf

4   Schneidman, Witney W., 'Africa: Obama's Three Objectives for Continent,' AllAfrica.com, available at http://allafrica.com/stories/200809291346.html

5   Driver, Anna 'Halliburton to pay $559 million to settle bribery probe,' Reuters, January 26, 2009, available at http://www.reuters.com/article/ousivMolt/idUSTRE50P5ZE20090126

6   Editorial, 'Harvesting Poverty: The long reach of king cotton,' *The New York Times*, August 5, 2003, available at http://www.nytimes.com/2003/08/05/opinion/harvesting-poverty-the-long-reach-of-king-cotton.html?sec=&spon=&pagewanted=2

7   Al-Arabiya, 'Al-Arabiya's Game Changing Interview with Barack Obama: A New Punctuation Point in US Foreign Policy,' Al-Arabiya, January 27, 2009, available at http://www.thewashingtonnote.com/archives/2009/01/alarabiyas_game/

Index